ArtScroll Series®

Rabbi Nosson Scherman / Rabbi Meir Zlotowitz

General Editors

ספר לימודי ניסן

RABBI
NISON

Published by

Mesorah Publications, ltd

Teachings of a great Rav
and Rosh Yeshivah

ALPERT

ON THE SIDRAH

Compiled by Rabbi Dovid Weinberger

Adapted from the Hebrew Limudei Nison
by Rabbi Dovid Hojda

FIRST EDITION
First Impression … October 2006

Published and Distributed by
MESORAH PUBLICATIONS, LTD.
4401 Second Avenue / Brooklyn, N.Y 11232

Distributed in Europe by
LEHMANNS
Unit E, Viking Business Park
Rolling Mill Road
Jarow, Tyne & Wear, NE32 3DP
England

Distributed in Israel by
SIFRIATI / A. GITLER — BOOKS
6 Hayarkon Street
Bnei Brak 51127

Distributed in Australia and New Zealand by
GOLDS WORLDS OF JUDAICA
3-13 William Street
Balaclava, Melbourne 3183
Victoria, Australia

Distributed in South Africa by
KOLLEL BOOKSHOP
Ivy Common
105 William Road
Norwood 2192, Johannesburg, South Africa

ARTSCROLL SERIES®
RABBI NISON ALPERT ON THE SIDRAH
© Copyright 2006, by MESORAH PUBLICATIONS, Ltd.
4401 Second Avenue / Brooklyn, N.Y. 11232 / (718) 921-9000 / www.artscroll.com

---

ISBN:
ISBN-10: 1-4226-0201-x
ISBN-13: 978-1-4226-0201-0

Typography by CompuScribe at ArtScroll Studios, Ltd.

Printed in the United States of America by Noble Book Press Corp.
Bound by Sefercraft, Quality Bookbinders, Ltd., Brooklyn N.Y. 11232

ספר
לימודי
ניסן

We feel privileged to join in dedicating this volume to

Rav Nison Alpert זצ״ל

הרב ניסן ליפא בן הרב שבתי זצ״ל

He was an inspiration to us, and changed our lives forever.

As the *talmid* of Maran HaGaon Rav Moshe Feinstein *zt"l*,
he personified his Rebbe — brilliant, humble, dedicated,
unselfish, devoted to Torah and Klal Yisrael.

Not pain, not fatigue, not worries —
there was nothing that could diminish his love of learning.
There was no darkness in his life, only opportunities
to learn, to teach, and to grow.

His memory lives with us always,

JAY AND SARI TEPPER
YITZY AND RECHI AND YECHIEL
AKIVA AND ADINA AND LEORA
NISSON
YONA
ALIZA

We are proud to dedicate this volume in memory of our parents

Philip and Evelyn Zuckerman z"l

פסח יהודה בן יצחק אייזיק ע"ה

ט"ו אייר תשמ"ח

חוה בת יהודה ליב ע"ה

י"א ניסן תשנ"ט

Our father came to America from Galicia at the age of 14.
From a penniless beginning he built a successful business,
but never forgot his origins. He went back to his shtetl to film it
for posterity, In 1933, he went to the defense of Jews in Leipzig,
and was beaten by Nazi Storm Troopers.

Torah learning and life was all-important to our parents.
In 1948, they were among the founders of the
Westchester Day School, and 12 years later they were
among the founders of the Young Israel of New Rochelle.
They arranged for me to learn privately with the gaonim
Harav David Feinstein and Harav Reuven Feinstein shlit"a.,
for which I am forever grateful.

During our 38 years in Great Neck, we have grown close to
Rabbi Wolf ל"ז, the pioneer of our Orthodox community, and to
Rabbi Lerner, Rabbi Polakoff, and Rabbi Axelrod.
They would often quote the insightful teachings of
Rabbi Nison Alpert,. We are honored, therefore, to help
bring his Torah to the English-speaking public.

STEVE AND SHELLIE ZUCKERMAN

This new adaptation of *Limudei Nison*,
the commentary of HaRav Nison Alpert, *zt"l*,
on the Torah, is dedicated to the memory of

הרב ניסן ליפא בן הרב שבתי זצ"ל

and his beloved parents

הרב שבתי בן הרב עוזר זצ"ל
ורעיתו גוטע יעכנא בת הרב ניסן ליפא ע"ה

Rav Nison devoted his life to Torah,
but was equally devoted to family and *Klal Yisrael*.
His *ahavas habrios*, smile and humor
pervaded everything he did.
Though a giant of Torah, he was the embodiment
of הצנע לכת, "walk humbly, with God."

His untimely passing at such a young age
deprived the world of an extraordinary Torah luminary.
In his absence, may his *divrei Torah*
serve as a light and guide to us all.

their devoted family

FRIEDA AND MORRIS LEWINTER
KAREN AND ALAN MAZURCK
MARK AND VICKY LEWINTER
DAVID AND LINDA LEWINTER
TOBY AND MICHAEL PARKER

Contents

Bereishis / בראשית

Shemos / שמות

Vayikra / ויקרא

Bamidbar / במדבר

Devarim / דברים

An Appreciation

abbi Nison Alpert זצ״ל was born in 1927 in Polunka, a small *shtetl* in Poland, and was named after his maternal grandfather, Rabbi Nison Lipa Joselowitz, rosh yeshivah in Lazday, Poland, and later the rabbi of Polunka. Rabbi Joselowitz passed away when he was only 47, leaving a widow with seven young children. The eldest child, Guta Yachne, married Rabbi Shabsai Alpert, a brilliant *talmid* of the Mirrer Yeshiva and cousin of the Chofetz Chaim; R' Shabsai became the new Polunker Rav and undertook to support his widowed mother-in-law and her other children.

The Alperts had four children — Rita, Sarah, Frieda, and Nison. Those years between the two world wars were very hard for the Jews of Eastern Europe. With unbelievable prescience of the gathering storm that was later to engulf Europe, R' Shabsai told his beloved wife that the family should prepare to come to America. Twice he traveled to the United States to lay the groundwork, while his wife secretly prepared all the necessary documents. But before they could leave, World War II erupted. She lost contact with her husband in America, and all the documents for the trip were destroyed.

A lesser person would have despaired, but not Rebbetzin Alpert. The story of how she succeeded in escaping from Poland in wartime with four small children could be a thrilling book on its own, and demonstrates the resourcefulness, wisdom, and determination of this remarkable woman — and her faith in Hashem. Learning that Lithuania would have a degree of independence, she decided that if the family could get to Vilna, they could contact R' Shabsai in America. But crossing the border was extremely dangerous. Violators could be shot, jailed or turned back. By now it was Chanukah, December 1939. Further delay was equally perilous.

Young Nison, 11 or 12 years old at the time, would often eavesdrop at the Polunka police station, where he heard that the Nazis would soon be coming to Polunka. He told his mother, "Now is the time to go." They decided that despite the frigid weather, they would leave Motza'ei Shabbos, but they had to be careful not to arouse suspicion. All Shabbos and at the regular shul Melavah Malkah, they had to act nonchalant, knowing they had to catch a train later that night. They drew the shades as if all were going to sleep, put on three layers of clothing, left the samovar on and set the table. With nothing but the "the clothes on their backs" and one copy of *Shaarei Olam*, R' Shabsai's *sefer*, they abandoned their home. Seven-year old Frieda's last memory was seeing her grandmother standing in a corner of the kitchen with tears rolling down her cheeks and a handkerchief stuffed in her mouth to muffle the sounds of her sobbing.

They made it to Vilna, dodging border guards and gunfire, attack dogs and even land mines. R' Shabsai sent travel documents — but then the door was slammed shut when the Soviet Union occupied Lithuania. Undaunted, Rebbetzin Alpert traveled to Kaunas (Kovno) and obtained one of the first visas from the righteous Japanese diplomat Chiune Sugihara. With her four children in tow, the rebbetzin made the dangerous journey across Russia to Japan, to San Francisco and finally to the Lower East Side of New York.

Shortly after they arrived, R' Shabsai became ill. Rebbetzin Alpert devoted herself tirelessly to caring for her husband and children; to help support the family, she took in boarders, refugees and foster children. The Alpert home became a warm haven for all in need. As R' Shabsai's health deteriorated, she cared for him devotedly, with true *mesirus nefesh*, for decades. Those lessons in commitment, loyalty, love and dedication to *Yiddishkeit* remained with the Alpert children.

It was recognized very early on that Nison was an exceptionally bright young man. Though he came to America at age 12 with no knowledge of English, he graduated high school as valedictorian of his class. His extraordinary intellect was matched by an equally extraordinary devotion to learning. Nison *lived* for learning, first at Mesivta Tifereth Jerusalem and then as Rosh Kollel at Yeshivas Rabbi Yitzchak Elchonon [RIETS]. In later years his *gadlus* in Torah was recognized by many *baleh batim* when they asked him to accept the position as Rav of Agudath Israel of Long Island.

It was this combination of brilliance and *hasmadah* (diligence) that had attracted the eye of Rabbi Moshe Feinstein, one of the greatest sages of the generation, who took young Nison under his wing. R' Nison became R' Moshe's closest disciple. The two were inseparable, learning together, walking together, performing mitzvos together. The relationship of *rebbe* and *talmid* became like that of father and son. For example, as a teenager R' Nison intercepted a letter from MTJ saying that he could not attend classes if tuition was not paid. Knowing his family's precarious financial situation, Rav Nison was in tears and locked himself in his room. Upon hearing the story, R' Moshe came to the apartment, embraced Nison and said, "Come, let us go to yeshivah. For you there is no need for tuition." At the *bris* of Rav Nison's oldest son, Mordechai, R' Moshe said, "It is customary to say about a young *talmid chacham* that he is growing to become a *gaon*. Regarding R' Nison, I can say that he is *already* a *gaon*."

In fact, Rebbetzin Shima Feinstein, the wife of HaGaon Rav Moshe Feinstein, arranged the *shidduch* between Rav Nison and Zeldie

Scheinberg, daughter of the esteemed *gaon*, HaRav Chaim Pinchus שליט"א, and Rebbetzin Basya Scheinberg, שתחי'.

Rebbetzin Zeldie Alpert epitomizes the true essence of an *eishes chayil*. She dedicated her entire being to allow Rav Nison to devote his whole life to learning and disseminating Torah and being עוסק בצרכי ציבור באמונה.

Rav Nison, and תבלחט"א Rebbetzin Zeldie Alpert, were from the first couples to join the Kollel Torah V'horaah of HaGaon HaRav Moshe Feinstein. The life they led was truly a life of *bitachon* and *mesirus nefesh*. With her staunch *emunah* in the *Ribono Shel Olam*, Rebbetzin Alpert encouraged and supported her husband to remain totally immersed in Torah literally the entire day and night, fulfilling והגית בו יומם ולילה. Together they raised a family of true *bnei Torah*. Their youngest son, Yeshaya Mendel, who was *nifter* at a young age, was a true עבד ה' and was מקדש שם שמים in every aspect of his life. He exemplified an אב בחכמה ורך בשנים and had the great *zechus* of being משמש Rav Moshe as did his father. He was indeed *zocheh* to אריכות ימים, as his father would explain — days that were long and fulfilling with Torah and *yiras Shamayim*.

Rav Nison's *hasmadah* was legendary. He would often learn in a tiny unheated shul or on his small apartment balcony, saying, "Where it is bitter cold, I stand little chance of falling asleep." Whether on a crowded subway, in a car or taxi, even when his health was precarious, Rav Nison continued his laser-like concentration and steadfast focus on learning Torah.

Like his *rebbe*, R' Moshe, Rav Nison was warm and outgoing. His sharp wit and sense of humor were disarming and enlightening. Patient and caring, never judgmental, R' Nison never talked down to anyone. He was the embodiment of Torah and *derech eretz*, wrapped in a cloak of humility motivated by the *middah* of *emes*.

R' Nison was one of the founders of Peylim, an organization dedicated to preventing Israeli children from being torn from their religious heritage. Thanks to Peylim, many young Jews, particularly

Sefardim, were inspired to live Torah-true lives. If the honor of Torah was involved, Rav Nison abandoned his personal humility and protested publicly and vigorously. Though he suffered great personal tragedies — his father's debilitating illness, the loss of his son Shaya at the age of 19, the loss of his *rebbe*, R' Moshe, and his own illness — he always lived by one word: *bitachon*, trust in Hashem, as defined by the Chazon Ish. *Bitachon* does not mean that everything will happen as I want it. It means that whatever Hashem does is right and good.

Sharp, brilliant and analytical, R' Nison filled many notebooks with his original Torah thoughts. Numerous *sefarim* of his *chidushim* have thus been published, making a mark in the *olam HaTorah*. With this publication, countless Jews, now and in the future, will read and absorb these outstanding *divrei Torah*, fulfilling R' Nison's only desire — that more people learn and enjoy Torah.

Introduction

A number of years have passed since I published the two-volume Hebrew work, *Limudei Nison*, presenting a selection of my late father-in-law's זצ"ל thoughts on the weekly *parashah*. It is now my honor to present this English adaptation of much of that *sefer*. When I began work on the Hebrew edition, I was ambivalent, because the writings that he left behind were mere notes, and were not meant for print. Once published, however, the positive response was overwhelming.

Rabbanim and *bnei Torah* were constantly using the *sefer*, often quoting it in their *derashos*. The gratification of so many individuals using this *sefer*, in addition to the many in the broader Torah community requesting an English edition, eased my conscience, and showed that the publication of the work was a proper *kavod* to my father-in-law.

The task of producing an English version was much more daunting and difficult. In the Hebrew edition, the language and style were maintained as close to the original as possible. In the English version, although the themes and *chidushim* have been maintained, the individual pieces very often had to be adapted for purposes of clarity and stylistic integrity. I bear total responsibility for any errors or misunderstanding in the text. Although I present this work with trepidation, it is my fervent *tefillah* to Hashem that the lessons gleaned from this *sefer* will indeed be a *zechus* and an *ilui neshamah* for my revered father-in-law. In this English version, I have omitted the more intricate *lomdus* that was meant for the Talmudic scholar. For the convenience of people researching particular themes, or for speakers, I have provided an index of topics and have added titles to all of the selections.

Numerous individuals must be publicly acknowledged for helping to bring the present work to fruition:

- **Rabbi Mordechai Alpert,** who meticulously read the manuscript and whose valuable comments are incorporated in the final draft;

- **Rabbi Dovid Alpert,** who wrote the initial draft for this *sefer*, based on the Hebrew text and his personal recollections;

- **Rabbi Eliyahu Alpert,** who continues to inspire his students with his father's teachings;

- **Rabbi Dovid Hojda**, a gifted writer and *talmid chacham* who painstakingly adapted the manuscript for publication;

- **Rebbetzin Zeldie Alpert**, my mother-in-law, whose encouragement and *mesirus nefesh* for Torah during all the years of their married life made it possible for my father-in-law to become a great *talmid chacham*, *darshan*, and *posek*. She truly epitomizes the concept of *eishes chaver k'chaver*. As Reb Nison himself once paraphrased, "All of my Torah belongs to my wife."

Finally, I express boundless appreciation to my wife **Adina** for her endless devotion to our family, and for affording me precious time to be *marbitz Torah* to the best of my ability, to our wonderful Kehillah, Congregation Shaaray Tefillah, and beyond.

I would like to personally thank **Mr. & Mrs. Jay Tepper, Mr. & Mrs. Steve Zuckerman,** my aunt and uncle, **Frieda & Morris Lewinter** and my cousins, **Karen & Alan Mazurek; Mark & Vicki Lewinter; David & Linda Lewinter** and **Toby & Michael Parker,** for being the major benefactors of this work.

In addition to the primary dedicators, the generosity of many others helped to make this publication possible. They are: Samuel Abramson, Rabbi Kenneth Auman, Elchonon Berkowitz, Daniel Blum, Dr. Blum, Barry Braude, Asher Breatross, Dr. Reuven Bulka, Mark Caller, Shaya Chefetz, Cong. Beth Shalom, Dr. Larry Eisenberg, Reuven Escott, Yaakov Finkelstein, David Frost, Jennifer Ganz, Norman Gras, Dr. Marcus Hanflaing, Dr. Seymor Huberfeld, Richard Jedwab, Philip Kazlow, Steven Kerner, Dr. Mark Klapholz, Stuart Lavenda, Efrem Lifschitz, Joel Mael, Mr. and Mrs. Vicky Mayer, Steven Miretzky, Ira Press, David Richmond, Dr. Allen Schwartz, Jonathan Silver, Isaac Stillman, Rabbi J. Tropp, Dr. Y. Twersky, Dr. Allen Uliss, Joseph Vann, Dr. Howard J. Wasserman, Ronald Weiss, Tzvi Werzberger, Ira Wiznitzer, Y. I. of New Rochelle, Y. I. of Lawrence / Cedarhurst, Y. I. of West Hempstead, Rabbi David Zlatin, and חי׳ לאה בת ליבש אליהו, דוד נח בן יקותיאל יהודה, פייגע בת ר׳ יהושע.

I am extremely grateful to my dear friends Rabbi Meir Zlotowitz and Rabbi Nosson Scherman for recognizing the value of this *sefer* for the broad Torah community, thereby perpetuating the memory of Rabbi Nison Alpert for generations. I would also like to thank the staff of Mesorah Publications for their help in making this work possible. I would like to thank Mendy Herzberg for coordinating the project; Mrs. Mindy Stern for her editing of the manuscript; Rabbi Avrohom Yoseif Rosenberg and Mrs. Faygie Weinbaum for their proofreading of both the Hebrew and English texts; Mrs. Esther Feierstein, Sury Reinhold and Sara Rifka Spira for entering the many revisions and corrections; Shevy Grossman for paginating the book; and Eli Kroen for the beautiful cover design.

I am grateful to them all, and to Hashem Yisbarach for His constant blessings.

Rabbi David Weinberger

Lawrence, New York.
Tishrei 5767/September 2006

בראטשית

"הִנֵּה כְתוּבָה עַל סֵפֶר הַיָשָׁר" (שמואל ב א:יח) – מַאי סֵפֶר הַיָשָׁר? אָמַר
רַבִּי חִיָּיא בַּר אַבָּא אָמַר רַבִּי יוֹחָנָן: זֶה סֵפֶר אַבְרָהָם יִצְחָק וְיַעֲקֹב שֶׁנִּקְרְאוּ
יְשָׁרִים, דִּכְתִיב בְּהוּ: (במדבר כג:י) "תָּמֹת נַפְשִׁי מוֹת יְשָׁרִים ..."

*"Behold this is written in the Sefer HaYashar" (II
Shmuel 1:18) — What is Sefer HaYashar? (In other
words, what sefer is it referring to?) R' Chiya bar
Abba said in the name of R' Yochanan: It is the Sefer
of Avraham, Yitzchak, and Yaakov, who were called
"yesharim," as it says regarding them (Bamidbar 23:10):
"May my soul die the death of the upright" (מוֹת יְשָׁרִים)
(Avodah Zarah 25a).*

Sefer Bereishis is also known as *Sefer HaYashar*, the Book of
Uprightness. One source for this idea is the verse in Shmuel
cited above, which carries a reference to something that is
"written in the *Sefer HaYashar*." Commentators to that verse
say that this *Sefer HaYashar* is *Sefer Bereishis*. The Gemara cited

above explains that *Bereishis* acquired this name by virtue of its being the book of the *Avos*, who were themselves known as *"yesharim."*

A hint to this idea can be found simply by rearranging the letters of the word בראשית. The letters can be reordered to read ישר אבת, *Yashar Avos.*

The most famous exposition of why *Sefer Bereishis* is called *Sefer HaYashar* is found in *Haamek Davar* by Rabbi Naftali Tzvi Yehudah Berlin, the *Netziv*, in its introduction to *Sefer Bereishis.*

I would like to expand upon this idea as well.

In order to do so, I would like to examine *Rashi's* very first comment to *Sefer Bereishis.*

He asks why the Torah begins with the story of Creation rather than with Israel's first commandment (*Shemos* 12:2): *This month shall be for you ... Rashi* cites the answer of R' Yitzchak, who said that the Torah began this way in order to demonstrate the Jewish people's right to Eretz Yisrael. When the nations accuse the Jews of theft, they can reply that Hashem, Who created the world, first gave Eretz Yisrael to the Canaanites. When they proved themselves unworthy, He took it from them and gave it to the Jews.

Apparently, R' Yitzchak would agree that the story of Creation belongs in the Torah; he wonders only why it was placed at the very beginning.

I find this answer of R' Yitzchak difficult to understand. Fine, let us say that the narrative of Creation had to appear in the Torah to refute the accusations of the nations, but the question remains — why did it have to come first? Once it is related in the Torah, it's in the Torah — and could then be pointed to, to counter any and all claims. It could be used no matter where it was to be found: beginning, middle, or end of the Torah.

As a way of resolving this difficulty, let us consider the well-known Mishnah (*Avos* 5:1) that says that the world was created with ten utterances. The Mishnah says that it could have been created with only one, but was created with ten in order to punish the wicked (who seek to destroy the world) and reward the righteous (who sustain the world). This seems to be saying that, while it would have been possible to create the world with one utterance, an extra nine were used so that more punishment would come to those who destroy Hashem's world. Why should they deserve this extra punishment, though? Does a shoemaker deserve ten day's pay when his job could have been completed in one?

Furthermore, the number ten does not seem quite accurate. The first utterance, וַיֹּאמֶר... יְהִי אוֹר , is followed by eight more, not nine. *Sefer Tehillim* (33:6), however, speaks of a tenth: בִּדְבַר ה' שָׁמַיִם נַעֲשׂוּ וּבְרוּחַ פִּיו כָּל צְבָאָם, *By the word of Hashem the heavens were made, and by the breath of His mouth all their hosts.* In other words, another utterance (not recorded) preceded the creation of light.

Maharsha (*Maseches Shabbos*) explains that because nothing existed prior to this first act of Creation (the world was created *ex nihilo* — *Yeish MeiAyin*), this *dibbur* could not have been heard. In other words, since there was nothing there, no thing or person could hear it. Once there were other entities, Hashem could say (in their presence), "Let there be light ... let there be a firmament, let the earth produce vegetation, etc."

We have now accounted for how there could have been ten utterances, although the Torah records only nine. And we see that the presence of Heaven and Earth gave license to Hashem's beginning to bring into creation all the subsequent forms of life, as expressed in the remaining utterances. They must therefore have been closely related — perhaps to the extent that one could say that the potential for all subsequent life forms was latent within the first created things.

Only a universe full of water was visible at first, with nothing resembling flora, fauna, or even light. It was a universe described as בֹּהוּ, *nothingness.* That בֹּהוּ, however, was really בּוֹ הוּא, meaning that the potential to become a world was in it.

And one could say that the world's potentiality was immeasurably greater than its actuality at that point, as we see from the many times that Hashem caused that nothingness to produce things, namely light, vegetation, birds, and so on. Further, a moment's reflection will show that the latent potentiality in the world is still far greater than the world that actually exists.

Thus the wicked "who destroy the world that was created with ten utterances" are punished not only for destroying the actual world we see, but also for destroying the far greater potentiality that may yet come into existence. Similarly, the righteous are rewarded not only for sustaining the existing world, but also for all the good that is destined to flourish in that world.

Let us now return to our earlier puzzlement over R' Yitzchak's question. We understood him to be conceding that, while it would have been more appropriate for the Torah to have begun with Yisrael's first mitzvah, it began instead with the account of Creation so that Israel could counter the nations' charge that Eretz Yisrael was stolen from them. While acknowledging the importance of countering the nations' claim, we wondered why their claim could not have been countered just as easily had the Creation story appeared anwhere else in the Torah. As we said, what difference would it make where it is positioned, as long as we could show that it appears.

I believe that we now have an answer. It is to be found in *Sefer Tehillim* (111:6): כֹּחַ מַעֲשָׂיו הִגִּיד לְעַמּוֹ לָתֵת לָהֶם נַחֲלַת גּוֹיִם, *The strength of His works He declared to His nation, to give them the heritage of the peoples.*

The Hebrew word כֹּחַ translates as "strength," just as we translated it in the above verse. However, it also translates as "potential."

Yes, the Torah's mitzvos are primary; they deserve to come first. However, before one can take the Torah into his life, he must first know of the כֹּחַ (the "strength," the "potential") that resides both within the Creation and within himself. His life in this world could be like *Gan Eden.* But, as in the narrative of *Gan Eden,* he has within himself the power, the כֹּחַ, through his wrongful deeds, to destroy it all.

Everything.

He has the כֹּחַ to sink to the lowest depths of depravity and corruption, to descend to the perversity of Sodom.

The converse is true as well: He can also strive to emulate the trait of Abraham, that of *chessed*, kindness.

Man has within himself the potential for all of the above.

Although his nature is to be influenced by his surroundings, it is within man's ability to fight against the world and emerge victorious, as did Abraham.

First, though, he must be aware of his latent כֹּחַ. That is a lesson he learns from *Ma'aseh Bereishis*. And that is why *Ma'aseh Bereishis* had to come first. And that is why R' Yitzchak, in his answer, quoted the verse in *Tehillim*: *The כֹּחַ of His works He declared to His nation.*

Sefer Bereishis teaches us the "כֹּחַ," the *potential* of our actions: We have within ourselves the כֹּחַ to make the world into a good place or a bad one. The peoples who occupied the Land of Canaan before us fell into such decadence that the Land vomited them out. It was then given to us, those who would observe the Torah.

בְּרֵאשִׁית בָּרָא אֱלֹהִים אֵת הַשָּׁמַיִם וְאֵת הָאָרֶץ
In the beginning of God's creating the heavens and the earth (1:1).

ר' אָסָא אוֹמֵר כ"ו דּוֹרוֹת הָיָה אָלֶ"ף קוֹרֵא תִגָּר לִפְנֵי הקב"ה לוֹמַר אֲנִי רִאשׁוֹן שֶׁל אוֹתִיּוֹת וְלֹא בָרָאתָ בִּי אֶת הָעוֹלָם אֶלָּא בְּבֵי"ת "בְּרֵאשִׁית בָּרָא אֱלֹהִים". אָמַר לוֹ הקב"ה חַיֶּיךָ שֶׁאֲנִי פּוֹרֵעַ לְךָ תּוֹרָה נִבְרֵאת לְפָנַי עַד שֶׁלֹּא נִבְרָא הָעוֹלָם אַלְפַּיִם שָׁנָה וּכְשֶׁאָבוֹא לִיתֵּן תּוֹרָה לְיִשְׂרָאֵל אֵינִי פוֹתֵחַ אֶלָּא בָּךְ שֶׁנֶּאֱמַר "אָנֹכִי ה' אֱלֹהֶיךָ" (יַלְקוּט שמעוני תּוֹרָה פָּרָשָׁה יִתְרוֹ).

his Midrash presents the image of the letter *aleph* questioning Hashem: "I am the first letter of the alphabet, yet, the world was created with a *beis* — בְּרֵאשִׁית בָּרָא אֱלֹהִים אֵת הַשָּׁמַיִם וְאֵת הָאָרֶץ. Why was I not given the privilege of being the first letter of the first word with which You created the world?"

Hashem answers, "You are right, but wait: It is true that I created the world with בְּרֵאשִׁית. But before I created the world, I created the Torah. When I give the Torah to the Jewish people, the Ten Commandments will begin with none other than yourself, as it says: אָנֹכִי ה' אֱלֹהֶיךָ" (*Shemos* 20:2).

Let us take another look at this encounter. And, let us examine the implications of Hashem's having used *beis* when He created the world, but when giving the Torah, He began instead with *aleph*.

Beis is *two*. *Two* signifies duality and opposites: man and woman, light and darkness, day and night, life and death, righteous and wicked.

By creating the world with the letter that represents an entity and its opposite, Hashem built into Creation from its outset the reality of free will. Choice is always there for us.

Our goal, however, is to achieve the *aleph*, that is, to fully acknowledge אָנֹכִי ה' אֱלֹהֶיךָ and to recognize that there is no life other than Torah and mitzvos.

And that is why it says, וַיְהִי עֶרֶב וַיְהִי בֹקֶר יוֹם אֶחָד, *And there was evening and there was morning, one day* (*Bereishis* 1:5). True, there is evening. And, there is morning. Two opposites.

Choice.

But, the goal is יוֹם אֶחָד, *one* day.

Perhaps we can now see a reason for the Torah's having commanded a father to bring his son into the Covenant of Abraham when the child is eight days old, at a stage when he cannot possibly comprehend what is being done with him.

Yes, there is free choice — the power to choose between the bad and the good. And that is where we start. But, every Jew is obligated to lead his fellow Jew toward the right path, that of אָנֹכִי.

And this holds true especially with regard to a father and his son. And, just as the father is commanded to bring his son into the Covenant, so must each of us, as well, strive to convince his brethren to follow the mitzvos, the path of recognizing אָנֹכִי.

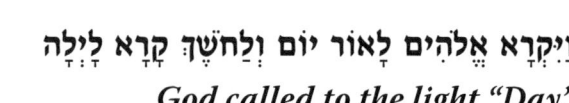

וַיִּקְרָא אֱלֹהִים לָאוֹר יוֹם וְלַחֹשֶׁךְ קָרָא לָיְלָה
God called to the light "Day,"
and to the darkness, He called "Night" (1:5).

אָ"ר אֶלְעָזָר לְעוֹלָם אֵין הקב"ה מְיַחֵד שְׁמוֹ עַל הָרָעָה אֶלָּא עַל הַטּוֹבָה, "וַיִּקְרָא אֱלֹהִים לָאוֹר יוֹם וְלַחֹשֶׁךְ קָרָא אֱלֹהִים לָיְלָה" אֵין כְּתִיב כַּאן, אֶלָּא "וְלַחֹשֶׁךְ קָרָא לָיְלָה" (בְּרֵאשִׁית רַבָּה פ' ג').

R' Elazar said: Hashem does not link His Name with the "bad," but only with the "good." It does not say: "God called the light 'Day,' and God called the darkness 'Night.'" It says only, " ... and the darkness He called 'Night'" (Bereishis Rabbah 3:6).

Bereishis Rabbah points out that God called the light "Day," but, when it came to naming the night, He did not use His Name. Instead, the verse merely states, ... *and the darkness He called "Night."* R' Elazar gives a reason: Hashem does not wish to link His Name with something that is "bad."

And darkness, apparently, is "bad."

This demands clarification. For, if God does not wish to have His Name linked with "bad" — and darkness, according to the Midrash, is "bad" — then why do we use His Name to bless the darkness every evening at *Maariv*? [We say, "Blessed are You ... Who by His word brings on evenings ... He causes day to pass and brings night."

And why does the Mishnah in *Berachos* (9:5) say: חַיָּיב אָדָם לְבָרֵךְ עַל הָרָעָה כְּשֵׁם שֶׁהוּא מְבָרֵךְ עַל הַטּוֹבָה, *One is "required" to make a blessing on the "bad" things just as on the "good" things?* If Hashem does not wish to have His Name associated with "bad," why would we do so anyway?

Perhaps the following might provide us with an answer:

Sifri to *Parashas Beha'aloscha* writes on the verse, אֶסְפָה לִּי שִׁבְעִים אִישׁ מִזִּקְנֵי יִשְׂרָאֵל, *Gather for Me seventy men from the elders of Israel* (*Bamidbar* 11:16) that wherever Hashem says לִי, *to Me,* its meaning is "for My Name, which endures for ever and ever," as in the verses, וְעָשׂוּ לִי מִקְדָּשׁ, *They shall make for Me a sanctuary* (*Shemos* 25:8), and קַדֶּשׁ לִי כָל בְּכוֹר, *Sanctify for Me every firstborn* (ibid. 13:2), among many other examples.

Certain things are directly associated with the Name of Hashem: the *Beis HaMikdash*, Kohanim, firstborn, and the Great Sanhedrin — which interprets the Torah of Hashem. And, we are commanded to accept their interpretations as if we had heard them directly from Hashem at Har Sinai.

Now, we also know that the Hebrew names the Torah assigns to things are not arbitrary and do not merely describe the items. Rather, they express their inner meaning and character.

We can now apply this to suggesting a way of understanding the association made by R' Elazar in *Bereishis Rabbah* between Hashem's Name and the the light created during Creation.

We might add that this association with the light created during Creation applies equally to spiritual light, the light of Torah and mitzvos, as it says כִּי נֵר מִצְוָה וְתוֹרָה אוֹר, *For a mitzvah is like a candle and Torah is light* (*Mishlei* 6:23). This physical light is the reflection of a spiritual light with which Hashem associates His Name.

And, anything called by His Name will, just like the Name Itself, remain for eternity.

On the other hand, certain things are created for the benefit of man, but do not reflect Hashem's essence, as we see in some of the

Midrashic readings of וַיַּרְא אֱלֹהִים אֶת כָּל אֲשֶׁר עָשָׂה וְהִנֵּה טוֹב מְאֹד, *And God saw* all *that He had made, and behold it was very good* (1:31). The word כָּל, *all,* is understood to intentionally include even the things with which He does not associate His Name, and therefore will not be eternal. They serve only temporary and transient roles.

Darkness would fall into that category, because in the World to Come the light of the moon will be likened to the light of the sun and the light of the sun will be seven times as powerful (see *Yeshayah* 30:26). Hashem will reveal the אוֹר הַגָּנוּז, *the hidden light,* and that light will overwhelm the darkness.

This applies only to the World to Come. But this world requires the darkness and the bad. Thus, it is incumbent upon us to bless them both. [As we say in the first of the Blessings of the *Shema,* "Blessed are You … Who forms light and creates darkness … "]

Nonetheless, Hashem does not associate His Name with these things. Therefore, Scripture says that *God called the light "Day"* but it does not say that God called the darkness "Night."

This tells us that "night" — and the "bad" — will, unlike His Name, be neither permanent nor eternal.

וַיִּקְרָא אֱלֹהִים לַיַּבָּשָׁה אֶרֶץ
God called to the dry land "Earth" (1:10).

The verse says that God gave the name *"Eretz"* (earth) to the *yabashah* (dry land). Why did He feel a need to rename the *yabashah*? Was there something not suitable about its name?

We have already learned that when God gives something its name, He tells us its nature, thereby revealing its true purpose and impact. It thus becomes essential that each thing be called by its appropriate name, the one that best describes its essential purpose. Any particular item might have multiple functions, but we could assume that certain ones are essential and others, subordinate.

It is incumbent upon us to learn to recognize the difference.

The word יַבָּשָׁה, *dry land,* appears to be related to the word יִשּׁוּב, *settlement.* Both contain the same letters, only in slightly different order. The Hebrew language has multiple examples of word pairs that use two different arrangements of the same letters and mean the same thing. [E.g., כֶּשֶׂב=כֶּבֶשׂ, שִׂמְלָה=שַׂלְמָה.]

After all, the world was created to be settled (יִשּׁוּב), and the emergence of dry land (יַבָּשָׁה) made human settlement possible. יַבָּשָׁה would therefore seem to be a very appropriate name for the earth.

So, why, then, was it given the name *"Eretz"*?

Let us suggest the following: While dry land, meaning suitable location, is certainly *one* prerequisite for human habitation, it is not the only one. Enormous amounts of continuous human effort are also required to develop and build the earth.

The word אֶרֶץ suggests this. It is similar to the words רָצוֹא, *running,* and רָצוֹן, *will.*

Our verse tells us וַיִּקְרָא אֱלֹהִים לַיַּבָּשָׁה אֶרֶץ, *God called to the dry land "Eretz."* What's the significance? It is saying that by doing this, by taking the dry land and calling it *"Eretz,"* Hashem was thereby taking the dry land's latent potential and actualizing it. "אֶרֶץ" is the process of "רָצוֹא," which we have translated as "running." Hashem was putting into the *yabashah* the next necessary process, the one that would truly allow human habitation. This would be the "running," the energy to do the רָצוֹן of Hashem.

This idea is elaborated upon in *Bereishis Rabbah 5*:

"וַיִּקְרָא אֱלֹהִים לַיַּבָּשָׁה אֶרֶץ", לָמָּה נִקְרָא שְׁמָהּ אֶרֶץ, שֶׁרָצְתָה לַעֲשׂוֹת רְצוֹן קוֹנָהּ

Why is the land called "אֶרֶץ"? Because it wanted (רָצְתָה) to do the will (רָצוֹן) of its Maker.

Now, since Man (אָדָם) was created from earth , (אֲדָמָה) he, like the earth, would have those same powers of רִיצָה and רָצוֹן.

And, through the correct use of these powers, he could then turn the primeval nothingness — תֹּהוּ — into inhabited settlement — יִשּׁוּב — for Mankind.

The above idea could also provide us with an insight into the blessing that we make over bread, בָּרוּךְ אַתָּה ה' ... הַמּוֹצִיא לֶחֶם מִן הָאָרֶץ, *Blessed are You, Hashem ... Who brings forth bread from the earth.* Is it the *bread* that is brought forth from the earth? Isn't it rather the wheat? And, there are so many steps and so much effort that must be expended to turn the raw wheat into bread! It must be cut, put into sheaves, threshed, winnowed, ground, kneaded, baked, etc.

The answer is as we have already suggested: The power put by Hashem into אֶרֶץ, namely רִיצָה and רָצוֹן (*active endeavor* as well as *desire*), passed on to אָדָם by virtue of his being formed from the אֲדָמָה, is the very thing that makes the production of bread possible.

It is absolutely appropriate, therefore, for us to say, just as is stated in the blessing, הַמּוֹצִיא לֶחֶם מִן הָאָרֶץ, *Who brings forth bread from the* אֶרֶץ.

<hr>

וַיֹּאמֶר אֱלֹהִים נַעֲשֶׂה אָדָם בְּצַלְמֵנוּ
God said, "Let us make man" (1:26).

A שׁוֹר, an *ox*, is known as a שׁוֹר already from the day it is born. Man, however, is not. What accounts for this difference? Perhaps the following:

Generally, an animal is fully formed at birth. Man, however, is not. Rather, he is born with a goal — the goal of actualizing his potential. He must develop his abilities, as best as he can, to their ultimate. This will be his lifelong task.

אָמַר רַבִּי אָבִין הַלֵּוִי: הַנִּפְטָר מֵחֲבֵרוֹ אַל יֹאמַר לוֹ לֵךְ בְּשָׁלוֹם, אֶלָּא לֵךְ
לְשָׁלוֹם. שֶׁהֲרֵי יִתְרוֹ שֶׁאָמַר לוֹ לְמֹשֶׁה "לֵךְ לְשָׁלוֹם" עָלָה וְהִצְלִיחַ; דָּוִד
שֶׁאָמַר לוֹ לְאַבְשָׁלוֹם "לֵךְ בְּשָׁלוֹם", הָלַךְ וְנִתְלָה.

R' Avin HaLevi said: When taking leave of one's fellow, one should not say, "לֵךְ בְּשָׁלוֹם, Go in peace," but rather, "לֵךְ לְשָׁלוֹם, Go to peace." For behold, Yisro said to Moses, "לֵךְ לְשָׁלוֹם" (Shemos 4:18), and Moses went "up," to great success. David said to Absalom, "לֵךְ בְּשָׁלוֹם" (II Samuel 15:9), and Absalom went on to be hanged (Berachos 64a).

Let us understand this as follows:

שָׁלוֹם, *Shalom,* is translated as "peace," but its root is שלם, which also means "complete."

We can now understand this Gemara in a new way, a way that sheds light on the question we originally asked, namely, about the distinction between Man and beasts, specifically as to the significance of Man's not being born fully formed.

Man must always keep himself fully convinced that he has not yet reached the level of *shleimus* (completion). Rather than feel self-satisfied, he should always strive to advance forward, step after step, on the path toward *shalom* in its second meaning, which is שָׁלֵם, *complete.*

This is a "completion" that has not yet been reached, and, in reality, never *will* be reached. Still, it must remain one's constant target.

When one realizes that he has "made it," that he is already "there," he will, in truth, have just announced the beginning of his own decline.

We can now see a deeper meaning in Hashem's pronouncement, "Let us *make* Man": He was proclaiming that Man must be *made,* or rather *remade.* He requires remaking, every day, by striving for perfection, by aspiring to fulfill his personal role within Creation.

A verse from *Iyov* (11:12) is quite pertinent to this approach: וְעַיִר פֶּרֶא אָדָם יִוָּלֵד, *Let one who is like a wild ass be reborn as a man. Ralbag* comments: ר"ל שֶׁהוּא נִמְשַׁל כַּבְּהֵמוֹת בְּעֵת הִוָּלְדוֹ, *That is to say, he is compared to the beasts at the moment he is born.*

This means that his *yetzer hara*, his evil inclination, is already within him from the moment that he first emerges into this world. If so, how is he to overcome it? How will he become who he needs to be?

It might be quite difficult, if not impossible, for him to achieve this on his own. Therefore, our verse reads, נַעֲשֶׂה, "*Let us make man.*" Note that "us" is plural.

Hashem is calling out to those who will surround this child — parents, teachers, and friends — telling them that this must be a joint endeavor, a joint responsibility. We are all called upon by Hashem; in fact, we could even consider ourselves His agents.

We must help this child along, help to *make* him an אָדָם, one who will advance along the path that is straight and good, the one that will lead to his ultimately becoming a great man.

וַיֹּאמֶר אֱלֹהִים הִנֵּה נָתַתִּי לָכֶם אֶת כָּל עֵשֶׂב
זֹרֵעַ זֶרַע אֲשֶׁר עַל פְּנֵי כָל הָאָרֶץ וְאֶת כָּל הָעֵץ
אֲשֶׁר בּוֹ פְרִי עֵץ זֹרֵעַ זָרַע לָכֶם יִהְיֶה לְאָכְלָה.
וּלְכָל חַיַּת הָאָרֶץ וּלְכָל עוֹף הַשָּׁמַיִם וּלְכֹל רוֹמֵשׂ עַל הָאָרֶץ
אֲשֶׁר בּוֹ נֶפֶשׁ חַיָּה אֶת כָּל יֶרֶק עֵשֶׂב לְאָכְלָה וַיְהִי כֵן

*God said, "Behold, I have given to you all
herbage yielding seed that is on the surface of
the entire earth, and every tree that has seed-
yielding fruit; it shall be to you for food. And to
every beast of the earth, to every bird of the sky,
and to everything that moves on the earth, within
which there is a living soul, all herbal greenery is
for food." And it was so (1:29,30).*

רש״י: לָכֶם יִהְיֶה לְאָכְלָה. וּלְכָל חַיַּת הָאָרֶץ – הִשְׁוָה לָהֶם הַכָּתוּב
בְּהֵמוֹת וְחַיּוֹת לְמַאֲכָל, וְלֹא הִרְשָׁה לְאָדָם וּלְאִשְׁתּוֹ לְהָמִית בְּרִיָּה
וְלֶאֱכֹל בָּשָׂר, אַךְ כָּל יֶרֶק עֵשֶׂב יֹאכְלוּ יַחַד כֻּלָּם, וּכְשֶׁבָּאוּ בְּנֵי נֹחַ הִתִּיר
לָהֶם בָּשָׂר, שֶׁנֶּאֱמַר (לְהַלָּן ט:ג) כָּל רֶמֶשׂ אֲשֶׁר הוּא חַי וְגו׳ כְּיֶרֶק עֵשֶׂב
שֶׁהִתַּרְתִּי לְאָדָם הָרִאשׁוֹן, נָמַתִּי לָכֶם אֶת כֹּל.

RASHI: IT SHALL BE TO YOU FOR FOOD. AND TO
EVERY BEAST OF THE FIELD — *He made animals and
beasts equal to them for food and He did not permit
Adam and his wife to put a creature to death and to
eat its meat. But any greenery, all of them will eat in
common. When the sons of Noah came (after having
survived the Flood), He allowed them meat, as it says
(9:3): "Every moving thing that lives etc., like herbal
greenery, which I allowed Adam, the first man, I give
you everything."*

---

*R*ashi explains that originally, at the time of Creation, both man and beast were allowed to eat greenery, but forbidden to kill animals for food. [According to *Mizrachi, Rashi* is saying that man was forbidden only to kill animals for food, but would be permitted to eat the meat of an animal that had died on its own.] This changed after the Flood, when the prohibition against killing animals was lifted. While *Rashi* tells us of the chronology, he does not seem to address the reason why the sons of Noah were permitted to kill wild animals and birds for food, while Adam was not.

Radak, one of the early Rishonim, offers the following:

> *They were not given permission to eat meat until after the Flood, but I don't know why. Maybe, because it was absolutely known to Him that the Flood would happen and that Noah would save, along with himself, the other living things. Hashem therefore said that He would give them to him, in exchange for his effort on their behalf. For He does not withhold reward from any of His creatures. How much more so from man.*

While *Rashi* seems to hold that Adam was prohibited only to kill animals for food, but allowed to eat the meat of those that had already died, *Radak* seems to be troubled as to why Adam would have been prohibited from eating the meat of all animals and birds, irrespective of whether he had killed them or not (see *Ramban*). And that is the question he addresses in his answer.

We would like to take *Radak's* question and suggest a different answer.

We know that Hashem's prohibitions are always tailored to the nature of the ones to whom they apply. The greater the power that someone has, the greater is the need to impose restraints on his use of it.

A king is forbidden to amass money, horses, or wives in excessive amounts, even though these things are permitted (though hardly encouraged) to ordinary people. Similarly, a king is commanded to personally write two *Sifrei Torah* and read from them every day of this life. The Torah, in *Devarim* 17:19-20, tells us why: ... לְמַעַן יִלְמַד לְיִרְאָה אֶת ה' אֱלֹהָיו לִשְׁמֹר אֶת כָּל דִּבְרֵי הַתּוֹרָה הַזֹּאת וְאֶת הַחֻקִּים הָאֵלֶּה לַעֲשֹׂתָם. ... לְבִלְתִּי רוּם לְבָבוֹ מֵאֶחָיו וּלְבִלְתִּי סוּר מִן הַמִּצְוָה יָמִין וּשְׂמֹאול, *so that he will learn to fear Hashem, his God, to observe all the words of this Torah and these decrees, to perform them, so that his heart does not become haughty over his brethren and not turn from the commandment right or left.*

Ordinary men would not need this level of checks and balances; but the king would, for Hashem felt that his added powers might lead to his straying from the correct path.

Adam was commanded to conquer the earth and to rule over all its creatures, whether they lived in the air, on land, or at sea. He was given the powers that would be commensurate with his task.

However, just as the Torah tells us that the added powers of the king necessitated additional checks and balances, lest these greater powers lead him astray, so too checks and balances needed to be imposed on Adam, so that his great powers would be used only to benefit the creatures of the world — and not to needlessly dominate them.

This is why it was necessary to forbid him from killing or eating any animal; they possess a נֶפֶשׁ חַיָּה, a *living soul*. Anything that had any semblance of the נֶפֶשׁ הָאָדָם, *the soul of man*, could not be eaten or killed. Only vegetation, which had no soul at all, would be permitted.

After the Flood, however, man's powers, as well as the control over the world that these powers gave him, were curtailed. His lifespan was diminished and he even needed an assurance that he not fear wild animals.

With these diminished powers, the prohibition against killing animals was no longer necessary. He could now be permitted to do so, according to his needs. The prohibition against eating the limb of a living animal would suffice as a reminder that he not have an inflated sense of the extent of his own dominion.

As man changed, so did the checks and balances.

We can apply the above thought in understanding why the Torah gives us the power to make vows and oaths. These serve as a means of protecting ourselves from situations that we recognize as being particularly fraught with temptation, every individual knowing for himself what holds the greatest appeal.

The Sages said (see *Rashi* on *Bamidbar* 6:2) that someone who sees a *sotah*, a woman proven by the test of the bitter waters to have been unfaithful to her husband, will then decide to swear off intoxicating wine.

Contemplation of that sight (albeit that he was not the one caught up in that particular temptation) will cause him to realize how close he, too, could have come to sinning under similar circumstances.

This, then, is a lesson for us all; each of us must take stock of the trials and temptations of his own time, and — recognize his own unique weaknesses.

Then each individual must decide, honestly and realistically, what limits and restraints he might best impose upon himself in order to resist the temptations.

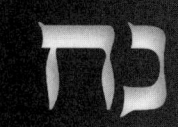

נֹחַ

אֵלֶּה תּוֹלְדֹת נֹחַ נֹחַ אִישׁ צַדִּיק
תָּמִים הָיָה בְּדֹרֹתָיו אֶת הָאֱלֹהִים הִתְהַלֶּךְ נֹחַ
These are the offspring of Noah, Noah was
a righteous man, perfect in his generations.
Noah walked with God (6:9).

W hy did the Torah write the name "Noah" three times in this
verse, when once would seem to have been sufficient?

Perhaps we can suggest the following: Every individual
has three different facets: the one that he chooses to show the world,
the one he chooses to show Hashem, and — the true self as it exists
on its deepest level.

The Torah here testifies that Noah was consistent, serving Hashem with all three facets, and truly was righteous and "straight"
with Hashem.

וַיְשַׁלַּח אֶת הָעֹרֵב וַיֵּצֵא יָצוֹא וָשׁוֹב עַד יְבֹשֶׁת הַמַּיִם מֵעַל הָאָרֶץ

He sent out a raven, and it kept going and returning until the drying of the waters from upon the face of the earth (8:7).

... מִכָּל בְּהֵמָה חַיָּה וְעוֹף שֶׁיֵּשׁ כָּאן אֵין אַתָּה מְשַׁלֵּחַ אֶלָּא לִי? אָמַר לוֹ: מַה צּוֹרֶךְ לְעוֹלָם בָּךְ – לֹא לַאֲכִילָה, לֹא לְקָרְבָּן. רַבִּי בֶּרֶכְיָה בְּשֵׁם רַבִּי אַבָּא בַּר כַּהֲנָא אָמַר: אָמַר לוֹ הַקָּדוֹשׁ בָּרוּךְ הוּא: קַבְּלוֹ, שֶׁעָתִיד הָעוֹלָם לְהִצְטָרֵךְ לוֹ. אָמַר לוֹ: אֵימָתַי? אָמַר לוֹ: "עַד יְבֹשֶׁת הַמַּיִם מֵעַל הָאָרֶץ", עָתִיד צַדִּיק אֶחָד לַעֲמוֹד וּלְיַיבֵּשׁ אֶת הָעוֹלָם וַאֲנִי מַצְרִיכוֹ לוֹ. הֲדָא הוּא דִכְתִיב (מלכים א:יז): "וְהָעוֹרְבִים מְבִיאִים לוֹ לֶחֶם וּבָשָׂר בַּבֹּקֶר וְלֶחֶם וּבָשָׂר בָּעֶרֶב" ... (בראשית רבה [וילנא] פרשה לג).

he Midrash (*Bereishis Rabbah* 33:5) relates that the raven boasted to Noah, "Of all the beasts and fowl here, I'm the only one you send."

"What use are you to the world," retorted Noah. "You're not fit for eating or for bringing as an offering."

Said Hashem to Noah, "There will come a time when the world will need the raven."

"When will that be?" Noah asked.

"There will be a time when water will dry up from the earth. A *tzaddik* [the prophet Eliyahu] will arise and cause a drought in the world and I will make him dependent on the raven, as the verse (*I Melachim* 17:6) says: *The ravens bring him bread and meat in the morning and bread and meat in the evening.*"

I have seen an interpretation of this Midrash that says that Noah's real objection to the raven was because it is a symbol of cruelty (supposedly, the raven abandons its young), and Noah felt that the trait of cruelty is of no use to the world. Once we see that the ravens embody cruelty, and since they are fit neither for food nor for a *korban*, we can conclude that there is no use for them at all.

In the case of most undesirable traits, there is room to say that we *do* benefit from them. Think of all the great public works whose existence is purely the result of some leader's excessive pride or greed.

When it comes to cruelty, though, what good does it do?

Therefore, when there is a *tzaddik* who dedicates himself to defending the honor of Hashem and to instilling fear of Him in the world, even cruel ravens are transformed into doers of kindness. In other words, they are seen as useful only *after* their trait of cruelty has been obliterated.

That is the basic idea behind the approach of this Midrash.

I would like to add a few thoughts of my own.

My question is this: Given that it was necessary for Eliyahu to be brought bread and meat, why, from among all of His creatures, did Hashem choose the raven? After all, שְׁלוּחִים הַרְבֵּה יֵשׁ לַמָּקוֹם, Hashem has many agents.

Why, then, the raven?

Perhaps it was in order to teach a lesson to mankind: There is no trait so evil or so fixed that it cannot be repaired and transformed.

How is that possible?

It all has to do with one's goals. In other words, it has to do with what one desires to do, with how one wishes to use a particular trait. Will it be for the good, toward service of Hashem? Or will it be for the bad, to attempt to defeat His wishes.

In the case of Eliyahu, the trait of cruelty was used for Man's ultimate benefit: Eliyahu caused a drought so that idolatrous beliefs would be uprooted and the Jews would realize that Hashem Alone rules the world. Although one could say that this was quite cruel, in that it caused great suffering and pain, Eliyahu's goals were entirely selfless and praiseworthy.

And they were appropriate. It could be compared to the work of a surgeon. He wishes to save the entire body. In order to do so, though, he must cut into the flesh and sometimes even needs to amputate a limb.

In other words, Elihayu demonstrated how even cruelty can be harnessed toward furthering the glory of Hashem.

And that is why the raven, specifically the raven, was chosen to be at his service. It was the raven, the legendary embodiment of cruelty, that would bring him his food and keep him alive.

And that was most fitting, so that we could learn this important lesson.

In other words, while it is certainly true that Hashem has many agents, in this case, the raven was the best choice.

―――

וַיֹּאמֶר ה' אֶל לִבּוֹ לֹא אֹסִף לְקַלֵּל עוֹד אֶת הָאֲדָמָה ...
בַּעֲבוּר הָאָדָם כִּי יֵצֶר לֵב הָאָדָם רַע מִנְּעֻרָיו
וְלֹא אֹסִף עוֹד לְהַכּוֹת אֶת כָּל חַי כַּאֲשֶׁר עָשִׂיתִי.

... and Hashem said in His heart:
I will not continue to curse again the ground
because of man, since the imagery of man's heart
is evil from his youth; nor will I again continue to
smite every living being, as I have done (8:21).

Perhaps the above verse hints at what we are trying to say. Perhaps Hashem is saying here that the time has now come for words that will be soft and reassuring, speech that will have the best chance of reaching man's heart.

Possibly, we can go even a step further — we can say that it is as if, in empathy, He needed to comfort Himself, as fulfillment of עִמּוֹ אָנֹכִי בְצָרָה, *I am with him in his distress* (*Tehillim* 91:15).

We are told that before the Flood the earth was so fertile that man needed to plant only once in forty years; the earth would then yield enough food to sustain him until the next planting forty years later.

Man barely needed to work.

Of course, this would certainly seem to be a wonderful blessing. Just think of what could be done with all the extra time!

However, to paraphrase *Kesubos* 59b, lack of work ultimately leads to sin.

Hashem decided that after the Flood, the earth would no longer offer the fantastic yields that were previously possible. Man would have to constantly toil now, as fulfillment of the Mishnah in *Avos* (2:2): יָפֶה תַלְמוּד תּוֹרָה עִם דֶּרֶךְ אֶרֶץ שֶׁיְּגִיעַת שְׁנֵיהֶם מַשְׁכַּחַת עָוֹן, *Great is Torah study combined with an occupation, for the exertion of them both makes sin forgotten.*

Immediately following the verse that was cited above (8:21), saying that Hashem said in His heart that He would no longer curse the earth, is the following verse: עֹד כָּל יְמֵי הָאָרֶץ זֶרַע וְקָצִיר וְקֹר וָחֹם וְקַיִץ וָחֹרֶף וְיוֹם וָלַיְלָה לֹא יִשְׁבֹּתוּ, *Continuously, all the days of the earth, seedtime and harvest, cold and heat, summer and winter, day and night, shall not cease.*

This cycle shall not cease. And man will not rest from his work.

וַאֲנִי הִנְנִי מֵקִים אֶת בְּרִיתִי אִתְּכֶם וְאֶת זַרְעֲכֶם אַחֲרֵיכֶם

As for Me, behold, I establish My covenant with you and with your offspring after you (9:9).

This section of the Torah is filled with hidden meanings and with multiple iterations of what seem to be essentially the same theme, stated in sequence, again and again over the course of the nine verses from 9:9 through 9:17. More than seven times Hashem tells Noah that He has made with him a covenant to never again destroy all flesh, and that a rainbow, placed within a cloud, will be its sign.

I have often tried to show that the Torah is written in a way that tells us not only of God's Divine Plan and of our commandments, but also demonstrates for us how that plan can be actualized.

Let us consider for a moment how the world might have looked from the perspective of the survivors of the Flood. Bewildered by the terrifying spectacle they had lived through, full of fear, overwhelmed by what had just happened to the world, perhaps they wished to withdraw from resettling it.

They were commanded by Hashem to "be fruitful and multiply," to build a new world, but were simply too weak, too overwhelmed to begin approaching the task they had just been given. They felt neither the strength, nor the drive, nor the energy.

Recognizing this, Hashem came to encourage them, to strengthen their spirits, and to offer His comfort. They need not fear. Nor should they simply give up.

Consolation involves approaching a person and easing the burden that is weighing on his heart. To successfully do so requires not only an appreciation of what those concerns might be, but also an insight as to how to constructively address them. One must empathize and find the right words, those to which his friend will be most receptive.

Upon finding the right words, he should tell them to his friend over and over again, reassuring him that he has a friend who understands him. He should continue until these words have found their way into the friend's heart.

The more one does so, the greater will be the effect.

וַיְהִי כָל הָאָרֶץ שָׂפָה אֶחָת וּדְבָרִים אֲחָדִים
The whole earth was of one language and of common purposes (11:1).

Superficially, this verse appears to be an introduction to that generation's plot and the punishment they suffered for it: They were of one language and one common purpose. In what way was this wrong? Is there something wrong with being of one language and working together in harmony?

In fact, there seems to have been another sin entirely.

It says in *Midrash Tanchuma* (*Parashas Noach* 21) that the people of that generation had in mind, "Why should Hashem choose the upper worlds for His dwelling and relegate us to the lower world. Let us go up to the heavens and smite Him with shovels."

This a very serious matter. Why is it not recounted openly in the Torah itself?

I would like to suggest that because they *intended* that, but were discreet enough not to say so openly, Hashem, Who is totally just, also showed discretion in not openly revealing their true intentions.

The fact is that they feared Him enough to be ashamed to discuss their thoughts against Him in the open, even among themselves. Thus, even though their sin was greater than that of the generation of the Flood, the Torah accords them the consideration of referring to their sins only obliquely.

This is alluded to in the verse: *The whole earth was of one language.* The word used here for language, שָׂפָה, literally means *lip*: Just as the lips are on the outside of the face, so was their plotting conducted only on the surface. In the depths of their hearts, they were of *common purposes* — in the plural — but not of one single purpose.

Each had a different motive for participating in the plot. Some wanted to make war against Hashem. Others wished to serve idols. Others wanted to dwell in peace with their fellows. And some believed that every 1,656 years there would be another flood, and therefore they wished to build a tower in order to escape from it. וַיְהִי כָל הָאָרֶץ שָׂפָה אֶחָת, *The whole earth was of one language* — but of different motives.

There are two ways to achieve unity in the world. One is by eliminating all the differences and special qualities that distinguish one individual from another. This ensures that no one will be better than anyone else in any way, since no one has more of anything than anyone else. When this happens, the common denominator shared by everyone will be no more than life itself. In fact, everyone eats, sleeps, and speaks "in one language."

Another way of achieving unity is by uniting everyone around a shared higher purpose. An example would be if everyone was given the task of conquering and climbing a particular mountain. The strong would reach the summit, while the weak would go only as high as their strength allowed. We don't say to the strong that they go no further than the weak; rather, everyone is to apply himself to conquering the mountain to the best of his abilities.

The people of Babel chose the first way, as we see from the verse, *The whole earth was of one language and of common purposes.* In their view, it was only the "earth," meaning, man's earthly origin and his physical nature, that united everyone into one mass. Everyone had דְּבָרִים אֲחָדִים, meaning "the same things." No one was allowed to have any greater abilities than anyone else; they refused to recognize the uniqueness of every human being. Instead, the whole emphasis was on the common features shared by everyone.

When the Jews arrived at Mount Sinai, the Torah relates (*Shemos* 19:2): וַיִּחַן שָׁם יִשְׂרָאֵל נֶגֶד הָהָר, *The people of Israel encamped facing the mountain.* Rashi comments that they were all "of one heart and like one man." They were united by the common purpose of preparing themselves to receive the Torah on the mountain that was facing them. This lofty goal brought out the best in each person, enabling each one to use his individual abilities to the fullest. It made the people as a whole worthy of being called Israel, the firstborn of Hashem.

The first approach requires the leveling of all individuals so that the strongest will be no better than the weakest. The second approach elevates even the lowest to the level of the greatest member of the group, in the sense that all will aspire to the highest possible goal.

This is the way of Hashem, as the Psalmist sang (113:7-8): מְקִימִי מֵעָפָר דָּל מֵאַשְׁפֹּת יָרִים אֶבְיוֹן לְהוֹשִׁיבִי עִם נְדִיבִים עִם נְדִיבֵי עַמּוֹ, *He raises the needy from the dust, from the trash heaps He lifts the destitute, to seat them with nobles, with the nobles of His people.*

וַיֹּאמֶר ה' אֶל אַבְרָם לֶךְ לְךָ מֵאַרְצְךָ...

Hashem said to Abram,
"Go for yourself from your land ..." (12:1).

רש"י: לֶךְ לְךָ – לַהֲנָאָתְךָ וּלְטוֹבָתְךָ, וְשָׁם אֶעֶשְׂךָ לְגוֹי גָּדוֹל, וְכָאן אִי
אַתָּה זוֹכֶה לְבָנִים. וְעוֹד שֶׁאוֹדִיעַ טִבְעֲךָ בָּעוֹלָם.

RASHI: Go for yourself — *For your pleasure and
for your benefit. There, I will make of you a great nation,
whereas here you do not merit having children. And
furthermore, you will benefit by going, for I will make your
name known in the world.*

*R*ashi comments that the word לְךָ, *for yourself,* indicates
that Hashem is telling Abraham to leave Haran in order
to receive some kind of personal benefit.

This is strange, for it seems to run counter to the Mishnah in *Avos* (1:3): אַל תִּהְיוּ כַּעֲבָדִים הַמְשַׁמְּשִׁין אֶת הָרַב עַל מְנָת לְקַבֵּל פְּרָס, *Be not like servants who serve their master for the sake of receiving a reward.*

Yet, it seems that, according to *Rashi*, Hashem is doing precisely what the Mishnah in *Avos* seems to be discouraging. How can this be?

One answer might be that Hashem must have had something else in mind.

He promises Abraham in the very next verse, וֶהְיֵה בְּרָכָה, *You shall be a blessing. Rashi* comments, paraphrasing *Bereishis Rabbah*:

רש"י: וֶהְיֵה בְּרָכָה – הַבְּרָכוֹת נְתוּנוֹת בְּיָדְךָ, עַד עַכְשָׁיו הָיוּ בְיָדִי, בֵּרַכְתִּי אֶת אָדָם וְאֶת נֹחַ וְאוֹתְךָ, וּמֵעַכְשָׁיו אַתָּה תְבָרֵךְ אֶת אֲשֶׁר תַּחְפּוֹץ.

RASHI: YOU SHALL BE A BLESSING — *The blessings are put into your hand. Until now, they were in My hand: I blessed Adam and Noah and you. But from now on, you will bless whomever you wish.*

With these words, Hashem was giving Abraham the power to bless others. Until that time, only Hashem had this power, and had used it to bless Adam and Noah. From now on, Abraham could bless whomever he wished.

In the aftermath of the Tower of Babel, humanity was scattered throughout many lands and separated into many different language groups, families and nations. This led to nationalistic rivalries and sectarian hatreds. The universal brotherhood and love that had once prevailed had disappeared.

Instead, it was כָּל דְּאַלִּים גְּבַר, *The strongest one wins* (*Gittin* 60b). Each group sought to conquer other peoples and their lands.

It was almost as if Hashem had been forgotten. Men turned toward idols and thirsted for the blood of their enemies. They chose to forget that all men are brothers, created by the same loving Creator, the One Who had commanded them to live together in peace, and Who still watched over them all and still desired their well-being.

They had forgotten their Father, the Father Who is King over all the world, the merciful Father over all creation.

These were the same conditions that caused the last of the prophets, Malachi, to cry out: הֲלוֹא אָב אֶחָד לְכֻלָּנוּ הֲלוֹא אֵל אֶחָד בְּרָאָנוּ מַדּוּעַ נִבְגַּד אִישׁ בְּאָחִיו לְחַלֵּל בְּרִית אֲבֹתֵינוּ , *Do we not all have one Father? Did not one God create us? Why do men betray each other and debase the covenant of our fathers?* (2:10).

Through the mouth of the same prophet (1:6), Hashem Himself asked, בֵּן יְכַבֵּד אָב וְעֶבֶד אֲדֹנָיו וְאִם אָב אָנִי אַיֵּה כְבוֹדִי וְאִם אֲדוֹנִים אָנִי אַיֵּה מוֹרָאִי, אָמַר ה׳ צְבָאוֹת, *A son honors his father and a servant his master. If I am a Father, then where is My honor; if I am a Master, then where is the fear of Me?*

This was the reason for Abraham's designation.

Abraham had been the one who strove to restore awareness of Hashem's presence. He was the one who reminded all of his brothers that Hashem was close by.

Abraham had set a personal example of seeking to emulate His ways. By going out among all of his brethren, concerning himself with their well-being, Abraham was embodying the very concept that had been forgotten — that Hashem is Father to all the nations.

By conducting himself with love and generosity — albeit only the tiniest shadow of what Hashem showers on His creatures — Abraham had begun to mend the tear that had been rent in the fabric of human society by generations of rebellion against Hashem.

This, then, is the meaning of the verse, וֶהְיֵה בְּרָכָה, *You shall be a blessing*: "Until now," said Hashem to Abraham, "the power to bless has been in My hands. I now give it to you, since you have made yourself into a father to My children, to those who wish to go in My ways. Use this power to bless them, to encourage them and inspire them, to strengthen them to learn My ways, to learn to be My people."

<hr />

... וְאַבְרָם בֶּן חָמֵשׁ שָׁנִים וְשִׁבְעִים שָׁנָה בְּצֵאתוֹ מֵחָרָן

... *Abram was seventy-five years old when he left Haran (12:4).*

Why does the Torah make no mention of Abraham's age until he reached the age of 75? Further, why is it that the Written Torah fails to make any explicit reference to the great miracle in Ur Kasdim, where Abraham was rescued from the furnace, thereby sanctifying Hashem's Name in front of the nations?

Let us suggest, by way of an answer, that the Torah does not choose to detail Abraham's achievements prior to his becoming father of the Jewish people.

Impressive as his deeds might have been prior to his arrival in the land of Canaan, their influence was limited to the nations among whom he dwelled, but did not extend to his future descendants. Therefore, the Written Torah records these events without a lot of detail. The Oral Torah, however, does fill in quite a bit of what happened.

As for the Written Torah, though, not even Abraham's age is mentioned, until this point. Similarly, the Torah relates almost nothing of what happened to Moses during his early years in Egypt or during the time he spent in Midian.

We see here a vital lesson for us as a nation in exile: While we must certainly be loyal citizens, we must be careful not to overly invest in developing the lands to which we are temporarily exiled. Those efforts are destined to eventually be swept away without a residue. Indeed, our enemies might even come to turn those efforts against us (Heaven forbid).

The only things we can count on are the sacrifices we make on behalf of the Jewish people; and they, without question, will endure forever. Anything else we do might fall into the category of "serving other gods."

Abraham went *to* himself, to his source. But, in order to reach the source of his soul, he first needed to uproot all influences that came from other lands.

As Abraham's descendants in a time of exile, we have the task of strengthening ourselves in Torah and purifying ourselves from the corrupting influences that surround us, and thereby freeing our souls so that we can accomplish our mission.

And, this is one more way of understanding the first verse in this *parashah,* וַיֹּאמֶר ה' אֶל אַבְרָם לֶךְ לְךָ מֵאַרְצְךָ וּמִמּוֹלַדְתְּךָ וּמִבֵּית אָבִיךָ אֶל הָאָרֶץ אֲשֶׁר אַרְאֶךָּ, *Hashem said to Abram, "Go out for yourself, from your land, from your relatives, and from your father's house to the land that I will show you."*

Go out for yourself, that is, for the sake of building up your new self, which will be for your own good and for your own benefit. *From your land, from your relatives, and from your father's house* — from the influences of the land in which you had been residing.

We could take this idea a bit further: *From your father's house* — This is what is being referred to in *Bereishis Rabbah* 39:

וַיֹּאמֶר ה' אֶל אַבְרָם לֶךְ לְךָ וגו' – ר' יִצְחָק פָּתַח: "שִׁמְעִי בַת וּרְאִי וְהַטִּי אָזְנֵךְ וְשִׁכְחִי עַמֵּךְ וּבֵית אָבִיךְ" (תְּהִלִּים מה:יא).

AND HASHEM SAID TO ABRAHAM, "GO OUT FOR YOURSELF" — *R' Yitzchak compared this to the verse in Tehillim 45:11, "Hear, O daughter, and see, and incline your ear: Forget your people and the house of your father."*

Take note that the verse in *Tehillim*, paralleling our verse here, urges the listener to leave her people and her father's house. It uses the feminine gender — "Hear, my daughter" rather than "Hear, my son" — for the Jewish people are often compared to a woman who is married to the Holy One, Blessed is He. The verse from *Tehillim* says explicitly that the Jewish people should "forget" its gentile origins. So now, the implied commandment to Abraham, in our interpretation, becomes clearer and more powerful.

<hr>

וַיֵּצְאוּ לָלֶכֶת אַרְצָה כְּנַעַן וַיָּבֹאוּ אַרְצָה כְּנָעַן
They embarked for the land of Canaan, and they came to the land of Canaan (12:5).

<hr>

סְפוֹרְנוֹ: וַיָּבֹאוּ אַרְצָה כְּנָעַן – לֹא כְעִנְיַן יְצִיאַת תֶּרַח "לָלֶכֶת אַרְצָה כְּנַעַן" (יא:לא) שֶׁלֹּא בָא אֶלָּא עַד חָרָן.

SFORNO: AND THEY CAME TO THE LAND OF CANAAN — *Not like the "going out" of Terah "to go to the land of Canaan" (11:31), for he did not come any further than Haran.*

<hr>

*S*forno notes a difference between Abraham's journey to Canaan and his father's: Abraham ultimately reached Canaan; Terah went no further than Haran.

What is the significance of this distinction?

We read at the end of *Parashas Noach* (11:31): וַיִּקַּח תֶּרַח אֶת אַבְרָם בְּנוֹ ..., וַיֵּצְאוּ אִתָּם מֵאוּר כַּשְׂדִּים לָלֶכֶת אַרְצָה כְּנַעַן וַיָּבֹאוּ עַד חָרָן וַיֵּשְׁבוּ שָׁם, *Terah took Abram his son ... and they departed with them from Ur Kasdim to go to the land of Canaan; they arrived at Haran and settled there.*

Some people emigrate from their homeland to some other place because of the perceived attractiveness of the destination. Were it not for whatever was drawing them to the new land, they might have contentedly remained wherever they were.

Others leave not because of what the new land has to offer, but rather in order to escape from the place that they are departing. They just have to get away — to any place other than the one they seek to flee. And that is their primary goal when they set out.

This is what distinguished Abraham's motives in leaving Ur Kasdim from those of his father.

Concerning Terah, the Torah says, וַיֵּצְאוּ ... מֵאוּר כַּשְׂדִּים, *they departed from Ur Kasdim.* The emphasis is on his leaving.

Terah's son had been thrown into the fiery furnace as punishment for rebelling against idol worship. Abraham survived, but his father was disgraced, a man now without a shred of the prestige he had previously enjoyed within his community of idolaters.

"Disgraced," he had to get out. His destination was Canaan, but the destination was only a secondary factor. He arrived in Haran, found that he could resettle there in peace, free from the humiliation of Ur Kasdim, and abandoned the original plan of moving to Canaan.

His needs were met just as well in Haran, and therefore he remained there until his death, never having reached the Holy Land.

Abraham, however, was different. Regarding his departure, the verse says וַיֵּצְאוּ לָלֶכֶת אַרְצָה כְּנַעַן, *they embarked* for *the land of Canaan.* His eyes were fixed on his destination, the land of Canaan, because he wished to be in the holiest of places, the Land of Israel.

Because his journey was driven by a desire to reach a certain goal, he, unlike Terah, did not wind up falling short. He succeeded.

Regarding Abraham, our verse says, וַיָּבֹאוּ אַרְצָה כְּנַעַן, *and they came to the land of Canaan.*

וַיָּשֶׁב אֵת כָּל הָרְכֻשׁ וְגַם אֶת לוֹט אָחִיו וּרְכֻשׁוֹ הֵשִׁיב וְגַם אֶת הַנָּשִׁים וְאֶת הָעָם

He brought back all the possessions; he also brought back his kinsman, Lot, with his possessions, as well as the women and the people (14:16).

This verse comes within the context of telling the story of Abraham's going to war in order to rescue Lot, his nephew, who had been taken captive. The previous verses tell us this quite explicitly:

וַיִּשְׁמַע אַבְרָם כִּי נִשְׁבָּה אָחִיו וַיָּרֶק אֶת חֲנִיכָיו יְלִידֵי בֵיתוֹ שְׁמֹנָה עָשָׂר וּשְׁלֹשׁ מֵאוֹת וַיִּרְדֹּף עַד דָּן. וַיֵּחָלֵק עֲלֵיהֶם לַיְלָה הוּא וַעֲבָדָיו וַיַּכֵּם וַיִּרְדְּפֵם עַד חוֹבָה אֲשֶׁר מִשְּׂמֹאל לְדַמָּשֶׂק,

And when Abram heard that his kinsman was taken captive, he armed his disciples ... and he pursued them as far as Dan. And he with his servants deployed against them at night and struck them (14:14-15).

It certainly seems, then, that the saving of Lot was clearly his motive for going to war.

Why, then, does our verse, when describing the rescue, give first mention to his having rescued *"the possessions"* and only after that, *"he also brought back his kinsman, Lot."* Was it the possessions that he was fighting for, or was it Lot?

I would like to suggest that the logical order is reversed here in order to reveal to us an insight into Abraham's character, and to show us that his motives here were absolutely and totally for the sake of Heaven.

He was not going to war for the sake of "family loyalty" or because of his personal identification with the plight of a family member.

Rather, he was doing so because he felt that this was what Hashem wanted, and therefore, it was the right thing to do.

This insight is learned from the Torah's first mentioning the possessions. Would one dream that Abraham did this for the sake of enriching himself with the plunder? And, that the rescue of the human beings was a mere afterthought?

Of course, Abraham retrieved the property for no reason other than to return it to its rightful owners. He had no personal interest in the booty. His motive was *kiddush Hashem*.

So too with the rescue of Lot: Just as the property was rescued purely as a means of sanctifying Hashem's Name, so too, Lot was brought out for no personal benefit, but only to sanctify Hashem's Name.

───═══───

אִם מִחוּט וְעַד שְׂרוֹךְ נַעַל וְאִם אֶקַּח מִכָּל אֲשֶׁר לָךְ וְלֹא תֹאמַר אֲנִי הֶעֱשַׁרְתִּי אֶת אַבְרָם

[Abram said to the king of Sodom :] "If so much as a thread to a shoestrap; or if I will take of anything of yours! So you shall not say, 'It is I who made Abram rich'" (14:23).

אִם מִחוּט – א"ר אַבָּא בַּר מַמָּל א"ל הקב"ה אַתְּ אָמַרְתְּ "אִם מִחוּט" חַיֶּיךְ שֶׁאֲנִי נוֹתֵן לְבָנֶיךָ מִצְוַת צִיצִית, הֵיךְ מַה דְּאַתְּ אָמַר (בַּמִּדְבָּר טו: לח) "וְנָתְנוּ עַל צִיצִת הַכָּנָף פְּתִיל תְּכֵלֶת" וּמִתַּרְגְּמִינָן חוּטָא דִתְכֵלְתָּא, "וְעַד שְׂרוֹךְ נַעַל", חַיֶּיךְ שֶׁאֲנִי נוֹתֵן לְבָנֶיךָ מִצְוַת יְבָמָה הֵיךְ מַה דְּאַתְּ אָמַר (דְּבָרִים כה:ט) "וְחָלְצָה נַעֲלוֹ מֵעַל רַגְלוֹ" (בְּרֵאשִׁית רַבָּה מ"ג).

IF SO MUCH AS A THREAD — ... *The Holy One, Blessed is He, said, "You said, 'If so much as a thread.' By your life, I will therefore give your children the mitzvah of the strings of tzitzis." And so it says in the Torah (Bamidbar 15:38), "... and they shall place upon the tzitzis of each corner a thread of turquoise wool." This is translated [by Onkelos] as "a string of turquoise." To a shoestrap — "By your life, I will therefore give your children the mitzvah*

*of yevamah." And so it says in the Torah (Devarim 25:9),
"she shall remove his shoe ... " [whereby a childless widow
frees her brother-in-law of the obligation to marry her,
through a ceremony that includes use of a shoe] (Bereishis
Rabbah 43).*

The verse describes Abraham declining the king of Sodom's offer to "allow" Abraham the privilege of leaving with the possessions that he had just rightfully won in war.

Meshech Chochmah quotes the above Midrash and describes it as an allusion to the saying of the Sages (*Yerushalmi Yevamos*) that the critical part of the procedure of *yibum* is the undoing of the shoestrap.

We see from the above Midrash that the Jewish people merited two mitzvos here: *techeiles* (the blue thread required in *tzitzis*) and *chalitzah,* whereby a childless widow frees her brother-in-law of the obligation to marry her, through a ceremony that includes use of a shoe.

What is the connection? What connects these two mitzvos to each other? And, what connects either of them to Abraham's statement in our verse?

Obviously, one could simply point out the linguistic association, and leave it at that. However, we believe that there is more to it.

Let us look at it again. Abraham made an oath to the king of Sodom not to derive benefit from two particular kinds of plunder. As a result, his descendants merited the mitzvah of *techeiles* as well as the mitzvah of *chalitzah.*

Perhaps we could explain this as follows:

Abraham was the first to reveal Hashem's greatness to the world. He told them of His total dominion over every aspect of life, from the smallest to the largest.

Techeiles reminds us of the sea and the sky, both of which have the same hue as Hashem's *Kisei HaKavod,* the Throne of Honor.

Abraham refused to take anything from the possessions of Sodom. This served to magnify Hashem's honor in the world. It won him the reward of *techeiles*, which is a striking symbol of Hashem's Throne of Honor, the very symbol of the fact that He rules over everything.

One person's loosening of another's shoestrap, on the other hand, dishonors him. In this case, it is the dishonor that is due someone who has refused to comply with Hashem's will that he marry his late brother's widow and thereby perpetuate his brother's name in Israel.

A person who has been forced to go barefoot has thereby lost much of his honor.

לְעוֹלָם יִמְכּוֹר אָדָם קוֹרוֹת בֵּיתוֹ וְיִקַּח מִנְעָלִים לְרַגְלָיו, *A person should sell the beams of his home (if necessary) in order to buy shoes (Shabbos* 129a).

One who fails to increase the honor of Hashem has thereby forfeited his own honor.

The connection now becomes much more clear:

Abraham was certainly entitled to accepting his share of the spoils of war. However, by doing so, it might seem as if he were honoring the king of Sodom, accepting his "magnanimity" and acknowledging his sovereignty.

That, necessarily, would have meant a diminution of the honor of Hashem in the eyes of the world, a "removal of the shoe," so to speak.

Therefore, he refused.

———

וְאַבְרָהָם בֶּן תִּשְׁעִים וָתֵשַׁע שָׁנָה בְּהִמֹּלוֹ בְּשַׂר עָרְלָתוֹ
Abraham was ninety-nine years old when he was circumcised on the flesh of his surplusage (17:24).

The Sages tell us that Abraham observed all the commandments of the Torah without being commanded to do so, including even Rabbinic decrees such as *eruv tavshilin*. Why then did Abraham wait to perform the mitzvah of *bris milah* until he was commanded to by Hashem?

Another even more puzzling question: At the beginning of *Para-shas Vayeira* (18:1), *Rashi* comments, paraphrasing a Midrash, that Hashem appeared to Abraham on the land of his friend Mamre because Mamre had given him advice concerning his circumcision:

רש"י :**בְּאֵלֹנֵי מַמְרֵא** – הוּא שֶׁנָּתַן לוֹ עֵצָה עַל הַמִּילָה, לְפִיכָךְ נִגְלָה עָלָיו בְּחֶלְקוֹ.

RASHI: IN THE PLAINS OF MAMRE — *He is the one who gave [Abraham] advice about the circumcision. That is why [God] was revealed [to Abraham] in his portion.*

Why should Abraham have asked Mamre's advice about this command more than about any of the others that he had received from Hashem?

When told to bring his beloved son as an offering, Abraham was so eager to fulfill Hashem's will that he rose early that morning, saddling his donkey himself, in his haste to be on his way. Why did *Rashi* think that when it came to this mitzvah, the sacred sign of Hashem's covenant with His people, Abraham would hesitate, going to seek advice?

There is a Midrash that might resolve these difficulties. In essence, the Midrash says that *milah* makes such a powerful impression, both on a man's body and his soul, that it creates a profound and obvious distinction between those who are circumcised and those who are not.

Abraham's apprehension was that, once he was on one side of the fence, so to speak, and the rest of the world on the other, he would no longer be able to fulfill his primary mission, which was to promulgate service of Hashem.

For this reason, he delayed doing this one mitzvah, even though he longed to observe it, until explicitly commanded to do so.

Even after having been explicitly commanded, though, his dilemma remained and he sought advice from Mamre as to how to best observe Hashem's commandment without compromising fulfillment of his mission.

If he circumcised himself in public, he would show the world how devoted he was to Hashem, but then others would not be able to relate to him as they had previously. If he did it in secret, he would lose out on the opportunity for *kiddush Hashem*, but fewer people would feel that they could no longer relate to him. A *bris milah* carried out privately would thus better enable him to change the world for the better.

Until Abraham reached the age of 99, Hashem had acquiesced to his reasons for delaying this mitzvah. Then, however, as the time for Isaac's birth drew close, the duty of establishing his dynasty — a nation of Hashem's servants — came to overshadow the mission of informing the world of Hashem's power and glory. The foundation for that nation had to be laid with total holiness and purity that was possible only through *milah*.

Furthermore, it was vital that the impressionable young Isaac see his father only as a sincerely committed and pure person, totally untainted by the wickedness of his contemporaries. Hashem therefore ordered Abraham to circumcise himself, even though this might diminish his influence on others.

We, too, often face these same dilemmas in regard to our own service of Hashem. No matter how strong we wish to be, unshaken in our beliefs, we must face the fact that Man is a social creature. All of us desire the company of others, and seek their acceptance. Our natural propensity is to be drawn to conforming with the way others think and act, lest we become an "outsider."

Even if a person is sincere in his service of Hashem, and however strong his initial resolution to insulate himself from his contemporaries' undesirable qualities, it is natural that, over the course of time, he will find excuses for their bad habits. It will then be only a few small steps before he, too, has adopted their ways, naturally following the path of least resistance.

When Hashem was about to give the Torah to Israel, the Ministering Angels protested. "Place Your glory in the Heavens," they said, implying that only the pure angels who dwell in the heavens were worthy of receiving the Torah, but not Man.

Answered Hashem, "But you yourselves ate milk together with meat!"

The angels claimed that they were the only ones capable of revealing the Torah's true beauty and glory. Man is too easily led into compromises, just to remain popular and in order to conform with his social environment.

Hashem reminded them of their meal of milk and meat. They could have found an excuse, but ate rather than seem different from the people around them. They therefore had no right to claim that man was unworthy of receiving the Torah simply because he was subject to social pressures of the moment.

וַיֵּרָא אֵלָיו ה' בְּאֵלֹנֵי מַמְרֵא
וְהוּא יֹשֵׁב פֶּתַח הָאֹהֶל כְּחֹם הַיּוֹם

Hashem appeared to him in the plains of Mamre
while he was sitting at the entrance of the tent in
the heat of the day (18:1).

רש"י: כְּחֹם הַיּוֹם – הוֹצִיא הקב"ה חַמָּה מִנַּרְתִּיקָה שֶׁלֹּא לְהַטְרִיחוֹ
בָּאוֹרְחִים, וּלְפִי שֶׁרָאָהוּ מִצְטַעֵר שֶׁלֹּא הָיוּ אוֹרְחִים בָּאִים, הֵבִיא
הַמַּלְאָכִים עָלָיו בִּדְמוּת אֲנָשִׁים.

RASHI: IN THE HEAT OF THE DAY — *The Holy One,*
Blessed is He, brought the sun out of its sheath so as
not to trouble [Abraham] with guests. Because [God]
saw [Abraham] aggrieved that there were no visitors
coming, He brought the angels to him in the form
of men.

ashi relates that Hashem made the day very hot, "taking the sun out of its sheath," so that Abraham would not be troubled with guests while recovering from his circumcision. However, upon seeing Abraham's distress at not having the opportunity to carry out the mitzvah of *hachnasas orchim* (receiving guests), He sent to Abraham three angels, disguised as men.

According to *Rashi*, then, Hashem wanted to give Abraham an opportunity to perform mitzvos. If so, why send disguised angels? Let Him send actual people! Let him give Abraham the actual mitzvos of *tzedakah* and *hachnasas orchim*!

Once it became clear that these were not men, it also became apparent that there never was a mitzvah! So what was the point?

Let us suggest that Hashem arranged this in order to teach a fundamental lesson regarding *hachnasas orchim* and all other forms of charity and kindness.

We might have mistakenly thought that the primary reason for the institution of *hachnasas orchim* and *tzedakah* is for the sake of the recipient: Were it not for our *tzedakah* dollars and the meal that we serve him, our guest would certainly have starved to death!

That is simply not the case. Hashem has many ways and many agents. Were the goal merely the allocation of resources, He would have had many other options.

Rather, the prime beneficiary of *tzedakah* is not the one who receives it; the prime beneficiary is the *giver*. This can be learned from the *malachim*.

Once we know that these "men" were actually *malachim,* we also know that they had no need for the food or the hospitality: By definition, *malachim* have no physical needs and receive no benefit whatsoever from the physical world.

Were these "guests" to be the sole beneficiaries of all of the activity, it would have been a pointless charade. This episode did nothing for them.

Rather, it must have all been for the benefit of Abraham.

So, too, with *hachnasas orchim* and *tzedakah* in general:

שָׁאַל טוּרְנוּסְרוּפוּס הָרָשָׁע אֶת רַבִּי עֲקִיבָא: אִם אֱלֹהֵיכֶם אוֹהֵב עֲנִיִּים הוּא,
מִפְּנֵי מַה אֵינוֹ מְפַרְנְסָם? א"ל: כְּדֵי שֶׁנִּיצוֹל אָנוּ בָהֶן מִדִּינָהּ שֶׁל גֵּיהִנָּם.

*Turnosrufus the evil one asked R' Akiva: "Why, if Hashem
so loves the poor, why doesn't He provide for them?" R'
Akiva answered that it is so that we be saved through
them, from the judgment of Gehinnom (Bava Basra 10a).*

וַיֵּרָא אֵלָיו
He appeared to him (18:1).

braham is not mentioned by name in any of the first
five verses of this *parashah*. This is despite the fact that
these five verses describe what seem to be highly significant events — all of which occurred only because of the greatness
of Abraham. Hashem appears to him in a prophetic vision, angels
miraculously arrive to visit him, and he engages the angels in conversation. Yet, he is not mentioned by name.

Then, verse 6 says, וַיְמַהֵר אַבְרָהָם הָאֹהֱלָה אֶל שָׂרָה ... , *Abraham hur-
ried to the tent, to Sarah,* followed by the next verse, וְאֶל הַבָּקָר רָץ
אַבְרָהָם, *Then Abraham ran to the cattle.*

It seems a bit strange that after not associating Abraham by name
with the great events that had just occurred, his name is suddenly
used here. His hurrying toward his wife's tent and running to the
cattle are activities that one would have to view as being somewhat
mundane, things that pale in comparison with communing with
God and being visited by angels.

It would certainly seem that if the prior events did not merit mention of his name, then neither should these. The Torah should have continued the stylistic pattern it had established until now.

Perhaps we can suggest an answer by contrasting the differences between the nature of the interactions that the first five verses describe and that which is described from verse 6 onward.

Let us also have a look at the name, "Abraham."

וַיִּפֹּל אַבְרָם עַל פָּנָיו וַיְדַבֵּר אִתּוֹ אֱלֹהִים לֵאמֹר. אֲנִי הִנֵּה בְרִיתִי אִתָּךְ
וְהָיִיתָ לְאַב הֲמוֹן גּוֹיִם. וְלֹא יִקָּרֵא עוֹד אֶת שִׁמְךָ אַבְרָם וְהָיָה שִׁמְךָ
אַבְרָהָם כִּי אַב הֲמוֹן גּוֹיִם נְתַתִּיךָ.

Abram threw himself upon his face, and God spoke with him, saying:

"As for Me, this is My covenant with you: You shall be a father of a multitude of nations; your name should no longer be called Abram, but your name shall be Abraham, for I have made you the father of a multitude of nations (17:3-5).

The first three verses of our *parashah*, beginning with the words וַיֵּרָא אֵלָיו ... , depict a personal visit, one that was made to Abraham as an individual, rather than as "the father of many nations" described in Chapter 17 and quoted above.

The next two verses, similarly, do not depict him in his leadership role. Instead, we see him reducing himself to the status of a servant attending to the personal needs of his master. The emphasis is on his self-effacement rather than on his prestige.

When he ran to his household, however, he did so in his capacity as "father of many nations." He took charge of the details, this time as a leader, instructing them as to what they should do. He invested all of his energy, as if the entire world depended on the performance of the mitzvah. It was as if he were acting on behalf of the entire world.

Thus, when he was being visited as an individual or hiding his greatness by acting like a simple servant, his aspect of "father of many nations," the basis of his being given the name "Abraham," was hidden.

Later, when he acted with great urgency and with leadership, as if the entire world rested on the outcome, he was showing himself as "Abraham."

Hence, the change.

＝＝＝＝

וַיִּשָּׂא עֵינָיו וַיַּרְא וְהִנֵּה שְׁלֹשָׁה אֲנָשִׁים נִצָּבִים עָלָיו ...
He lifted his eyes and saw: and behold! three men were standing over him (18:2).

The story, as brought by *Rashi* from *Chazal,* is familiar to us all: Abraham was aggrieved that no visitors were coming. Hashem therefore presented him with three angels in the form of Arabs, so that Abraham's wish to do acts of kindness would be fulfilled.

That story has always bothered me. Was there a shortage of actual poor people at that time? Was there really a need for Abraham's food and hospitality to go to waste on angels who neither eat nor drink instead of being used for needy, hungry human beings?

I would like to propose an answer.

Hashem introduced His covenant with Abraham by saying (17:1): אֲנִי אֵל שַׁדַּי הִתְהַלֵּךְ לְפָנַי וֶהְיֵה תָמִים, *I am the All-powerful God; go before Me and be perfect.* The *Torah Temimah* commentary, basing itself on a Midrash, says that שַׁדַּי means, "I am the One Who said to the world, 'Enough!'" The Midrash says that Hashem was saying to Abraham, "It is sufficient that only I and you are in the world; if you do not accept my commandment to circumcise yourself, then it is enough that My world has survived until now. I will now bring it to an end."

What does this mean?

Growth and expansion can be measured in quantity or in quality. During the first six days of Creation, the main growth was in quantity. On the seventh day, Hashem said "Enough!" and rested from His "work." He wished to give the forces He had created time to grow and expand in quality. This is perhaps alluded to in the Midrash that says that even though Hashem rested from all of His "work" on Shabbos, this refers only to *His* work of Creation, but not to the "work" of the *reshaim* and the "work" of the *tzaddikim*. With respect to them, the work goes on (see *Bereishis Rabbah* 11).

I believe that Abraham's life contains an interesting parallel.

For the first 99 years of his life, Abraham directed his energies to transmitting to the multitudes the message of pure faith. He traveled from place to place, proclaiming Hashem's Name. Then, he received a new directive from Hashem, "Enough of going to as many people as possible and traveling as far and wide as possible. The time has now come to focus on the *qualitative* expansion of yourself. True, you will now be dealing with only the few. And, it may very well be that you won't even come into contact with a single individual who will be receptive to your message. Still, this is what must be done; your energies must now be directed toward building up yourself, a *qualitative* expansion. It is enough that I and you are in the world."

Perhaps, this was Hashem's intent when He said, "Go before Me and be perfect." Perfect yourself qualitatively, make yourself perfect.

Abraham's quality of lovingkindness had reached a new plane, to the extent that, quite ironically, the level of *chessed* he was now operating on was beyond the grasp of the masses. Only the angels could appreciate what Avraham had become and the quality of his *chessed*. From their perspective, it was almost as if they were in contact with the *Shechinah*.

By bringing this mitzvah to its fullest possible expression (ed. note: Perhaps this refers to Abraham's willingness to treat like royalty even those of the seemingly lowest status — that, despite his own physical discomfort), Abraham expanded the qualitative power of *chessed* throughout the world.

<hr>

וַיֹּאמַר אֲדֹנָי אִם נָא מָצָאתִי חֵן בְּעֵינֶיךָ אַל נָא תַעֲבֹר מֵעַל עַבְדֶּךָ

He said, "My Lord, if I find favor in your eyes, please do not pass away from your servant" (18:3).

*R*ashi gives two explanations for why the plural word אֲדֹנָי is followed by a singular verb, תַעֲבֹר, "pass." According to the first (which would translate אֲדֹנָי in the plural, as "masters") Abraham was speaking to his three visitors; he first addressed them collectively as "my masters" and then addressed the leader of the trio in the singular. According to *Rashi's* second explanation, however (which would translate אֲדֹנָי as "My Lord"), Abraham was asking Hashem to wait while he went to see to the needs of his guests.

From this latter interpretation, the Sages derived the teaching that hospitality to guests is more important that receiving Hashem's Presence.

How is it that Abraham knew this principle?

Perhaps he knew it from having encountered it in the course of his Torah study; perhaps, however, he was being taught the lesson only at this very moment.

Consider the following. On the verse, וְהוּא יֹשֵׁב פֶּתַח הָאֹהֶל, *he* [Abraham] *was sitting at the entrance of the tent. Rashi* comments:

<hr>

יֹשֵׁב – יָשַׁב כְּתִיב, בִּקֵּשׁ לַעֲמוֹד, אָמַר לוֹ הַקָּדוֹשׁ בָּרוּךְ הוּא: שֵׁב וַאֲנִי אֶעֱמוֹד, וְאַתָּה סִימָן לְבָנֶיךָ, שֶׁעָתִיד אֲנִי לְהִתְיַצֵּב בַּעֲדַת הַדַּיָּינִין וְהֵן

יָשֵׁב is spelled without a *vav*, meaning that it could be read as *yashav*, sat, rather than *yosheiv*, sitting. Abraham wanted to stand up, out of respect for Hashem. However, Hashem insisted that Abraham sit while He stood. This was to teach Abraham's descendants a lesson: "You are a signpost for your descendants; in the future I will stand in the council of judges, while they, the judges, will sit, as it says (*Tehillim* 82:2): *God stands in the Divine assembly* (among judges who assemble to seek truth and justice)."

The obvious question is what *Rashi's* comment has to do with our verse, since Abraham was not in any way sitting as a judge.

The Sages taught that Hashem's visit to Abraham was in the nature of a visit to a sick person. Presumably, they drew this conclusion from the fact that the verses do not relate that Hashem said even a single word to Abraham; there was no verbal message. Rather it must be that His mere appearance was sufficient to show honor to the sick Abraham. This explains also why the verse says merely "to him" and not "to Abraham," since Hashem visited him as He would have any other sick person. There was therefore no reason to include Abraham's name.

From the fact that Hashem put aside all His other affairs to see to Abraham's needs the Sages learned that the needs of a fellow human being have precedence over Hashem's needs.

In visiting Abraham, thereby showing him how important it is to be attentive to the needs of one's fellow man, Hashem also revealed to him another secret: "You are a symbol to your descendants that in the future I will stand in the council of judges."

Let us understand how this can be inferred.

The Torah was given to man, and not to the angels. Whatever the judges of Israel decree on earth is followed as well in the Heavenly Court. There is no greater form of respect than that which Hashem gives to humankind by allowing them to render true judgments rather than to keep this role for Himself. When He delays Heavenly judgment until a judgment has been rendered on earth, it is as if Hashem "stands" in waiting for the judges to issue a ruling.

There are two lessons for us here. One is that attending to the needs of one's fellow man can sometimes be more important than attending to so-called holy matters that seem to be in conflict with performing this mitzvah. Another is that, at times, Hashem "stands" and waits until a judgment has been rendered on earth, meaning that having us personally right the wrongs done by one person to another is a vital part of our service of Hashem.

Thus, to return to our original question, it was from being taught this halachah that Abraham learned that it would be proper to ask Hashem to wait for him until he had seen to the needs of the three guests who were presenting themselves to him. This also clarifies why *Rashi* saw fit to compare Hashem's standing over Abraham to Hashem's standing in a council of judges.

וַיֹּאמֶר ה' אֶל אַבְרָהָם לָמָּה זֶּה צָחֲקָה שָׂרָה לֵאמֹר
הַאַף אֻמְנָם אֵלֵד וַאֲנִי זָקַנְתִּי. הֲיִפָּלֵא מֵה' דָּבָר ...

Then Hashem said to Abraham,
"Why is it that Sarah laughed, saying:
'Shall I in truth bear a child, though I have aged?'
Is anything beyond Hashem?!" (18:13-14).

ashem is asking Abraham why Sarah had laughed at the news that he and Sarah would have a child. It is understood that Hashem seems to be reproaching her. Yet, we see that when told the same news, Abraham himself seems to have reacted in a similar fashion.

וַיֹּאמֶר אֱלֹהִים אֶל אַבְרָהָם ... וּבֵרַכְתִּי אֹתָהּ וְגַם נָתַתִּי מִמֶּנָּה לְךָ בֵּן וּבֵרַכְתִּיהָ וְהָיְתָה לְגוֹיִם מַלְכֵי עַמִּים מִמֶּנָּה יִהְיוּ. וַיִּפֹּל אַבְרָהָם עַל פָּנָיו וַיִּצְחָק וַיֹּאמֶר בְּלִבּוֹ הַלְּבֶן מֵאָה שָׁנָה יִוָּלֵד וְאִם שָׂרָה הֲבַת תִּשְׁעִים שָׁנָה תֵּלֵד.

And God said to Abraham, "... I will bless her; indeed, I will give you a son through her: I will bless her and she will give rise to nations; kings of peoples will rise from her." And Abraham threw himself on his face and laughed; and he thought, "Shall a child be born to a hundred-year-old man? And shall Sarah — a ninety-year-old woman — give birth?" (17:15-17).

And, despite his seemingly having an identical reaction, Abraham was not reproached. Even more curiously, Sarah expressed her disbelief after being told the news by a stranger whom she took to be an itinerant non-Jew. Abraham, on the other hand, reacted as he did after being told directly by Hashem!

Surely, if anyone is going to be reproached, it should have been Abraham!

An answer to this question can be found in the words of *Ramban*, based on the following two verses:

וַתִּצְחַק שָׂרָה בְּקִרְבָּהּ לֵאמֹר אַחֲרֵי בְלֹתִי הָיְתָה לִּי עֶדְנָה וַאדֹנִי זָקֵן

And Sarah laughed at herself, saying, "After I have withered shall I again have delicate skin? And my husband is old?" (18:12).

וַתְּכַחֵשׁ שָׂרָה לֵאמֹר לֹא צָחַקְתִּי כִּי יָרֵאָה וַיֹּאמֶר לֹא כִּי צָחָקְתְּ.

Sarah denied it, saying, "I did not laugh," for she was frightened. But he said, "No, you laughed, indeed." (18:15).

רמב"ן: וַתְּכַחֵשׁ שָׂרָה לֵאמֹר – אֲנִי תָמֵהַּ בַּנְּבִיאָה הַצַּדֶּקֶת ... לָמָּה לֹא הֶאֱמִינָה לְדִבְרֵי מַלְאֲכֵי אֱלֹהִים. וְהַנִּרְאָה בְעֵינַי כִּי הַמַּלְאָכִים הָאֵלֶּה הַנִּרְאִים כַּאֲנָשִׁים בָּאוּ אֶל אַבְרָהָם, וְהוּא בְחָכְמָתוֹ הִכִּיר בָּהֶם ... וְשָׂרָה שׁוֹמַעַת, וְלֹא יָדְעָה כִּי מַלְאֲכֵי עֶלְיוֹן הֵם ... וְאוּלַי לֹא רָאֲתָה אוֹתָם כְּלָל.

וַתִּצְחַק בְּקִרְבָּהּ לִלְעַג ... והקב"ה הֶאֱשִׁים אוֹתָהּ לְאַבְרָהָם לָמָּה הָיָה הַדָּבָר נִמְנַע בְּעֵינֶיהָ וְרָאוּי לָהּ שֶׁתַּאֲמִין, אוֹ שֶׁתֹּאמַר "אָמֵן כֵּן יַעֲשֶׂה ה'":

RAMBAN: SARAH DENIED IT, SAYING — *I wonder about the righteous prophetess: ... How could she not have trusted the words of the angels of God? It seems to me that these angels, who appeared to be men, came to Abraham, and he, in his wisdom recognized [that they were actually angels, not men] ... And Sarah heard, but did not know that they were angels ... perhaps, she did not even see them.*

She therefore laughed within herself, with derision (Ramban now brings proofs as to why this type of laughter, laughing within herself, indicates derision, or total dismissal) ... And Hashem accused her to Abraham as to why the matter should have been an impossibility in her opinion. She should have either believed it or [at the very least not totally discounted it, even if she thought the source of the blessing to be unreliable] say, "Amen, so should it be done by God."

Ramban says that the fact that Sarah laughed within herself, וַתִּצְחַק שָׂרָה בְּקִרְבָּהּ, demonstrates that she had totally rejected the possibility that these "men" could have been correct in their telling her that she would soon become pregnant and give birth to a son. While it might have been understandable, given the circumstances, that she be skeptical, she should have at least accepted the blessing and recognized that there is nothing that is too difficult for Hashem.

She was therefore reproached.

Along the lines of *Ramban*, I would like to make one other point. The use of the word לֵאמֹר in both of the above verses would seem to support *Ramban's* idea.

לֵאמֹר indicates not only "to say," but to do so with conviction. This would be an additional proof that Sarah laughed because she was certain that it was impossible for her to give birth. Thus Hashem reproved her with the same word, לֵאמֹר, for being so certain, thereby dismissing the possibility that even Hashem could help her.

We can now understand Sarah's denial upon being accused. It is not that, God forbid, she was pretending that she had never doubted the angel's words. Of course she had.

Rather, she was denying the aspect of לֵאמֹר . She was saying, "It's true that I was skeptical. But, never did I think the matter to be impossible, never did I believe with absolute certainty that such a thing would be impossible for Hashem!"

וַה' אָמָר הַמְכַסֶּה אֲנִי מֵאַבְרָהָם אֲשֶׁר אֲנִי עֹשֶׂה
And Hashem said, "Shall I conceal from Abraham what I do" (18:17).

The wording here could give the impression that Hashem had been deliberating whether to reveal to Abraham what He intended to do to Sodom or whether to conceal it from him; ultimately He decided to let him know.

Hashem does not change His mind. This verse must therefore be understood as a lesson for man, that upon being faced with a similar situation we, too, would be expected to carefully deliberate whether to say anything.

What was it about this episode that demanded such discretion? And how, in particular, would it be especially pertinent to us?

Abraham personified the trait of kindness:

תִּתֵּן אֱמֶת לְיַעֲקֹב חֶסֶד לְאַבְרָהָם, *Give truth to Jacob, kindness (chessed) to Abraham ... (Michah 7:20).*

The precondition to being a *baal chessed* is to be absolutely convinced of the intrinsic greatness that is within each and every human being, including those of the absolutely lowest status: מֵאַשְׁפֹּת יָרִים אֶבְיוֹן ... , *From the dumps will I raise the impoverished (I Shmuel 2:8).*

From the *baal chessed's* perspective, every individual must be seen as possessing a spark of Godliness from which could be kindled a great light. Otherwise, how could the *baal chessed* continue reaching out to those whose value is least apparent?

What if he were to be shown that, in fact, there are people in the world who have lost their humanity and are really no better than wild animals? What effect would this sobering realization have on the *baal chessed*? To what extent would it dampen his enthusiasm for extending himself to those of the lowest rank, those who are actually the greatest in need? Would there now be a nagging doubt that, perhaps, all his efforts will be in vain? Would he now hesitate?

One might therefore reason that it very well might have been best that Hashem not tell Abraham of the level of depravity that had been reached by the people of Sodom. In fact, Hashem had given up hope for them; they were beyond returning to humanity. They had to be destroyed.

Perhaps it would have been best to conceal this from Abraham. Let him think that Sodom was being destroyed as a dramatic warning to others that they should repent. Or, let him think that they were not yet deserving of such punishment, but were being allowed to die now like the rebellious son, who is executed because of what he may turn into rather than because of what he has already done.

These considerations all seem to be quite reasonable. But this is so only when we are dealing with private citizens. We need their idealism, even though it might sometimes be misplaced. Must they become jaded? Let them continue showing *chessed* to even the most unlikely subjects.

Abraham's case was different, however. As one who was destined to be "the father of many nations," it would be his responsibility to guide future generations. His vision needed to be much more clear. He would be making fateful decisions that would affect great nations.

He therefore had to be taught to acknowledge the bitter reality that predatory creatures with human forms inhabit society, and that showing them kindness would be tantamount to acting with cruelty toward those who are most vulnerable. The only proper course for such people would be strict judgment — and suitable, merciless punishment.

And that is what is meant by the following:

> הַמְכַסֶּה אֲנִי מֵאַבְרָהָם אֲשֶׁר אֲנִי עֹשֶׂה. וְאַבְרָהָם הָיוֹ יִהְיֶה לְגוֹי גָּדוֹל ...
> כִּי יְדַעְתִּיו לְמַעַן אֲשֶׁר יְצַוֶּה אֶת בָּנָיו וְאֶת בֵּיתוֹ אַחֲרָיו וְשָׁמְרוּ דֶּרֶךְ ה'
> לַעֲשׂוֹת צְדָקָה וּמִשְׁפָּט

> *... Shall I conceal from Abraham what I do, now that Abraham is surely to become a great and mighty nation ... For I have loved him, because he commands his children and his household after him that they keep the way of Hashem, doing charity and justice (18:17-19).*

As we can now see, Hashem is clearly stating His reason for telling Abraham of His intentions with regard to Sodom: Abraham will be the father of a great nation. And, that responsibility is specifically directed toward instituting a system of צְדָקָה וּמִשְׁפָּט, *charity and justice*.

That is, there must be charity, but there will also be occasions calling for מִדַּת הַדִּין, *strict judgment*, accompanied by suitable, merciless punishment.

And that is a lesson that is ultimately most relevant to those who will head the society rather than those who will function within it. Let the rest of us, however, remain as innocents.

≈

וַיְהִי אַחַר הַדְּבָרִים הָאֵלֶּה וְהָאֱלֹהִים נִסָּה אֶת אַבְרָהָם
And it happened after these things that God tested Abraham (22:1).

רש"י : אַחַר הַדְּבָרִים הָאֵלֶּה – יֵשׁ מֵרַבּוֹתֵינוּ אוֹמְרִים אַחַר דְּבָרָיו שֶׁל שָׂטָן, שֶׁהָיָה מְקַטְרֵג וְאוֹמֵר מִכָּל סְעוּדָה שֶׁעָשָׂה אַבְרָהָם לֹא הִקְרִיב לְפָנֶיךָ פַּר אֶחָד אוֹ אַיִל אֶחָד, אָמַר לוֹ כְּלוּם עָשָׂה אֶלָּא בִּשְׁבִיל בְּנוֹ, אִילוּ הָיִיתִי אוֹמֵר לוֹ זְבַח אוֹתוֹ לְפָנַי לֹא הָיָה מְעַכֵּב.

RASHI: AFTER THESE THINGS — *There are those among our Rabbis who say this means after the word of the Satan, who was accusing Abraham and saying, "Out of the entire banquet that Abraham made, he did not offer before You even one bull or one ram." God said to him, "Did he make the banquet for any reason at all other than for his son? If I were to say to him, 'Sacrifice him before me,' he would not refrain from doing it."*

Rashi, based on the Gemara in *Sanhedrin* 89b, understands the phrase אַחַר הַדְּבָרִים הָאֵלֶּה, *after these things*, to actually mean, "after these *words*," meaning that the event of the sacrifice happened in response to the *words* said by the Satan. To wit: Satan spoke certain accusatory words (דְּבָרִים) regarding the festive meal that Abraham had made without also offering a sacrifice to Hashem. [See 21:8

Parashas Vayeira / 79

— *Abraham made a great feast on the day Isaac was weaned.*] In response to this accusation, Hashem commanded Abraham to sacrifice his son.

But, hadn't this banquet taken place thirty-five years earlier? Why was the Satan's accusation suddenly reawakened now? And, shouldn't we also wonder whether Satan might have had a point? Why didn't Abraham bring a thanksgiving offering?

In answer to the first question, perhaps we could say that Satan made his accusation immediately after the feast, but society had been giving Abraham the benefit of the doubt. And, as long as society had not accepted this libel, Hashem offered His protection.

Abraham had achieved a position of great prominence and had become "a father of many nations." Abimelech even found it necessary to enter into a covenant with him. The old charges reappeared. The nations said that even they would have made an offering to their gods in gratitude for happy or miraculous events. Why were Abraham and his God any different? Wouldn't one expect at least that minimal standard?

They had waited, fully expecting that he had been planning to bring the offering. Perhaps he had postponed the sacrifice during the twenty-six years that he had dwelled in the land of the Philistines because he considered the place too impure, unfit for the bringing of a sacrifice.

But after he had already been living in Hebron for twelve years and still had not demonstrated that he was about to fulfill what the nations would have considered to be an obligation, the complaints came to the forefront. In their eyes, it was a desecration of Hashem's Name! The Satan's earlier charge was reinstated and, in retrospect, seemed justified.

That is why the response came only after thirty-five years.

As to the second question, why in fact Abraham had not offered a sacrifice, let us make a suggestion: Perhaps Abraham thought that he had already done so.

Hashem had informed him that his descendants would be as numerous as the dust of the earth and would inherit all of the lands around him. In response, he built an altar (see 13:14-18), even though none of this had yet occurred. All he had was a promise.

But, for Abraham, that promise was enough: Once Hashem promised something, in Abraham's eyes it was as if He had already fulfilled it. Therefore, Abraham already had brought a sacrifice thanking Hashem for his son's birth. It's just that he did it before the event!

When Isaac was born, Sarah voiced praise and gratitude to Hashem, but Abraham did not. As far as he was concerned, once Hashem had announced Isaac's birth to him, Isaac was as good as born.

וַיְהִי אַחַר הַדְּבָרִים הָאֵלֶּה וְהָאֱלֹהִים נִסָּה אֶת אַבְרָהָם
And it happened after these things
that God tested Abraham (22:1).

רש"י : **אַחַר הַדְּבָרִים הָאֵלֶּה** ... וְיֵשׁ אוֹמְרִים אַחַר דְּבָרָיו שֶׁל יִשְׁמָעֵאל שֶׁהָיָה מִתְפָּאֵר עַל יִצְחָק שֶׁמָּל בֶּן שְׁלֹשׁ עֶשְׂרֵה שָׁנָה וְלֹא מִיחָה, אָמַר לוֹ יִצְחָק בְּאֵבֶר אֶחָד אַתָּה מְיָרְאֵנִי, אִילוּ אָמַר לִי הַקָּדוֹשׁ בָּרוּךְ הוּא זְבַח עַצְמְךָ לְפָנַי לֹא הָיִיתִי מְעַכֵּב.

RASHI: AFTER THESE THINGS — *And there are those who say that it means after the words of Ishmael who would pride himself over Isaac because he underwent circumcision at the age of thirteen and did not object. (Isaac was eight days old at his bris and had no choice in the matter.) Isaac said to him, "Do you try and instill fear in me with what you did with only one body part? If the Holy One, Blessed is He, would say to me, 'Sacrifice yourself before Me,' I would not refrain from doing so."*

*I*n addition to the opinion quoted in our previous comment, *Rashi* brings a second approach in commenting on the phrase, "after these things," again understanding it as "after these words." This time he says that Ishmael had boasted to Isaac that while Isaac's circumcision had taken place when he was too young to object to it, Ishmael had willingly allowed himself to be circumcised at the age of 13. Isaac replied that Ishmael offered only one body part, while he, Isaac, would gladly be willing to sacrifice his entire body.

One might think that there would appear to be a significant weakness in this version of events: If it were correct, shouldn't the Torah have rather stated that Hashem tested Isaac? It says that Hashem tested Abraham, but, according to this version, Isaac was really the one who was being subjected to a test, a test for which he had asked!

We could answer this, however, by suggesting that any time a son is given some kind of spiritual challenge, his father is being tested as well: What type of education did the child receive? What kind of values? What type of priorities? Did the father educate him well enough to successfully withstand this spiritual trial?

So, when the Torah reports that Hashem tested Abraham, it is really telling us that Isaac would certainly be tested, but he would not be the only one. It would also, perhaps ultimately, be a test for his father.

Returning now to our original question, as to why Isaac was not mentioned, perhaps the phrase וְהָאֱלֹהִים נִסָּה אֶת אַבְרָהָם contains an acknowledgment of the fact that this was a dual test. Perhaps, when the verse says אֶת אַבְרָהָם, it could be understood as meaning that Hashem tested not just Abraham, but also the one who was subordinate to him: his son.

The one who was עִם אַבְרָהָם, with Abraham.

Isaac.

וַיְהִי אַחַר הַדְּבָרִים הָאֵלֶּה וְהָאֱלֹהִים נִסָּה אֶת אַבְרָהָם

And it happened after these things that God tested Abraham (22:1).

This verse describes, of course, the trial known as *Akeidas Yitzchak*, the call for Abraham to sacrifice Isaac, his son. The Mishnah in *Pirkei Avos (5:4)* tells us that there were, in fact, ten trials that were given to Abraham. If so, what is so unique about this one that it, and no other, is explicitly identified by the Torah as being "a trial"?

One reason could be that *Akeidas Yitzchak* is considered by some Rabbinic sources to be the final trial. The previous nine could then be considered mere preparations for this one, which would be the ultimate test. It would be a test of whether a person would be willing to give everything he has — only in order to fulfill Hashem's will.

The first trial Abraham faced, that of being cast into the fiery furnace in Ur Kasdim, showed that he was willing to sacrifice his body for Hashem's sake. This test, however, would be different. He was being called upon to bind his beloved son, place him on the altar, and demonstrate his willingness to give up an entire life-time's worth of spiritual achievements in order to obey Hashem's command.

Abraham had devoted his life to bringing love of Hashem into the world. His defined mission was to persuade others that Hashem desired only what would be good for the world; He would certainly have no desire for human sacrifice!

Now, suddenly, Hashem tested him by ordering him to chance the possibility of casting away all of this goodwill. Were he to sacrifice his only son, upon the demand of this God Who, he had claimed, only desired the good, the world might possibly think that he had, in fact, been wrong all along — perhaps even insane!

Such was the nature of this trial. And, all that he had endured up to now would come as his preparation.

Perhaps this is why Hashem put so many qualifiers in his commands to Abraham: "Please take your son, your only one, whom you love — Isaac."

Some people are willing to give up all their physical possessions for Hashem's sake, and are even prepared to give up their lives, but are unwilling to let go of their spiritual accomplishments, even though they know that Hashem desires it of them.

Perhaps the fact that Isaac was to be brought as a *korban olah*, an elevation-offering, totally consumed on the altar with nothing left for any person, symbolizes this demand, namely that one be prepared to offer his entire self, spiritual as well as physical, before Hashem.

וַיֹּאמֶר אַבְרָהָם אֶל נְעָרָיו שְׁבוּ לָכֶם פֹּה עִם הַחֲמוֹר
וַאֲנִי וְהַנַּעַר נֵלְכָה עַד כֹּה וְנִשְׁתַּחֲוֶה וְנָשׁוּבָה אֲלֵיכֶם

And Abraham said to his young men,
"Stay here by yourselves with the donkey,
while I and the lad will go yonder;
we will worship and we will return to you" (22:5).

The Sages interpreted Abraham's order as a slur against his servants, insinuating that they were somewhat like donkeys.

Isaiah the prophet said (1:3): יָדַע שׁוֹר קֹנֵהוּ וַחֲמוֹר אֵבוּס בְּעָלָיו, *An ox knows its owner and a donkey knows the feeding-trough of its master.*

In other words, the animal relates to its owner only in the very limited sense of the owner's being the provider of his food. But, nothing beyond that.

The animal does not recognize his human master's inherent superiority or see him in any capacity beyond the very limited physical sense.

So, too, with these servants of Abraham, whose vision of their master did not extend to following him as he went on a mission of the spirit.

When it came to a mission of the spirit, therefore, they had to remain behind.

וַיִּהְיוּ חַיֵּי שָׂרָה מֵאָה שָׁנָה וְעֶשְׂרִים שָׁנָה
וְשֶׁבַע שָׁנִים שְׁנֵי חַיֵּי שָׂרָה

Sarah's lifetime was one hundred years,
twenty years, and seven years;
the years of Sarah's life (23:1).

רַבִּי עֲקִיבָא הָיָה יוֹשֵׁב וְדוֹרֵשׁ וְהַצִּבּוּר מִתְנַמְנֵם בִּקֵּשׁ לְעוֹרְרָן אָמַר מָה
רָאֲתָה אֶסְתֵּר שֶׁתִּמְלוֹךְ עַל שֶׁבַע וְעֶשְׂרִים וּמֵאָה מְדִינָה אֶלָּא תָּבֹא
אֶסְתֵּר שֶׁהָיְתָה בַּת בִּתָּהּ שֶׁל שָׂרָה שֶׁהָיְתָה ק׳ וכ׳ וז׳ וְתִמְלוֹךְ עַל ק׳ וכ׳
וז׳ מְדִינוֹת.

R' Akiva was teaching and his audience was tired. He
decided to spark their interest. He said, "How was it that
Esther merited to rule over 127 provinces? It was because
she descended from Sarah who lived 127 years" (Bereishis
Rabbah, Parashas Noach 3).

*W*hat is the meaning of this Midrash? Why the association between Esther and Sarah? How is it that Sarah's having lived 127 years should translate into Esther's having ruled 127 provinces?

We could try to understand this by recalling the following Gemara in *Berachos* 13a:

שָׂרַי הִיא שָׂרָה, בַּתְּחִלָּה נַעֲשֵׂית שָׂרַי לְאוּמָתָהּ, וְלַבְּסוֹף נַעֲשֵׂית שָׂרָה לְכָל הָעוֹלָם כּוּלוֹ, *Sarai is Sarah: Initially, she was minister (*שָׂרַי *could translate as "my minister") over her own nation; in the end she was minister (*שָׂרָה translate as "its minister") over the entire world.*

The Gemara tells us that Sarai's name was altered to Sarah because she had dominion over the entire world.

And, just where do we see that Sarah ruled the world? Quite the opposite seems to be the case! Wasn't she taken against her will by Pharaoh and Abimelech? She didn't even own a place for her interment! And, Abraham had to pay "full price" for it!

Perhaps the meaning of Sarah's having dominion over the entire world is as follows. The Hebrew word "Sarah" has multiple meanings, among them *to rule*, but also to prevail, to maintain, to rest, and to dwell.

Sarah remained the same — unscathed and unaffected — no matter what happened to her and no matter where she happened to be. Whether she was in the house of Abraham, that of Abimelech, or of Pharaoh, she was always steadfast, consistently maintaining the same spiritual level. Her faith neither faltered nor diminished. She would not allow the immorality and depravity of her surroundings to affect her.

Even as a woman who was childless for many years, she still showed the same faith that she would express once she was blessed with a child.

That is the meaning of her name and the meaning of the statements of our Sages. She was Sarah because she ruled the world in the sense of her always staying above it. And, she never allowed the world to "rule" her. That is why she was a "Sarah."

Now we can explore how this could be connected with a particular merit or trait that Esther is said to have received from her, according to the Sages.

Like Sarah, Esther was taken from a place of righteousness to a place that was quite the opposite. Esther was taken from the house of Mordechai to the palace of the wicked Ahasuerus. She went from an environment that was at the extreme of righteousness to another at its opposite. Yet, she remained unscathed and untarnished. She maintained the same faith and fear of God.

This is the significance, then, of Esther's dominion over the world. She was queen of 127 provinces and never allowed any of those provinces — or their influences — to rule over her.

Sarah, our mother, blazed the trail. She transformed this great capability from the potential to the actual.

Once it was actively used by Esther, this powerful characteristic could then become an inherent part of the Jewish soul for all generations to follow.

We now have the ability to emulate these great women and we possess the strength that they have passed down to the soul of our nation, to find the resources and the desire to maintain our faith and to withstand the corruption of our surroundings.

מֵאָה שָׁנָה וְעֶשְׂרִים שָׁנָה וְשֶׁבַע שָׁנִים שְׁנֵי חַיֵּי שָׂרָה

One hundred years, twenty years, and seven years; the years of Sarah's life (23:1).

רש"י: וַיִּהְיוּ חַיֵּי שָׂרָה מֵאָה שָׁנָה וְעֶשְׂרִים שָׁנָה וְשֶׁבַע שָׁנִים – לְכָךְ נִכְתַּב שָׁנָה בְּכָל כְּלָל וּכְלָל, לוֹמַר לְךָ שֶׁכָּל אֶחָד נִדְרָשׁ לְעַצְמוֹ, בַּת מֵאָה

כְּבַת עֶשְׂרִים לְחֵטְא, מַה בַּת עֶשְׂרִים לֹא חָטְאָה, שֶׁהֲרֵי אֵינָהּ בַּת עוֹנָשִׁין, אַף בַּת מֵאָה בְּלֹא חֵטְא, וּבַת עֶשְׂרִים כְּבַת שֶׁבַע לְיוֹפִי.

RASHI: SARAH'S LIFETIME WAS ONE HUNDRED YEARS, TWENTY YEARS, AND SEVEN YEARS — *This is why "years" was written at each category, to say to you that each one is expounded on its own: when she was 100 years old, she was like 20 years old with respect to sin; just as one who is 20 years old is considered as if she had not sinned, for she is not liable to punishment, so too, when Sarah was 100 years old she was without sin. And when she was 20 years old, she was like 7 years old with respect to beauty.*

*R*ashi comments that the word "year" is repeated with each numerical unit to tell us that each one has a different meaning: At the age of 100 Sarah was as free of sin as a 20-year-old (who is not yet punished for her sins), and at 20 she was as beautiful as a 7-year-old.

Let us try to examine the significance of this statement.

A person's life can be viewed as a succession of phases, each with its own purpose and goal. As one moves from one phase to the next, he must try to extract the essence and purpose of the previous stage and carry it forward to the new one.

Childhood is the phase in which a person's beauty shows itself. A child is full of the joy of life, brimming with faith and confidence, and free of the impurities of sin. He is spontaneous and unaffected, showing all his emotions on the surface.

Youth is a time of education and training to assume the responsibilities of life.

The next phase could be called one's active years, when one must fulfill his tasks and bear life's burdens.

The challenge of youth is to retain the purity and sincerity of childhood even as one is being trained for the life that lies ahead.

The mature years are marked by the challenge of continuing to grow and strive toward one's purpose despite numerous burdens and responsibilities. One must continue to ascend to higher and higher levels and not allow himself to stagnate.

This is the way that we can now understand *Rashi*. Each person develops as an individual unit, a distinct world unto himself. His purpose and mission in life, as determined by his soul and his abilities, is to be himself (and to serve Hashem as the person he is). He should not pretend to be anyone or anything other than himself.

In stating that these were חַיֵּי שָׂרָה , *the years of Sarah's life*, the Torah is telling us that she made her life into *Sarah's life*; everything she did, she did as *Sarah* — and not as someone else.

Of her and others like her, the Psalmist wrote (37:18): יוֹדֵעַ ה' יְמֵי תְּמִימִם וְנַחֲלָתָם לְעוֹלָם תִּהְיֶה, *Hashem attends the days of the perfect; their inheritance will last forever.*

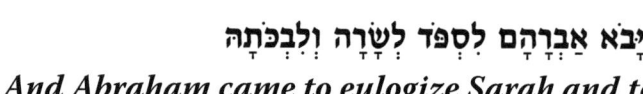

וַיָּבֹא אַבְרָהָם לִסְפֹּד לְשָׂרָה וְלִבְכֹּתָהּ
And Abraham came to eulogize Sarah and to bewail her (23:2).

וַיָּבֹא אַבְרָהָם לִסְפֹּד לְשָׂרָה – מֵהֵיכָן בָּא, רַבִּי לֵוִי אָמַר מִקְּבוּרָתוֹ שֶׁל תֶּרַח לְשָׂרָה בָּא, אָמַר לוֹ ר' יוֹסֵי וַהֲלֹא קְבוּרָתוֹ שֶׁל תֶּרַח קָדְמָה לִקְבוּרָתוֹ שֶׁל שָׂרָה שְׁתֵּי שָׁנִים אֶלָּא מֵהֵיכָן בָּא מֵהַר הַמּוֹרִיָּה וּמֵתָה שָׂרָה מֵאוֹתוֹ צַעַר לְפִיכָךְ נִסְמְכָה עֲקֵידָה לְ"וַיִּהְיוּ חַיֵּי שָׂרָה".

AND ABRAHAM CAME TO EULOGIZE SARAH — *From where had he come? R' Levi said he was coming from the burial of his father Terah to that of Sarah. R' Yose objected: "But Terah's burial preceded Sarah's by two years! Rather, from where had Abraham come? He had* *come from Mount Moriah. And, Sarah had died due to her distress. And that is why the Torah juxtaposes Akeidas Yitzchak to the words, 'and these were the days of Sarah'" (Bereishis Rabbah, Parashas Noach).*

The verse emphasizes that Abraham "came," but fails to tell us from where he had come and, more importantly, why this "coming" was of sufficient importance to merit its being mentioned in the Torah. Obviously, since Abraham was now in Hebron, he had to have "come" from some other place. Why, then, does the Torah need to tell us? It seems to be superfluous.

The Midrash in *Bereishis Rabbah* deals with this question.

R' Levi said he was coming from burying his father, Terah. R' Yose objected, saying that Terah had died two years earlier and argued that he must have been coming from Mount Moriah, where he had nearly brought his son Isaac as an offering. Sarah's death was brought on by the distress she felt upon hearing of this incident.

Upon thinking about what it was that led each of these sages to give the answers they did, I would like to tell you that Hashem has opened my eyes to a wonderful allusion that explains the source for both opinions.

The phrase that raised the question here is וַיָּבֹא אַבְרָהָם. Let us separate the phrase into its two component words: וַיָּבֹא and אַבְרָהָם. Now let us read each of these words from *left to right* rather than right to left, as we would normally read Hebrew.

We get the word אָבִיו (*his father*) from וַיָּבֹא, and מֵהַר בָּא (*he came from the mountain*) from אַבְרָהָם.

Now let us look again at the two opinions in light of the observation that we have just made. R' Levi reasons that only the word וַיָּבֹא is superfluous, since the Torah had to mention Abraham but did not need to tell us that he had come. R' Levi reversed that superfluous word and concluded that Abraham's coming was connected with his father.

R' Yose, however, thought that the two-year gap made the first interpretation, based on וַיָּבֹא , implausible. He therefore looked at the next word, אַבְרָהָם, and concluded that he must have "come" from what had happened on the mountain, Mount Moriah.

———

וְאַבְרָהָם זָקֵן בָּא בַּיָּמִים וַה' בֵּרַךְ אֶת אַבְרָהָם בַּכֹּל
Now Abraham was old, well on in years,
and Hashem had blessed Abraham
with everything (24:1).

———

רש"י: בֵּרַךְ אֶת אַבְרָהָם בַּכֹּל – בַּכֹּל עוֹלֶה בְּגֵימַטְרִיָּא בֵּן, וּמֵאַחַר שֶׁהָיָה לוֹ בֵן הָיָה צָרִיךְ לְהַשִּׂיאוֹ אִשָּׁה.

RASHI: HAD BLESSED ABRAHAM WITH EVERYTHING
— *The numerical value of* בַּכֹּל *equals that of* בֵּן, *"son."*

Rashi points out that the *gematria* of בַּכֹּל, *with everything,* is equal to בֵּן, *son.* Therefore, when the Torah is telling us that Abraham was blessed with "everything," it really means to tell us that he had been blessed with a son, Isaac.

We might therefore ask: If that is what the Torah intended to tell us, why didn't it just do so, without having us resort to *gematrias*? Let the verse have simply said, וַה' בֵּרַךְ אֶת אַבְרָהָם בְּבֵן, *Hashem blessed Abraham with a son!*

An examination of two opposite personality types that we find within our community might yield some insight into resolving our question.

Every community knows of individuals who wholeheartedly devote themselves to public service, spending nearly all their available waking hours in activities that benefit the community. These individuals sometimes wind up allowing themselves very little time for the raising of their own children.

Conversely, we see others who are quite the opposite, putting all their energy and available time into their children, with almost no time left over for the wider community's needs.

Both extremes are incorrect.

The first group should not be neglecting their own children; the second should not be turning their backs on the community.

While it is certainly important to give the highest priority to one's own children, one must not forget that there are also other children in the world: Hashem's children. The verse (*Devarim* 14:1) says, בָּנִים אַתֶּם לַה' אֱלֹהֵיכֶם, *You are children to Hashem, your God.*

All of us have the same Father.

Fortunate is the one who can successfully strike a balance, fulfilling both responsibilities, neglecting neither his own children nor Hashem's.

How can this best be achieved? Perhaps by training one's own children to consistently engage in acts of kindness, and to always be attuned to the needs of the poor and disadvantaged. And, especially, to visit and give moral support to the elderly and infirm.

Now, we can return to our original question: What is meant by saying that Abraham was blessed בַּכֹּל (*with everything*) which is בְּבֵן (*with a son*)? The answer goes back to what we have just said. It refers to the way Abraham related to both his son and to the world at large.

He was given the name Abraham because he would be "a father to many nations." *Tikkun HaOlam* (repair of the world) would be his life's mission.

Even so, he would also merit to personally raise his own child, assuring that he, too, would follow in His ways.

וַיֵּלְכוּ שְׁנֵיהֶם יַחְדָּו, *and the two of them walked together* (22:6). The two of them walked together, father and son, Abraham and Isaac, on the same path, like father like son.

And, Abraham would also be "a father to many nations."

לֹא אֹכַל עַד אִם דִּבַּרְתִּי דְּבָרָי
I will not eat until I have spoken my piece (24:33).

hy did Eliezer refuse to eat what was offered him by Laban? Doesn't this seem to be inconsistent with the the well-known statement in *Pesachim* 86b, כָּל מַה שֶׁיֹּאמַר לְךָ בַּעַל הַבַּיִת עֲשֵׂה, חוּץ מִצֵּא, *Do whatever your host asks of you, except to leave?*

This is a question that has been asked numerous times. *Maharil Diskin* says in the name of his father that once the time has arrived for doing a mitzvah, one may not eat. Another reason that has been given is that one who is about to betroth a woman is forbidden to eat, lest he become intoxicated and not have the required presence of mind. This is one of the common explanations for why a groom fasts on his wedding day. Since Eliezer was acting as Isaac's agent to betroth Rebecca, according to this explanation this would have applied to him as well.

I would like to offer another suggestion.

We learn from the Sages that when someone is given more honor than his position in life would justify, he is obligated to tell his hosts that they must be mistaken. We learn this from the case of the murderer who flees to the City of Refuge. If he passes through a city and its citizenry wishes to somehow honor him, thinking that it is due him, he must disclose his true situation, that he is actually a murderer en route to a City of Refuge.

If we look at the two previous verses (31-32), we see the kind of reception given to Eliezer by Laban and the context within which the food was offered:

וַיֹּאמֶר בּוֹא בְּרוּךְ ה' לָמָּה תַעֲמֹד בַּחוּץ וְאָנֹכִי פִּנִּיתִי הַבַּיִת וּמָקוֹם לַגְּמַלִּים. וַיָּבֹא

הָאִישׁ הַבַּיְתָה וַיְפַתַּח הַגְּמַלִּים וַיִּתֵּן תֶּבֶן וּמִסְפּוֹא לַגְּמַלִּים וּמַיִם לִרְחֹץ רַגְלָיו וְרַגְלֵי הָאֲנָשִׁים אֲשֶׁר אִתּוֹ, *He said, "Come, O blessed of Hashem! Why should you stand outside when I have cleared the house, and place for the camels?" So the man entered the house, and unmuzzled the camels. He gave straw and feed for the camels, and water to bathe his feet and the feet of the men who were with him.*

They then placed food in front of him, serving him in an honored place, offering him food before having any themselves. Eliezer began to suspect that perhaps these people had things a bit confused. Maybe Laban thought that he had Abraham himself sitting there, rather than a servant. (Why else would Laban have called this guest, a mere servant, "O blessed of Hashem"?)

Eliezer therefore said, לֹא אֹכַל עַד אִם דִּבַּרְתִּי דְּבָרָי , *I will not eat until I have spoken my piece.* And then, וַיֹּאמַר עֶבֶד אַבְרָהָם אָנֹכִי , He said, "A servant of Abraham am I."

I am neither Abraham, nor a free man. I am Abraham's servant, and not worthy of your special treatment.

Their attitude toward Eliezer changed immediately: וַיֹּאכְלוּ וַיִּשְׁתּוּ הוּא וְהָאֲנָשִׁים אֲשֶׁר עִמּוֹ, *They ate and drank, he and the men who were with him* (24:54).

With him, it says in the verse, meaning in a way that was equal to him. He was now repositioned, placed together with the servants who had accompanied him, and was no longer the beneficiary of honor that was never due him.

Now he could eat.

וַיֹּסֶף אַבְרָהָם וַיִּקַּח אִשָּׁה וּשְׁמָהּ קְטוּרָה. וַתֵּלֶד לוֹ אֶת
זִמְרָן וְאֶת יָקְשָׁן וְאֶת מְדָן וְאֶת מִדְיָן וְאֶת יִשְׁבָּק וְאֶת שׁוּחַ
... וְאֵלֶּה תֹּלְדֹת יִשְׁמָעֵאל בֶּן אַבְרָהָם אֲשֶׁר יָלְדָה הָגָר
הַמִּצְרִית שִׁפְחַת שָׂרָה לְאַבְרָהָם ... וְאֵלֶּה תּוֹלְדֹת יִצְחָק בֶּן
אַבְרָהָם אַבְרָהָם הוֹלִיד אֶת יִצְחָק

*Abraham proceeded and took a wife whose name
was Keturah. She bore him Zimran, Jokshan,
Medan, Midian, Ishbak, and Shuah ... These are
the descendants of Ishmael, Abraham's son, whom
Hagar the Egyptian, Sarah's maidservant, bore to
Abraham ... These are the offspring of Isaac, son of
Abraham — Abraham begot Isaac (25:1-2,12,19).*

While Ishmael is referred to in the Torah (ibid., quoted
above) as יִשְׁמָעֵאל בֶּן אַבְרָהָם, *Ishmael son of Abraham*, a
descendant of Abraham, the children of Keturah are not,
even though Abraham was their father. Similarly, their offspring are
not listed, while those of Ishmael are (ibid., quoted above).

This distinction is even more interesting when one considers that
Ishmael and the sons of Keturah shared not only the same father
(Abraham), but also, according to *Rashi*, the same mother! While
the Torah (16:15) identifies Ishmael's mother as being Hagar, *Rashi*
to 25:1 says that Hagar and Keturah are one and the same:

וַתֵּלֶד הָגָר לְאַבְרָם בֵּן וַיִּקְרָא אַבְרָם שֵׁם בְּנוֹ אֲשֶׁר יָלְדָה הָגָר יִשְׁמָעֵאל

*Hagar bore Abram a son and Abram called the name of
his son that Hagar bore him "Ishmael" (16:15).*

וַיֹּסֶף אַבְרָהָם וַיִּקַּח אִשָּׁה וּשְׁמָהּ קְטוּרָה

*Abraham proceeded and took a wife whose name was
Keturah (25:1).*

RASHI: KETURAH — *This is Hagar.*

What would be the significance of this differentiation? For one, we do know that Ishmael, unlike his siblings, did inherit some of his father's spiritual qualities. Nonetheless, Abraham was not the major influence on his life. Rather, it was his mother who was the stronger influence. Therefore, when the Torah lists Ishmael's descendants, instead of again calling him son of Abraham, it instead refers to him as the son of an Egyptian woman named Hagar: וְאֵלֶּה תֹּלְדֹת יִשְׁמָעֵאל בֶּן אַבְרָהָם אֲשֶׁר יָלְדָה הָגָר הַמִּצְרִית שִׁפְחַת שָׂרָה לְאַבְרָהָם, *These are the descendants of Ishmael, Abraham's son, whom Hagar the Egyptian, Sarah's maidservant, bore to Abraham* (25:12).

Hagar is called "the Egyptian" to stress that she was not yet cleansed from the contamination of Egypt. However, she was also "*the maidservant of Sarah*," subordinate to her mistress, Sarah, and therefore an indirect conduit of Sarah's influence as well.

The description indicates an internal conflict within Hagar, a contention of alternating dominance between Egyptian culture and the influence of Sarah. As she was Ishmael's major influence, this resulted in his becoming פֶּרֶא אָדָם, *a wild ass of a man* (16:12), someone with no clear course in life.

The word פֶּרֶא is similar to the word רפא, which means to be weakened. There were times when he would try to subdue his evil inclination and allow himself to repent. An example of this type of behavior would be when, after Abraham's death, he acknowledged the spiritual superiority of his younger brother, deferring to him by allowing him to take the lead in the burial of their father. There were other times when, quite the opposite, he was consumed with hatred of Isaac. He could pray to Hashem five times, but murder and steal as well.

In contrast, regarding Isaac, the Torah says: וְאֵלֶּה תּוֹלְדֹת יִצְחָק בֶּן אַבְרָהָם אַבְרָהָם הוֹלִיד אֶת יִצְחָק, *These are the offspring of Isaac, son of Abraham; Abraham begot Isaac* (25:19).

As the verse indicates, he was entirely the son of Abraham, a model and beloved companion of his father who inherited all his father's lofty spiritual qualities. When the verse reiterates that *Abraham begot Isaac*, it is is not doing so in order to merely present us with a biological fact, especially one that we already know.

Rather, when it says that he *begot* him, it also means that he molded him, working with him daily, as if he were "fathering" him anew every day, to the point that they became as one soul. וַיֵּלְכוּ שְׁנֵיהֶם יַחְדָּו, *and the two of them walked together* (22:6).

Therefore, when linking the list of Isaac's progeny with the fact that Abraham had begot Isaac, we are being told not only that these descendants of Isaac's would also be physical descendants of Abraham, but that Abraham's spiritual accomplishments would continue through these offspring.

In a sense, by fathering progeny who would be spiritual Abrahams, one could almost say that the son was now "giving birth" to the father, unlike Abraham's sons through Keturah.

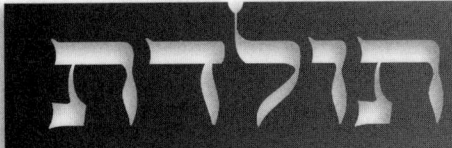

וְאֵלֶּה תּוֹלְדֹת יִצְחָק בֶּן אַבְרָהָם אַבְרָהָם הוֹלִיד אֶת יִצְחָק

These are the offspring of Isaac, son of Abraham;
Abraham begot Isaac (25:19).

T he word תּוֹלְדוֹת, which means *offspring* and is pronounced "*toledos*," could be spelled תּוֹלְדֹת, תֹּלְדוֹת, תּוֹלְדוֹת or תֹּלְדֹת. Each of these four spellings appears in the Torah. The first spelling has a *vav* after the *tav* and after the *dalet;* the last has no *vav* at all; the other two have the *vav* missing either after the *tav* or the *dalet*. The first type of spelling is full, complete, and is called מָלֵא; the other three are called *defective* or חָסֵר.

Rabbi Naftali Tzvi Yehudah Berlin of 19th-century Volozhin, who is known by his acronym "*Netziv*," writes that whenever the Torah uses the defective form, חָסֵר, it is suggesting that it is not only the spelling that is missing something, but that the word itself does not carry its full meaning.

I would like to present an example of how to apply this approach.

In our case, the word in question is תּוֹלְדוֹת. Following the *Netziv's* approach, the instances where it is spelled missing one of the *vavs* are telling us that there was also something defective about the offspring.

As you can see, the word תּוֹלְדֹת in our verse, which refers to the offspring of Isaac, has a *vav* following the *tav* but no *vav* after the *dalet*. When speaking of the offspring of Jacob, however, אֵלֶּה תֹּלְדוֹת יַעֲקֹב (37:2), the spelling is reversed. Concerning Ishmael, וְאֵלֶּה תֹּלְדֹת יִשְׁמָעֵאל (25:12), both *vavs* are missing.

What is the significance of these disparate spellings?

Let us start with the case of Ishmael. There, the *vav* is missing completely, both at the beginning and at the end. Perhaps this is telling us that Ishmael did not leave his "stamp" on his offspring, neither when they were first formed nor after they were born.

Let me explain.

It is natural and expected that parents will pass on to their children certain proclivities and character traits that are unique to that family chain. These characteristics are generally passed from father to son and to succeeding generations. Ishmael never developed a set of fixed characteristics. He was "a wild ass of a man," without defined traits that would become a part of his nature, uniquely his own. Upon having his own children, he therefore had nothing of "himself" to pass on; his children were born with nothing of their parents stamped into their souls.

Even after they were born, he made no systematic attempt to rear them toward pursuing any particular way in life. The totally defective spelling of the word תֹּלְדֹת is a reflection of the reality of the defectiveness of his offspring, both *vavs* missing to show that the lacking was at two stages, when they were first created and then throughout their existence.

Nonetheless, there was some minimal relationship of child to father, which decreased with each successive son. Therefore, the following verse, which lists Ishmael's sons in birth order, spells תּוֹלְדֹת using the first *vav:* "וְאֵלֶּה שְׁמוֹת בְּנֵי יִשְׁמָעֵאל בִּשְׁמֹתָם לְתוֹלְדֹתָם",

These are the names of the sons of Ishmael with their names by their births.

As regards the offspring of Isaac, תּוֹלְדֹת is written with the first *vav* but not the second. Perhaps this reflects the fact that Jacob was considered a worthy heir to Isaac, but Esau was not. Alternatively, we could interpret this spelling to suggest that Jacob and Esau, at the time of their birth, had an equal share in their parents' potential for spiritual achievement. Only later did they part ways — Jacob to become a *tzaddik* and Esau to follow the path of wickedness. Obviously this difference was also manifest in the way they brought up their own children and to what extent Esau's offspring would receive any of the spiritual inheritance, the *vav* of Isaac.

Let us now deal with the verse describing the offspring of Jacob: אֵלֶּה תֹּלְדוֹת יַעֲקֹב יוֹסֵף בֶּן שְׁבַע עֶשְׂרֵה שָׁנָה הָיָה רֹעֶה אֶת אֶחָיו בַּצֹּאן ... , *These are the offspring of Jacob: Joseph, at the age of seventeen years, was a shepherd ...* (37:2).

Following the logic that we have just presented, we must account for why it would be that the first *vav* in תֹּלְדוֹת is missing, but the last is present. Perhaps, we could suggest that while all of Jacob's offspring grew to be blessed with their father's spiritual greatness, only Joseph truly inherited his father's lofty soul from the outset.

אַבְרָהָם הוֹלִיד אֶת יִצְחָק
Abraham begot Isaac (25:19).

*W*e see from here that the education a father gives his son must be so solid that it will impact not only the son, but also the son's sons. This is implied by the words *Abra-*

ham begot Isaac. We could perhaps interpret this to mean that Jacob ultimately played a part in the formation of Isaac's children.

This idea of impressing one's Torah onto succeeding generations is also expressed in the following verses from *Yeshayah*:

וַאֲנִי זֹאת בְּרִיתִי אוֹתָם אָמַר ה' רוּחִי אֲשֶׁר עָלֶיךָ וּדְבָרַי אֲשֶׁר שַׂמְתִּי בְּפִיךָ לֹא יָמוּשׁוּ מִפִּיךָ וּמִפִּי זַרְעֲךָ וּמִפִּי זֶרַע זַרְעֲךָ אָמַר ה' מֵעַתָּה וְעַד עוֹלָם.

... My words that I have placed in your mouth shall not be withdrawn from your mouth nor from the mouth of your offspring, nor from the mouth of your offspring's offspring, said Hashem, from this moment and forever (Yeshayah 59:21).

בֵּית יַעֲקֹב אֲשֶׁר פָּדָה אֶת אַבְרָהָם

The House of Jacob, who redeemed Abraham (ibid. 29:22).

The latter verse seems to be saying that Abraham was redeemed because of Jacob, meaning that Abraham was redeemed because the foundation that he gave Isaac was so strong that it carried over to Isaac's son, Jacob.

We also find support for this in the words of our Sages, based on *Mishlei* 17:6:

עֲטֶרֶת זְקֵנִים בְּנֵי בָנִים וְתִפְאֶרֶת בָּנִים אֲבוֹתָם

The crown of the aged is grandchildren, and the splendor of children is their fathers.

"עֲטֶרֶת זְקֵנִים בְּנֵי בָנִים", רַבִּי שְׁמוּאֵל בַּר רַב יִצְחָק אָמַר: אַבְרָהָם לֹא נִיצַל מִכִּבְשַׁן הָאֵשׁ אֶלָּא בִּזְכוּת שֶׁל יַעֲקֹב.

The crown of the aged is grandchildren — R' Shmuel son of Rav Yitzchak said, "Abraham was saved from the

furnace of Kasdim due to the merit of Jacob"
(*Bereishis Rabbah* 63).

וַיֶּעְתַּר יִצְחָק לַה' לְנֹכַח אִשְׁתּוֹ כִּי עֲקָרָה הִוא
וַיֵּעָתֶר לוֹ ה' וַתַּהַר רִבְקָה אִשְׁתּוֹ

*Isaac entreated Hashem opposite his wife
because she was barren. Hashem allowed
Himself to be entreated by him,
and his wife Rebecca conceived* (25:21).

Rather than tell us that Rebecca was barren and that her
barrenness ultimately led to Isaac's prayer on her behalf,
the Torah first mentions the prayer and only afterward its
catalyst. We would have expected the opposite.

This change of order is in line with the well-known idea expressed
by the Sages:

הַקָּדוֹשׁ בָּרוּךְ הוּא מִתְאַוֶּה לִתְפִלָּתָן שֶׁל צַדִּיקִים, *the Holy One, Blessed is
He, desires the prayers of the righteous,* and therefore provides them
with reason to pray. In our case, the reason would be Rebecca's
childlessness. The order of the verse hints at this idea — that the
purpose of the barrenness was to inspire Isaac's prayer, rather than
the other way around.

Let us also have a look at *Rashi*:

רש"י: וַיֵּעָתֶר לוֹ – לוֹ וְלֹא לָהּ, שֶׁאֵין דּוֹמָה תְּפִלַּת צַדִּיק בֶּן צַדִּיק
לִתְפִלַּת צַדִּיק בֶּן רָשָׁע לְפִיכָךְ לוֹ וְלֹא לָהּ.

**RASHI: HE ALLOWED HIMSELF TO BE ENTREATED
BY HIM** — *But not by her, for the prayer of a righteous
person who is the child of a wicked person is not*

> *comparable to the prayer of a righteous person who is the child of a righteous person. Therefore,* לוֹ, *"by him" and not* לָהּ, *"by her."*

Rashi comments that Isaac's, not Rebecca's, prayer was decisive for Hashem (לוֹ וְלֹא לָהּ) because the prayers of a *tzaddik,* son of another *tzaddik,* do not resemble those of a *tzaddik,* son of a wicked person.

Both of the statements quoted above, regarding whose prayer is most efficacious and regarding Hashem's making *tzaddikim* suffer so that He can then listen to their prayers, demand further explanation.

Why would the desire of Hashem to hear the prayers of Isaac justify the barrenness of Rebecca? And, why would the prayers of a *tzaddik* who is the son of a *tzaddik* be more effective than those of a *tzaddik* who is the son of a wicked person? If anything, the reverse should be true, as the Sages taught: מָקוֹם שֶׁבַּעֲלֵי תְשׁוּבָה עוֹמְדִין, צַדִּיקִים גְּמוּרִים אֵינָם עוֹמְדִין, *In the place where baalei teshuvah (those who have repented of the wrongs they did) stand, even perfect tzaddikim cannot stand (Berachos* 34b).

Let us suggest a possible answer: The Hebrew word for prayer, לְהִתְפַּלֵּל, is related to a word that means justice — פְּלִילִים. This indicates that prayer is really a process of doing justice with oneself, recognizing that, in terms of strict justice, one is not worthy of having his requests answered.

One must therefore ask Hashem to grant his request as he would ask for an undeserved gift, as a servant would ask a favor from his master. (Thus the word חוֹנֵן, *supplicate,* is related to the word חִנָּם, *free of charge.*) It is the Divine will that, despite one's clear recognition that he is unworthy of having his request granted, he must make that request anyway, with the belief that Hashem will answer his prayer, as a Father Who has mercy on His children. This is the basis of the Sages' dictum (*Pirkei Avos* 2:18): וּכְשֶׁאַתָּה מִתְפַּלֵּל אַל תַּעַשׂ תְּפִלָּתְךָ

קֶבַע אֶלָּא רַחֲמִים וְתַחֲנוּנִים לִפְנֵי הַמָּקוֹם שֶׁנֶּאֱמַר (יואל ב:יג): כִּי חַנּוּן וְרַחוּם הוּא אֶרֶךְ אַפַּיִם וְרַב חֶסֶד וְנִחָם עַל הָרָעָה, *... and when you pray, do not make your prayer a set routine, but rather [beg for] compassion and supplication [רַחֲמִים וְתַחֲנוּנִים] before the Omnipresent, "... for He is gracious and merciful, slow to anger and of great kindness, and relents of evil"* (*Yoel* 2:13) .

There is still another aspect of prayer, in addition to that of requesting mercy, and it has to do with justice. One should ask Hashem to fulfill his requests because His doing so would increase His honor in the world and would thereby lead to greater justice.

Along the same lines, one could also say that just as any increase in Hashem's honor in the world will necessarily lead to greater justice, so too, when Hashem listens to our prayers and grants our wishes, as the result of His mercy, this leads to an increase in the amount of mercy in the world.

With these concepts, we can now address the two questions we asked earlier. The reason Hashem desires the prayers of *tzaddikim* is that, through their prayer, they are bringing themselves closer to His Presence. Their being drawn closer to Him will then cause an increase in the Divine Emanation from above to below.

And, if they are praying not for their own personal needs, but purely for the honor of Heaven, the effect will be even more powerful.

Perhaps this could provide an insight as to why Hashem is more receptive to the prayer of a *tzaddik* son of a *tzaddik* than one offered by a *tzaddik* son of a *rasha*. And it could shed some light on the specific case of Isaac's prayer apparently being more efficacious than Rebecca's.

As the son of a *tzaddik*, we could say that Isaac was more likely to have prayed purely for the sake of Heaven, rather than requesting a response to his own personal needs. Perhaps we could say that Rebecca, daughter of the wicked Bethuel and sister of the wicked Laban, was less likely to free her intentions from personal interest.

Thus Hashem would ultimately respond to his prayers, rather than hers, as stated by *Rashi*.

As a continuation to what we have just suggested, let us examine verse 22, וַיִּתְרֹצֲצוּ הַבָּנִים בְּקִרְבָּהּ, *the children agitated within her*. Perhaps, we could apply what we have just learned to gain a new insight into the dynamics of this struggle.

To the extent that we would be permitted to suggest such an idea, and bearing in mind the absolute greatness of our matriarchs and patriarchs to a degree that is beyond anything we can perceive, let us suggest the following: Rebecca's intentions were a combination of a desire to fulfill her own personal needs and a desire to advance the cause of Heaven. Isaac's were purely for the sake of Heaven.

Since their prayers were somewhat different, Hashem separated not only their prayers but also what came as a result of their prayers. Hashem wanted Jacob to develop into a completely pure, whole *tzaddik*, free of internal conflict between opposing forces. Rebecca's component, being a mixture of self-interest and desire for the honor of Heaven, might have compromised Jacob's wholeness.

Therefore, the seed was split in two: there would be not one son, but two. There would be another son, Esau.

Because his existence was due to a component of Rebecca's intentions, namely her desire for both self-fulfillment and the honor of Heaven, Esau was himself beset with conflict, a collision of internal forces with which he would struggle throughout his life. Esau would have to contend with an internal force that drew him to advance the cause of Heaven as well as another internal force which drew him to satisfy his own personal interests.

Unquestionably, he had the strength within him to overcome his base urges, but he rarely used it.

Let us now try to apply what we have just learned to our own lives. Let us see from here how the influence that a parent will have on his children's spiritual makeup begins even before conception. It begins from the thoughts they had when first praying for the children that they would eventually bring into the world.

וַתֹּאמֶר אִם כֵּן לָמָּה זֶּה אָנֹכִי
... and she said, "If so, why is it that I am?" (25:22).

רש"י: **לָמָּה זֶּה אָנֹכִי** – מִתְאַוָּה וּמִתְפַּלֶּלֶת עַל הֵרָיוֹן.

RASHI: WHY IS IT THAT I AM? *Desiring and praying for pregnancy.*

אִבְּן עֶזְרָא: וְהִיא שָׁאֲלָה לְנָשִׁים שֶׁיָּלְדוּ אִם אֵרַע לָהֶם כָּכָה, וַתֹּאמַרְנָה לֹא. וְטַעַם וַתֹּאמֶר אִם כֵּן הַדָּבָר וְהַמִּנְהָג, לָמָּה זֶּה אָנֹכִי בְּהֵרָיוֹן מְשׁוּנֶּה.

IBN EZRA: *It is a question that was posed to women who have given birth, whether they experienced the same thing. They said, "No." This means, then, that she was saying, "If that's true (that your experience is different), why is it that my pregnancy is so strange?"*

רמב"ן: ... וְהַנָּכוֹן בְּעֵינַי כִּי אָמְרָה אִם כֵּן יִהְיֶה לִי, לָמָּה זֶּה אָנֹכִי בָּעוֹלָם, הַלְוַאי אֵינֶנִּי, שֶׁאָמוּת אוֹ שֶׁלֹּא הָיִיתִי.

RAMBAN: (After having rejected the interpretations of *Rashi* and of *Ibn Ezra*, *Ramban* now gives his own interpretation) *In my opinion, she was saying, "If this is the way it will be for me, why am I in the world? I wish that I would no longer be, that I should die or that I never was."*

amban argues that the word "אָנֹכִי" does not refer to the pregnancy and therefore rejects the interpretations of both *Rashi* and *Ibn Ezra*.

I would like to offer a suggestion of my own, bearing in mind that we are trying to derive a lesson for ourselves from the actions of our matriarchs and patriarchs, whose greatness is beyond our comprehension.

Perhaps the Torah is trying to show us that the inner conflict we sometimes see in our children — the agitation, the uncertainty, the way they sometimes act as if they are being pulled in opposite directions — is actually a reflection of what is happening within the psyche of their parents.

Perhaps the parents are themselves conflicted, torn between two different value systems which are, in truth, incompatible. The Book of *Kings* already warns about this: וַיִּגַּשׁ אֵלִיָּהוּ אֶל כָּל הָעָם וַיֹּאמֶר עַד מָתַי אַתֶּם פֹּסְחִים עַל שְׁתֵּי הַסְּעִפִּים אִם ה' הָאֱלֹהִים לְכוּ אַחֲרָיו וְאִם הַבַּעַל לְכוּ אַחֲרָיו וְלֹא עָנוּ הָעָם אֹתוֹ דָּבָר, *Elijah approached all the people and said, "How long will you dance between two opinions? If Hashem is the God, go after Him! And if the Baal, go after it!"* (I *Kings* 18:21).

Perhaps, then, this is what was being felt by Rebecca. Within her womb, she sensed conflict. Her first thought was, "Why am I thus? Is there something about my own self, about my own soul, that is out of sorts? What is the discord that is within my womb telling me about myself?

"Is there something about אָנֹכִי that is conflicted, needing to be reevaluated, reexamined, reconciled, and resolved so that I can be more whole in my service of Hashem?"

וַיַעֲקֹב אִישׁ תָּם יֹשֵׁב אֹהָלִים

Jacob was a wholesome man,
dwelling in tents (25:27).

רש"י: יֹשֵׁב אֹהָלִים – אָהֳלוֹ שֶׁל שֵׁם וְאָהֳלוֹ שֶׁל עֵבֶר.

RASHI: ABIDING IN TENTS — *The tent of Shem and the tent of Eber.*

מִדְרָשׁ תַּנְחוּמָא פ' וַיִּשְׁלַח ט': אֵין לְךָ אָדָם שֶׁהָיָה יָגֵעַ בַּתּוֹרָה כְּאָבִינוּ יַעֲקֹב, כְּמָא דְאַתְּ אָמַר "וַיַעֲקֹב אִישׁ תָּם יֹשֵׁב אֹהָלִים" (כה:כז), אֵין כְּתִיב כַּאן יוֹשֵׁב אֹהֶל, אֶלָּא "יֹשֵׁב אֹהָלִים", יוֹצֵא מִבֵּית מִדְרָשׁוֹ שֶׁל שֵׁם, וְהוֹלֵךְ לְבֵית מִדְרָשׁוֹ שֶׁל עֵבֶר, וּמִבֵּית מִדְרָשׁוֹ שֶׁל עֵבֶר לְבֵית מִדְרָשׁוֹ שֶׁל אַבְרָהָם.

MIDRASH TANCHUMA: *There has never been anyone who has toiled in Torah like our father Jacob, as it is written, "Jacob was a wholesome man, dwelling in tents." It does not say there, "dwells in a tent," but rather "dwells in tents": He would leave the Study Hall of Shem and go to the Study Hall of Eber; from the Study Hall of Eber to the Study Hall of Abraham.*

The text refers to Jacob as a man who was "dwelling in tents," a description whose meaning and significance is unclear. *Rashi* explains these "tents" to be the Study Houses of Shem and Eber, based on what he saw in the words of the Midrash, whose Sages taught that Jacob went from the Study Hall of Shem to that of Eber to that of Abraham.

Now that we have *Rashi*, who in turn had the *Midrash Tanchuma*, we can finally understand what the Torah really means when it tells us that Jacob dwelled in tents. We can thereby learn an important lesson — Jacob put incredible effort into learning Torah.

This certainly seems to be an important and inspiring fact for us to know. If so, why didn't the Written Torah tell it to us explicitly? Why say that he "dwelled in tents" and then force us to rely on the Midrash? Why shouldn't the Written Torah have spelled out all of this and said, "Jacob our Father was a wholesome man, who learned Torah day and night, with tremendous diligence"? Then, his incredible commitment to Torah would be spelled out, black and white, for all to see.

The way that it stands now, from the way that the verse is written, it is as if Jacob's defining characteristic has been concealed, with no clear rationale as to why.

Let us suggest the following: What if the Torah had explicitly written that Jacob studied Torah day and night, without letup? Would we be any closer to appreciating the extent to which Jacob's dedication to Torah was his defining characteristic, what drove his very being?

I submit that we would not, the reason being that the truest measure of a person's dedication to Torah is not something that can be quantified based solely on the number of hours per day, the number of days per year, and the number of years in his lifetime that he spent in study. Rather, one must consider the extent to which he integrated Torah into his everyday life.

The extent to which Torah is his life.

The extent to which his life is Torah.

The greatness of Jacob was not the fact that he spent a lot of time learning. Rather, it was that he "pitched his tent" within the walls of the House of Study. Or, more accurately, the House of Study *was* his tent, the place he called home.

The word *"yeshivah"* comes from the same root as ישׁב *to sit, to dwell.* A *ben yeshivah* is someone who "lives there." It is not only his principal abode, it is the place where he feels most "at home."

How much more accurate, then, was the Torah's depicting Jacob as "a dweller in tents (of Study)" rather than simply stating that he clocked lots of hours there. From the language the verse uses, we see that Torah was *his life* and that his life was *Torah.*

וְיַעֲקֹב אִישׁ תָּם יֹשֵׁב אֹהָלִים
Jacob was a wholesome man, dwelling in tents (25:27).

Note that the word, יֹשֵׁב, although pronounced *yosheiv,* is spelled without a *vav.* Words that are pronounced with a *vav* but spelled without one are called חָסֵר, for they are spelled in the "*defective*" form.

As we have noted in the past, the great Rabbi Naftali Tzvi Yehudah Berlin of Volozhin says that the fact that a word is spelled חָסֵר indicates that it is חָסֵר, lacking some aspect of the fullest sense of that particular word.

How could this possibly apply, though, to Jacob, who certainly seems to have been the absolute paradigm of a "*yosheiv*" in the tents of Torah study? He sat day and night!

For an answer, let us look at the rest of the verse. Besides being known as a יֹשֵׁב אֹהָלִים, Jacob was also an אִישׁ תָּם, *a wholesome person.* So, he was *both* a person who was *whole* and a person who was lacking something as to his being a *yosheiv.* How can this be understood?

Perhaps his wholeness was directly related to his being lacking. What do I mean by this? Perhaps his wholeness came as a result of his always sensing, even within the walls of the Houses of Study of Shem and Eber, that something was *lacking* — he did not consider himself to be "complete," to have "made it," to have already achieved in Torah everything that he could possibly have hoped for, to have already become as great in Torah as he could ever be.

No. He felt himself incomplete. He wanted more — even as he was being *yosheiv* in these very great places.

And, that is one of the ways that he and Esau differed. Esau considered himself already "complete." He was one who "*knew*." Nothing was missing from his sense of completeness.

At least in his own eyes.

Unlike Jacob.

Which is the reason why Jacob was the one who became whole.

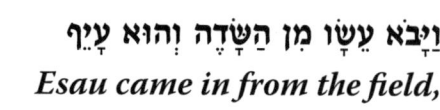

וַיָּבֹא עֵשָׂו מִן הַשָּׂדֶה וְהוּא עָיֵף
Esau came in from the field, and he was exhausted (25:29).

אָמַר רַבִּי יוֹחָנָן: חָמֵשׁ עֲבֵירוֹת עָבַר אוֹתוֹ רָשָׁע בְּאוֹתוֹ הַיּוֹם: בָּא עַל
נַעֲרָה מְאוֹרָסָה, וְהָרַג אֶת הַנֶּפֶשׁ, וְכָפַר בָּעִיקָר, וְכָפַר בִּתְחִיַּית הַמֵּתִים,
וְשָׁט אֶת הַבְּכוֹרָה.

Rabbi Yochanan said, "On that day, that evil one (Esau) committed five transgressions: he seduced a betrothed maiden, he killed someone, he denied Hashem's existence, he renounced the resurrection of the dead, and he scorned his birthright (Bava Basra 16b).

O n the day that Abraham passed away, Esau committed a host of serious transgressions, including murder, *gilui arayos,* and denial of the very foundations of the Jewish faith. So writes the Gemara, as quoted above. These are some of the most terrible sins that a man could possibly commit.

And, what does the Written Torah have to say about this particular day in the life of Esau? That he was "exhausted." Exhausted!?

That's how one describes him? He was a spiller of blood! A violater of the laws of family decency! A heretic! "Exhausted"?

By way of an answer as to why the Written Torah omits information that is told to us by the Gemara, one could suggest that the Written Torah relates only the external aspect of things. This statement of that external aspect will then serve as a key to deriving the inner meaning.

Let us demonstrate this principle using our own verse.

The Torah says here that "He *was exhausted*," not that "Esau came in from the field exhausted." Is there some significance to the depiction of the situation in this particular way?

Had the Torah used the latter phrase, rather than the former, we might have puzzled over why we would need to be kept abreast of Esau's experiences at the "office" that day. But, the Torah says that he was tired, rather than that his workday was tiring, telling us that we are not learning about his workday, but, rather, about him.

Esau's total being, from beginning to end, was characterized by exhaustion. Tiredness was him, as the Sages say about the phrase, הוּא אֲחַשְׁוֵרוֹשׁ, *He is Ahasuerus* (*Esther* 1:1). Ahasuerus was always Ahasuerus, totally and consistently, wicked from beginning to end.

When a person's entire life is characterized by "exhaustion," to the extent that he lacks even a trace of enthusiasm and vitality, and has withdrawn from society, if we can assume that it is more than a matter of utter depression, we must look for what might have been its catalyst. Why is it that he has cut himself off?

Perhaps, we could say that the murder, the sexual transgressions, and the heresy were either the symptoms of the emptiness of his life or maybe even the cause of his feelings of "exhaustion." The Written Torah, then, records his state of mind; the Oral Torah records how and why he got there.

For another example of the relationship between the Written Torah's account and that of the Oral Tradition, consider the verse,

וְיַעֲקֹב אִישׁ תָּם יֹשֵׁב אֹהָלִים, *Jacob was a wholesome man, dwelling in tents* (25:27).

The Written Torah records the external aspect, that which was apparent to the eye, namely that Jacob sat in tents. It is then left up to the Oral Tradition and to ourselves to look more deeply and to recognize that he wasn't just "sitting," but that his "sitting" was the process through which he would become great in Torah.

וַיֵּצֵא יַעֲקֹב מִבְּאֵר שָׁבַע וַיֵּלֶךְ חָרָנָה
And Jacob departed from Beer-sheba
and went toward Haran (28:10).

רש"י: **וַיֵּצֵא יַעֲקֹב מִבְּאֵר שָׁבַע** – לֹא הָיָה צָרִיךְ לִכְתּוֹב אֶלָּא וַיֵּלֶךְ יַעֲקֹב
חָרָנָה, וְלָמָּה הִזְכִּיר יְצִיאָתוֹ, אֶלָּא מַגִּיד שֶׁיְּצִיאַת צַדִּיק מִן הַמָּקוֹם עוֹשָׂה
רוֹשֶׁם, שֶׁבִּזְמַן שֶׁהַצַּדִּיק בָּעִיר הוּא הוֹדָהּ הוּא זִיוָהּ הוּא הֲדָרָהּ, יָצָא
מִשָּׁם פָּנָה הוֹדָהּ פָּנָה זִיוָהּ פָּנָה הֲדָרָהּ.

RASHI: AND JACOB DEPARTED — *It need only have
written, "And Jacob went to Haran." Why does it mention
his departure? To tell us that the departure of a righteous
person from a place makes an impression; for at the time
that a righteous person is in the city, he is its magnificence,
he is its splendor, he is its grandeur. Once he has departed
from there, its magnificence has gone away, its splendor
has gone away, its grandeur has gone away.*

*R*ashi, as quoted above, tells us of the negative impact that Jacob's departure had on Beer-sheba: Just as the presence of a righteous person in a city makes an impression (for what it adds to the city), so does his going away (for what is lost). This principle is derived from the case of Jacob.

Jacob was not the first of the forefathers to have departed a city. Both Abraham and Isaac also left to go from one place to another. Presumably, a void was created by their departure, just as in the case of Jacob. Why, then, did the Torah choose to teach this principle from Jacob, rather than from the other forefathers?

I remember seeing an answer to this question, as follows.

The Midrash is replete with references to Abraham's active role in bringing the local population closer to monotheism, and also describes the aura of greatness that surrounded Isaac. There is no question that their departure would have left a tremendous void.

With Jacob, however, we might not have been so certain. It's not that he was any less great, but we are told that Jacob, unlike the other forefathers, was totally immersed in learning. Rather than involving himself with the outside world, he "dwelled in the tents" of Shem and Eber. We might think that his departure, therefore, would never have been noticed.

Yet, the Torah tells us this assumption is not correct. Rather, when Jacob left, so did the city's magnificence, its splendor, and its grandeur.

וַיֵּצֵא יַעֲקֹב מִבְּאֵר שָׁבַע וַיֵּלֶךְ חָרָנָה
Jacob departed from Beer-sheba and went toward Haran (28:10).

רש"י: **וַיֵּצֵא יַעֲקֹב** – עַל יְדֵי שֶׁבִּשְׁבִיל שֶׁרָעוֹת בְּנוֹת כְּנַעַן בְּעֵינֵי יִצְחָק אָבִיו הָלַךְ עֵשָׂו אֶל יִשְׁמָעֵאל, הִפְסִיק הָעִנְיָן בְּפָרָשָׁתוֹ שֶׁל יַעֲקֹב וּכְתִיב

(כח:ו) וַיַּרְא עֵשָׂו כִּי בֵרַךְ וגו', וּמִשֶּׁגָּמַר חָזַר לָעִנְיָן הָרִאשׁוֹן.

RASHI: JACOB DEPARTED — *Due to ... (the fact that) the daughters of Canaan were evil in the eyes of Isaac, his father, Esau went to Ishmael (to take a wife). Scripture interrupted the subject of the episode of Jacob and wrote, "And Esau saw that [Isaac] had blessed ... ." And, once it completed (its point regarding Esau), it went back to its original topic (Jacob's departure).*

This verse describes Jacob's departure from Beer-sheba, in accordance with his parents' earlier request that he go to the house of Laban to take a wife. However, there are four intervening verses which tell the story of Esau's having gone to take a non-Canaanite wife, unlike his other wives. He did this because he realized that his father did not approve of the Canaanite wives.

Rashi says that Esau's action was a direct reaction to Isaac's admonition to Jacob not to take a Canaanite wife. The episode with Esau, then, is a digression from the main story. Now that we have finished the digression, we can continue with the original story, which is Jacob's departure.

I would like to suggest a different approach as to why the Torah's description of Jacob's "departure" is told here, immediately following its telling us of Esau's actions. Specifically, why is it that Jacob is leaving only now? Esau had been burning with resentment for some time already, yet Jacob had not felt it necessary to flee. What has changed?

I would like to suggest the following. As long as Esau was Esau, openly burning with resentment, the danger was not really so great. The danger was there for all to see and Jacob knew to always maintain his guard. Now, however, Esau is professing to be a *baal teshuvah*, heeding his father's warning to Jacob and therefore taking a non-Canaanite wife. He is presenting himself as a changed man, a man of peace.

And that is why the time has come to leave — and fast!

He's actually a lot more dangerous now. Jacob could find himself lulled into complacency, forgetting who Esau really is — and then letting his guard down.

And so, *"Jacob departed from Beer-sheba and went to Haran."*

Let us not forget this lesson of our forefather as we look around today, witnessing the modern-day Jacob-hating Esaus who also seek to impress the world with their professed changes of heart, but all the while coming "in peace" to mask their true hatred of the Jewish nation.

May Hashem protect us from Jew-haters everywhere, especially those who falsely claim to come "in peace."

<hr>

וַיִּפְגַּע בַּמָּקוֹם

He encountered the place (28:11).

מַהוּ וַיִּפְגַּע? צָלִי ... אָמַר רַבִּי יְהוֹשֻׁעַ בֶּן לֵוִי אָבוֹת הָרִאשׁוֹנִים הִתְקִינוּ
שָׁלֹשׁ תְּפִלּוֹת, אַבְרָהָם תִּקֵּן תְּפִלַּת שַׁחֲרִית, שֶׁנֶּאֱמַר (יט:כז) "וַיַּשְׁכֵּם
אַבְרָהָם בַּבֹּקֶר אֶל הַמָּקוֹם אֲשֶׁר עָמַד שָׁם וגו' ", וְאֵין עֲמִידָה אֶלָּא
תְּפִלָּה ... יִצְחָק תִּקֵּן תְּפִלַּת מִנְחָה, שֶׁנֶּאֱמַר (כד:סג) "וַיֵּצֵא יִצְחָק לָשׂוּחַ
בַּשָּׂדֶה", וְאֵין שִׂיחָה אֶלָּא תְּפִלָּה שֶׁנֶּאֱמַר (תהלים קמב) "אֶשְׁפֹּךְ
לְפָנָיו שִׂיחִי". יַעֲקֹב תִּקֵּן תְּפִלַּת עַרְבִית, שֶׁנֶּאֱמַר "וַיִּפְגַּע בַּמָּקוֹם", וְאֵין
פְּגִיעָה אֶלָּא תְּפִלָּה, שֶׁנֶּאֱמַר (ירמיה ז:טז) "וְאַל תִּשָּׂא בַעֲדָם וגו' וְאַל
תִּפְגַּע בִּי".

What is וַיִּפְגַּע? Prayer ... R' Yehoshua ben Levi said: The forefathers instituted the three prayer services:

Abraham established the morning service, as it says (19:27):"Abraham arose early in the morning to the place

where he had stood before Hashem." And the word, עֲמִידָה,
stood, has no meaning other than prayer ...

Isaac enacted the afternoon service, as it says (24:63)
"Isaac went out to converse in the field toward evening."
And there is no meaning for the word "converse" other
than prayer ...

Jacob established the evening service, as it says (in
our verse) וַיִּפְגַּע בַּמָּקוֹם. And the word פְּגִיעָה, encounter,
has no meaning other than prayer ... " (Bereishis
Rabbah 68:9).

A ccording to the Midrash quoted above, the prayers
of the three forefathers set the precedent for each of
the three fixed prayers that we have today. If you read
the Hebrew version quoted above, you will notice that while it
says that all three prayed, three different verbs are used for each of
these prayers. Abraham's prayer is termed עֲמִידָה, standing; Isaac's
prayer is called שִׂיחָה, conversation; Jacob's prayer is labeled פְּגִיעָה,
encountering.

We would like to explore the significance of these descriptions.
We can assume that by gaining some insight into what was unique
about each of these types of prayer, we will also gain some added
insight into some of the characteristics that were unique to each of
the forefathers.

We will start with Abraham, whose prayer was called עֲמִידָה, standing.

Abraham's life goal was to disseminate faith in God. As part of
this mission, he would have to confront and uproot the idol worship
that pervaded every place to which he traveled. He faced a world
that resisted whatever he had to say and tried to pull him in the opposite direction.

He faced these dangers alone. He tried to influence the people.
And they tried to influence him. It was Abraham against the world.

The sides were decidedly unequal.

Yet, he won.

How?

He won because he could not be shaken. He was absolutely determined, unequivocally resolute, and totally focused. He would not and could not be moved.

In other words, it was because he stood. He was עוֹמֵד, just as the Midrash and Torah verse describe him.

His success did not derive from an enthusiasm that would be so infectious as to captivate the hearts and minds of his audience. Nor was it in the logic or eloquence of his presentation. Rather, the greatest strength that one could have is a resolve not to budge from what he is determined to accomplish.

When one is being immovable, he is utilizing the power of the earth itself, which is also immovable. The earth existed before man. It exists now. And it will exist in the future, long after any individual man has already become part of its dust.

This was the power of עֲמִידָה that characterized Abraham. All who came into his midst would recognize that Abraham's prayer would not be one that would float away to become vapor. Nor did it stem from an emotional enthusiasm that was sure to be extinguished. Nor was he a person who would eventually give up and fade into oblivion.

Rather, they saw in him a single-minded determination to reach his goal and they realized that he would not stop before he got there. He stood in that one place, remained standing in that one place, and would continue standing in that one place until he would accomplish his goal.

This was a power they could not possibly defeat.

כָּל הַנְּחָלִים הֹלְכִים אֶל הַיָּם, *All rivers flow to the sea* … (*Koheles* 1:7).

דּוֹר הֹלֵךְ וְדוֹר בָּא וְהָאָרֶץ לְעוֹלָם עֹמָדֶת, *A generation comes and a generation passes, but the world* stands *forever* (ibid. 1:4).

The deep and mighty rivers whose waters powerfully flow along the earth, thundering as they pass, *flow to the sea* and are eventually swallowed into the great sea, where their roar will be silenced, never to be heard from again. They are now just a few more drops when compared with the vastness of the ocean.

But the earth, calm and voiceless, never traveling from place to place, will never be absorbed and assimilated, even by the ocean, despite the ocean's far greater mass.

Why? Because the earth is עָמְדָת, *standing*. It has the power of עֲמִידָה, not relinquishing its place, for whatever reason.

It therefore merits to continue its existence, long after the demise of all the living, mobile creatures who have walked its surface.

With this we can understand the Gemara that states: כָּל הַקּוֹבֵעַ מָקוֹם לִתְפִלָּתוֹ, אֱלֹהֵי אַבְרָהָם בְּעֶזְרוֹ, *Whoever designates a set place for his prayers, the God of Abraham will assist him* (*Berachos* 6b).

Many are those who pray with great concentration and enthusiasm, but only the one who sets a "fixed place" for his prayer will merit the assistance of the God of Abraham. Why? Because Abraham's supplication was a prayer that was "fixed," "set," grounded, and immovable. Abraham did not move from his place until he had completed doing everything possible to actualize the Divine will within the world.

And this is why the word עֲמִידָה, *standing*, is so closely identified with Abraham.

Let us continue with Isaac, whose prayer is called שִׂיחָה, *conversation*.

Isaac's prayer took on another dimension. Abraham was the trailblazer, the one who first introduced the world to the idea that there was no God other than Hashem and that He, alone, was Creator of the Universe. And, Abraham succeeded. His message and his fame spread throughout the world.

Isaac certainly was an asset to his father's life work. After Abraham died, Isaac accepted the responsibility of continuing his father's holy mission, with all of the attendant self-sacrifice. He, too, would further the cause of spreading the knowledge of Hashem throughout the world.

However, as noble as it very well might be (especially where the son has this kind of father), it is not a simple thing for a son to follow in his father's footsteps. And when the father is one such as Abraham, the challenge could be even greater.

The son must ask himself: "Why I am I doing this? What is my real motivation? Am I doing it simply in order to follow in my father's ways? By force of habit? Or, do I really believe in it? That is, do I really feel, deep inside of me, that this is something of value, independent of whether or not my father believed in it? Is this really an expression of my own life's passion?"

Answers to these questions can be arrived at only through constant, deep introspection — self-examination of the deepest recesses of the heart.

Isaac regularly went out to the fields precisely for this purpose. He left the bustling city's distractions behind him. There, in the fields, he could pour out his heart. He could speak to Hashem with the greatest of privacy, regarding his most intimate thoughts.

He could also learn about himself. And, he could relate to Hashem in his own individual and personal way, rather than through force of habit, doing what his father had always done and passed on to his loyal son — as important as that might be as one of the components of his own spiritual choices.

This, then, was the prayer of our father Isaac — שִׂיחָה, *conversation*. Silent contemplation and conversation. Prayer of the type that only a man's own soul could possibly sense its meaning and intent.

And this is why the word שִׂיחָה, *conversation,* is so closely identified with Isaac.

Jacob was fleeing from the wicked Esau, who was lying in ambush to kill him, to the house of Laban, who imperiled his faith. It was as if he were going through fire and water — from the immediate physical threat posed by Esau to the spiritual danger soon to be posed by Laban.

While residing in Laban's house, through what merit would Jacob be able to withstand being drawn into the sinfulness of Laban's ways? How would Jacob be able to return to his father's house whole, spiritually intact, on a spiritual level comparable to the one he had left?

True, fourteen years of this interval had been spent immersed in learning in the study halls of Shem and Eber. Still, he was apprehensive. The real-life challenges soon to be upon him would be most formidable.

וַיִּפְגַּע בַּמָּקוֹם, *And he encountered the place.* His desire was to increase his merits before facing Laban. The proper thing to do would be to offer a sacrifice. "But, which type of sacrifice," he thought to himself, "could I offer that has not already been brought in the past?"

וַיִּפְגַּע בַּמָּקוֹם, *And he encountered the place.* What place does the verse speak of? Says *Rashi*, it was Mount Moriah, future site of the Holy Temple of Jerusalem.

Here he was, in the very place where the Heavenly Presence would dwell, Mount Moriah, and he could not think of something new. But, he felt that he must.

Could he possibly presume to reach the level of selflessness displayed by his predecessors, Abraham and Isaac, who had stood here at the *Akeidah?* He could not even presume to offer a sacrifice of selflessness. Perhaps one of *chessed,* lovingkindness? How could he even imagine that he could achieve merit through the virtue of *chessed?* Again, he could not possibly compare himself to Abraham, his predecessor.

וַיִּפְגַּע בַּמָּקוֹם — but the place was already built and perfected. There was no house for *chessed* like that of Abraham's. And, he could not possibly approach the self-sacrifice of his father and grandfather at the *Akeidah*. How would he earn the personal merit that this dangerous situation would demand? How would he be able to continue the task of developing the Jewish nation?

These thoughts enveloped him even as he slept: וַיַּחֲלֹם וְהִנֵּה סֻלָּם מֻצָּב אַרְצָה וְרֹאשׁוֹ מַגִּיעַ הַשָּׁמָיְמָה וְהִנֵּה מַלְאֲכֵי אֱלֹהִים עֹלִים וְיֹרְדִים בּוֹ, *And he dreamt, and behold! A ladder was set earthwards and its top reached heavenward; and behold! Angels of God ascending and descending on it* (8:12).

Startled from his sleep, he said (28:17): אֵין זֶה כִּי אִם בֵּית אֱלֹהִים וְזֶה שַׁעַר הַשָּׁמָיִם, ... *this is none other than the abode of God and this is the gate of the heavens!*

Hashem was showing him that his estimation was correct: He could not hope to acquire merit by trying to match the *mesirus nefesh* and *chessed* of his predecessors.

However, that did not mean that he had no alternative other than to innovate new *korbanos*. The dream that he had of סֻלָּם מֻצָּב אַרְצָה וְרֹאשׁוֹ מַגִּיעַ הַשָּׁמָיְמָה, *A ladder was set earthwards and its top reached heavenward*, would, in fact, be the key to where his contribution would lie.

The Jewish people were destined to suffer greatly. Tragedy and oppression would inundate them. They would be physically humiliated, degraded, relegated to "civilized" society's lowest rung. Yet, even as their physical selves would be degraded, lacking any status whatsoever, their "heads" would be somewhere else.

Their "heads" would be involved in the life of Torah.

And Jacob would be their role model. He would be the סֻלָּם מֻצָּב אַרְצָה וְרֹאשׁוֹ מַגִּיעַ הַשָּׁמָיְמָה, the *ladder that was set earthwards and its top reached heavenward*.

He would be living in the house of Laban the Aramean, but his "head" would still be reaching for the heavens:

רש"י: עִם לָבָן הָרָשָׁע גַּרְתִּי וְתַרְיַ"ג מִצְוֹת שָׁמַרְתִּי וְלֹא לָמַדְתִּי מִמַּעֲשָׂיו הָרָעִים.

RASHI: *I sojourned with Laban, the evil one, yet I kept the 613 commandments and did not learn from his evil actions (32:5).*

He would merit to be father to the twelve tribes of Hashem, from whom would develop the Jewish nation — even as he sat in the house of Laban.

And Jacob would thereby reveal the true nature of our holy Torah: that it is a *living Torah,* a Torah of real, practical day-to-day life — and not in the heavens. Man, through his own free choice, could aspire to commune with Hashem — even as he sits in a situation of מַצָּב אַרְצָה, of being "earthbound."

Jacob looked around him, from within his own physical existence, amidst the physical world, and said (28:17): אֵין זֶה כִּי אִם בֵּית אֱלֹהִים וְזֶה שַׁעַר הַשָּׁמָיִם, ... *this is none other than the abode of God and this is the gate of the heavens!* He understood that the time had come to demonstrate that the entire world is בֵּית אֱלֹהִים, God's abode.

This, then, would be his unique contribution. Abraham was called *har, mountain.* Isaac was called *sadeh, field.* Only the few, those who had the luxury of being able to separate themselves from society, could possibly emulate Abraham's and Isaac's way of attaining a "foothold" on the upper rung of Hashem's ladder. Jacob, however, showed the Jewish people that the entire world was *Beis Elokim,* even the lowest rung. And from there one could climb. Right up to the *Shaar HaShamayim,* the Gates of Heaven.

And that is why Jacob's prayer is called פְּגִיעָה, *encountering.* He had no need to add to or innovate anything, as he had already arrived at the right place. The place was already fully ready, prepared in advance by Abraham and Isaac. The "groundwork" had already been laid.

Jacob's role would be to show that the path of Hashem circled the physical world. All of man's deeds, every aspect of his daily life, wherever he might find himself and whatever his occupation, there, in that very place, he could find Hashem. The possibility of living a Torah life would be there, no matter what an individual's status, whatever his "station in life."

Because the Torah encompasses all of life.

All of it. In all of its totality.

And this is why the word פְּגִיעָה, *encountering,* is so closely identified with Jacob.

עִם לָבָן גַּרְתִּי

I have sojourned with Laban (32:5).

רש"י: גַּרְתִּי – לֹא נַעֲשֵׂיתִי שַׂר וְחָשׁוּב אֶלָּא גֵּר, אֵינְךָ כְּדַאי לְשָׂנוֹא אוֹתִי עַל בִּרְכוֹת אָבִיךָ שֶׁבֵּרְכַנִי (כז:כט) "הֱוֵה גְבִיר לְאַחֶיךָ", שֶׁהֲרֵי לֹא נִתְקַיְּמָה בִּי. דָּבָר אַחֵר "גַּרְתִּי" בְּגֵימַטְרִיָּא תַּרְיַ"ג, כְּלוֹמַר עִם לָבָן הָרָשָׁע גַּרְתִּי וְתַרְיַ"ג מִצְוֹת שָׁמַרְתִּי וְלֹא לָמַדְתִּי מִמַּעֲשָׂיו הָרָעִים.

RASHI: I HAVE SOJOURNED — *I did not become a dignitary or a notable, but a mere sojourner. It does not befit you to hate me over the blessings of your father who blessed me, "Be a lord to your brothers," for it has not been fulfilled in me.*

Alternatively, the numerical value of גַּרְתִּי *is 613, as if to say, "I sojourned with Laban, the evil one, yet I kept the 613 commandments and did not learn from his evil actions."*

*R*ashi's two approaches seem to be mutually contradictory. In fact, though, the dichotomy illustrates an important lesson as to the nature of our existence in exile and, specifically, as to how we should conduct ourselves toward the nations of the world.

But, it is more than an illustration of how to conduct ourselves vis-à-vis the nations. It is also an illustration of how we should conduct ourselves toward *ourselves.*

Let me explain.

Our situation is such that, at this period in time, Esau is our "master." We are required to acknowledge this reality and to demonstrate our deference.

However, our permission to do this is contingent on our constantly reminding ourselves of our own inherent preeminence.

On the one hand, we are living in the lands of the nations and must not fail to show our subordination. That, in fact, is our reality.

But, it is only our *external* reality.

Together with what we must do externally, we must prevent ourselves from confusing a reality that is situational, based upon our temporarily being in exile, with what is inherently true. Otherwise, we could fall into the trap of forgetting our unique greatness and simply assimilate into our surroundings.

This is what is meant by the two opinions that are brought down by *Rashi.* The first opinion teaches what it is that we must say to them : *I did not become a dignitary or a notable, but a mere sojourner.* The second opinion, "*I sojourned with Laban, the evil one, yet I kept the 613 commandments and did not learn from his evil actions,*" is what we must always say to ourselves.

וַיָּקָם בַּלַּיְלָה הוּא וַיִּקַּח אֶת שְׁתֵּי נָשָׁיו וְאֶת שְׁתֵּי שִׁפְחֹתָיו
וְאֶת אַחַד עָשָׂר יְלָדָיו וַיַּעֲבֹר אֵת מַעֲבַר יַבֹּק

But he got up that night and took his two wives,
his two handmaidens, and his eleven sons and
crossed the ford of the Jabbok (32:23).

Why was Jacob so anxious to take his wives, his children, and all that he had and cross the Jabbok in order to approach Esau? And, in the middle of the night, no less!

What would have happened had he stayed where he was and met Esau right there?

See the *Rashbam* to our verse. I would like to suggest a different answer.

It seems to me that when Jacob heard that Esau was going to meet him with 400 men, he was reminded of the prophecy expressed to Abraham in 15:13: יָדֹעַ תֵּדַע כִּי גֵר יִהְיֶה זַרְעֲךָ בְּאֶרֶץ לֹא לָהֶם וַעֲבָדוּם וְעִנּוּ אֹתָם אַרְבַּע מֵאוֹת שָׁנָה, *Know with certainty that your offspring shall be sojourners in a land not their own, they will enslave them, and they will oppress them four hundred years.*

Jacob thought that Esau's intent was to prevent him from entering the Land of Israel. Therefore, Jacob rushed toward Eretz Yisrael, in an attempt to meet up with Esau only *after* arriving in the Land.

But, it was not to be: Esau's ministering angel intervened, preventing Jacob from carrying out his plan: וַיִּוָּתֵר יַעֲקֹב לְבַדּוֹ וַיֵּאָבֵק אִישׁ עִמּוֹ עַד עֲלוֹת הַשָּׁחַר, *And Jacob was left alone and a man wrestled with him until the break of dawn (32:25).*

רש"י: וַיֵּאָבֵק אִישׁ – ... וּפֵירְשׁוּ רַבּוֹתֵינוּ ז"ל שֶׁהוּא שָׂרוֹ שֶׁל עֵשָׂו.

RASHI: AND A MAN WRESTLED — ... *Our Rabbis explained that he was the ministering angel of Esau.*

Parashas Vayishlach / 129

Another thought I had as to why Jacob was rushing: He wanted to rectify the sin of not having returned to Eretz Yisrael until now:

רש"י: שָׁכַח פַּכִּים קְטַנִּים וְחָזַר עֲלֵיהֶם.

RASHI: *He had forgotten some small jars and went back for them.*

Perhaps this reference to Jacob's delay for the sake of some small jars is an allusion to the generations who have remained outside of Eretz Yisrael for no reason other than their "small jars."

Another thought I had as to why Jacob was rushing: *Rashi* to the next verse emphasizes Jacob's role in moving things from one side of the river to the other:

רש"י: עָשָׂה עַצְמוֹ כְּגֶשֶׁר, נוֹטֵל מִכַּאן וּמֵנִיחַ כַּאן

RASHI: *He made himself like a ferryman (the Hebrew word כְּגֶשֶׁר could also be read to mean "like a bridge") who takes from one side and sets things down on the other.*

Perhaps Jacob felt that Esau's primary power would be outside Eretz Yisrael. Jacob therefore wanted their meeting — whether it be to negotiate peace or to wage battle — to take place where that power was least effective — in the Holy Land.

וַיִּוָּתֵר יַעֲקֹב לְבַדּוֹ וַיֵּאָבֵק אִישׁ עִמּוֹ עַד עֲלוֹת הַשָּׁחַר.
וַיַּרְא כִּי לֹא יָכֹל לוֹ וַיִּגַּע בְּכַף יְרֵכוֹ וַתֵּקַע ...
עַל כֵּן לֹא יֹאכְלוּ בְנֵי יִשְׂרָאֵל אֶת גִּיד הַנָּשֶׁה
אֲשֶׁר עַל כַּף הַיָּרֵךְ עַד הַיּוֹם הַזֶּה

And Jacob was left alone and a man wrestled with him until the break of dawn. When he perceived that he could not overcome him, he struck the ball of his thighbone; and the ball of his thighbone became dislocated ... (32:26) Therefore the Children of Israel are not to eat the displaced sinew on the ball of the thighbone to this day (32:32).

Four Questions:
- What is it that caused Jacob to be "left alone"? According-ing to the Sages, it was due to his having returned for small pitchers.
- Who was the "man" who was "fighting" with him?
- Why did he succeed in injuring Jacob's thigh more than any other body part?
- What is the reason we may not eat the displaced sinew of the hip-socket?

It seems to me that this episode informs us of the consequences of the exile and its impact upon the Jewish nation.

Jacob spent twenty years with Laban. During this time, he wavered neither from his faith nor from his way of life. This was the challenge he had been given up to this point in his life. He would now be on his way to encounter Esau, his brother and archenemy.

While it is true that the Torah writes: וְרַב יַעֲבֹד צָעִיר, *and the elder* [brother] *will serve the younger* (25:23), this would only be on condition that the younger would follow the ways of Hashem. Were he to assimilate the values and ways of the nations, however, then the words of Hashem to Esau would apply: וְאֶת אָחִיךָ תַּעֲבֹד וְהָיָה כַּאֲשֶׁר תָּרִיד וּפָרַקְתָּ עֻלּוֹ מֵעַל צַוָּארֶךָ,... *your brother you shall serve; yet it shall be that when you will be aggrieved, you may remove his yoke from upon your neck* (27:40).

It is for this reason that *Rashi* writes:

רש"י : עם לָבָן גַּרְתִּי – גַּרְתִּי בְּגִימַטְרִיָּא תַּרְיַ"ג, כְּלוֹמַר עִם לָבָן הָרָשָׁע גַּרְתִּי וְתַרְיַ"ג מִצְוֹת שָׁמַרְתִּי וְלֹא לָמַדְתִּי מִמַּעֲשָׂיו הָרָעִים.

RASHI: I HAVE SOJOURNED WITH LABAN
— *The numerical value of* גַּרְתִּי *is 613, as if to say, "I sojourned with Laban, the evil one, yet I kept the 613 commandments and did not learn from his evil actions."*

The intent here is to say that the time for *"... yet it shall be that when you will be aggrieved ..."* has not yet arrived.

When Jacob returned to retrieve the "small pitchers," he found that the angel of Esau was there, ready to challenge him. Why? Because now he was vulnerable. His return for these "small pitchers" was, perhaps, indicative of a larger issue, of his having lost certain values, of having given in to materialism, a desire to amass sheep and cattle.

With his aspirations now turned toward material acquisition, toward a desire for the "fat of the land," he would be no better than Esau. His automatic, given "right" to best Esau could no longer be justified.

So, now the process of inquiry into Jacob's life in exile would begin. The questions would be asked: How, exactly, has he been affected? What effect have the influences of the exile had upon him?

The "man" struggled with him, and the dust went as high as the Throne of Glory.

Rabbi Yaakov Moshe Charlap explains that the "man," Esau's angel, wished to erase the image of Jacob that had been engraved onto the Divine Chariot. He wished to demonstrate that this was not the same Jacob as the one portrayed on the Chariot: He had a diminished resolve for achieving greatness in Torah study, holiness, and good deeds. Instead, his aspirations were directed toward "small pitchers."

Jacob's response was that the charge was false. He had lost nothing of his idealism. His desire for Truth remained uncompromised. His service of Hashem was still faithful. He was unaffected by Laban. His sole aspiration remained the same: to ascend the "ladder."

As hard as he looked, Esau's angel could not find an area where he could wound Jacob. That is, until he saw the thighbone, which allows for the body's mobility. That was where Esau's "opportunity" would be. Here, he could see a deficiency, something that was lacking, slightly amiss.

It wasn't that Jacob had compromised his thinking, but rather that he had lost something of his enthusiasm. He had worked fourteen years in order to marry his two wives. Six more years were spent for the sake of his property. Were it not for Laban's deceptions, Jacob might have remained in the land of the exile for an even longer period of time. He would not have felt particularly compelled to return to the land of his fathers, the place of holiness.

Jacob's exit from the *galus* had become somewhat of a burden, to the extent that he had lost some of his former apprehension about being outside of the Land.

Therefore, this joint was dislocated. It would remind future generations that even those who would be most filled with fear of Hashem and love for mitzvos could be susceptible to becoming a bit too complacent with their situation of *galus.*

The Jewish people were to avoid eating this joint, meaning that they should never destroy or disable their power of movement; that is, they should never allow their enthusiasm for leaving the exile for the Land of Israel to be dampened. They should not become paralyzed and debilitated, merely for the sake of the "small pitchers" that they feel they simply cannot leave behind.

＝＝＝

וַיַּרְא כִּי לֹא יָכֹל לוֹ וַיִּגַּע בְּכַף יְרֵכוֹ וַתֵּקַע ...
עַל כֵּן לֹא יֹאכְלוּ בְנֵי יִשְׂרָאֵל אֶת גִּיד הַנָּשֶׁה
אֲשֶׁר עַל כַּף הַיָּרֵךְ עַד הַיּוֹם הַזֶּה

When he perceived that he could not overcome
him, he struck the ball of his thighbone; and the
ball of his thighbone became dislocated ... (32:26).

Therefore the Children of Israel are not to eat
the displaced sinew on the ball of the thighbone
to this day (32:32).

hy is it that Esau's ministering angel specifically chose to dislocate this particular part of Jacob's body?

There is a Midrashic explanation which says that it was due to Jacob's having married two sisters. In order to fully appreciate what is meant by this, we must point out that prior to the giving of the Torah, this was permissible. So, it is not a simple matter of his being punished for having committed a transgression. And, even if he were being punished, we still have not answered why the punishment would have taken this particular form. The Midrash must therefore have had something else in mind.

Let me suggest the following: It is not that the marrying of two sisters constituted a sin, but rather that it was the indirect cause of the discord that would mark the relations between his sons.

Esau's angel sought to wound Jacob himself, but could not: וַיַּרְא כִּי לֹא יָכֹל לוֹ ... , *he perceived that he could not overcome him.* But, sensing his vulnerability due to having married two sisters, he went instead for the "thigh," which is symbolic of going after his offspring: וַיִּגַּע בְּכַף יְרֵכוֹ, *he struck the ball of his thighbone.*

Let me explain. Each sister had her own firstborn: Reuben was Leah's and Joseph was Rachel's. Joseph, being a child of Jacob's old age, was more like his father, both spiritually and physically, than was Reuben. This would cause a rift between the two sets of offspring. Perhaps, it could even have the long-term consequence of jeopardizing the very future of the Jewish people.

And, that is what Esau's angel had in mind.

Upon seeing this vulnerability, he went for it.

עַל כֵּן לֹא יֹאכְלוּ בְנֵי יִשְׂרָאֵל אֶת גִּיד הַנָּשֶׁה אֲשֶׁר עַל כַּף הַיָּרֵךְ עַד הַיּוֹם הַזֶּה, *Therefore the Children of Israel are not to eat the displaced sinew on the ball of the thighbone to this day.*

Given what it symbolizes, the place that was the source of Esau's hopes for disunity and discord among the Jewish nation, we are commanded to avoid the גִּיד הַנָּשֶׁה אֲשֶׁר עַל כַּף הַיָּרֵךְ. Or, rather, we are commanded to try and restore it, to not consume it but put it back into its place, as a symbol of our aspirations for the unity of the Jewish people. The unity of the brothers is the key to our continuity and eternity.

A further thought: the circumstances of Jacob's struggle seem to hint at this same idea.

וַיִּוָּתֵר יַעֲקֹב לְבַדּוֹ וַיֵּאָבֵק אִישׁ עִמּוֹ עַד עֲלוֹת הַשָּׁחַר, *And Jacob was left alone and a man wrestled with him until the break of dawn* (32:25).

When Jacob was *alone*, separated from the sons, only then did the angel of Esau come to struggle with him.

וַיַּרְא כִּי לֹא יָכֹל לוֹ וַיִּגַּע בְּכַף יְרֵכוֹ וַתֵּקַע ...

When he perceived that he could not overcome him, he struck the ball of his thighbone; and the ball of his thighbone became dislocated ... (32:26).

Many answers have been given as to why Esau's ministering angel chose this particular part of Jacob's body, finding a weakness there and nowhere else.

I would like to suggest one more.

It would seem to me that prior to meeting Esau, Jacob had to engage in a serious process of self-evaluation: How had the time spent in the house of Laban affected him? Had he been tainted, even in the slightest way, by his contact with Esau? What about his having been outside of the Land, away from his father's house?

If there was even the slightest blemish, through what merit would he be able to counter Esau now?

The angel of Esau also checked Jacob very carefully. He found nothing amiss. No sign of weakness. Neither in any physical sense nor in a spiritual sense. Jacob was healthy and whole — untarnished:

וְשַׁבְתִּי בְשָׁלוֹם אֶל בֵּית אָבִי ...

And I will return in peace to my father's house ... (28:21).

רַשִׁ"י: בְּשָׁלוֹם – שָׁלֵם מִן הַחֵטְא, שֶׁלֹּא אֶלְמַד מִדַּרְכֵי לָבָן

RASHI: IN PEACE — *Whole from sin, that I should not learn from the ways of Laban.*

However, there was one flaw to be found by Esau's angel: Jacob's life outside of Eretz Yisrael had caused a slight weakening in his resolve to return to the Land, back to the house of his father. He had completed the fourteen years required from him in order to earn the rights to his two wives, but then stayed an additional six, in violation of the vow that he had made.

As we know, a man's hipbone is what enables him to stand and allows him to quickly move toward his destination.

עַל כֵּן לֹא יֹאכְלוּ בְנֵי יִשְׂרָאֵל אֶת גִּיד הַנָּשֶׁה אֲשֶׁר עַל כַּף הַיָּרֵךְ עַד הַיּוֹם הַזֶּה ,... *Therefore the Children of Israel are not to eat the displaced sinew on the ball of the thighbone to this day ...*

The bone that became displaced from its socket, the symbol of losing mobility (or more precisely, the impetus to move along), is what we should always remember, so that we free ourselves of the impediments that needlessly keep us in the Diaspora, holding us back from fulfilling our commandment to return to the Holy Land.

וַיֵּשֶׁב יַעֲקֹב בְּאֶרֶץ מְגוּרֵי אָבִיו
And Jacob settled in the land
of his father's sojournings (37:1).

רש"י: וְעוֹד נִדְרַשׁ בּוֹ "וַיֵּשֶׁב" בִּקֵּשׁ יַעֲקֹב לֵישֵׁב בְּשַׁלְוָה, קָפַץ עָלָיו רוֹגְזוֹ
שֶׁל יוֹסֵף. צַדִּיקִים מְבַקְשִׁים לֵישֵׁב בְּשַׁלְוָה אוֹמֵר הַקָּדוֹשׁ **בָּרוּךְ** הוּא לֹא
דַּיָּן לַצַּדִּיקִים מַה שֶׁמְּתוּקָן לָהֶם לָעוֹלָם הַבָּא, אֶלָּא שֶׁמְּבַקְשִׁים לֵישֵׁב
בְּשַׁלְוָה בָּעוֹלָם הַזֶּה.

RASHI: *A further comment was expounded on this*
verse: "And Jacob settled" — Jacob sought to dwell in
tranquility. But, the ordeal of Joseph sprung upon him.
The righteous seek to dwell in tranquility. But, the Holy
One said, "The righteous do not consider that which is
prepared for them in the World to Come to be enough for
them, but they seek to dwell in tranquility in this world,
as well."

*J*acob sought to dwell in tranquility, but Hashem had other ideas: The episode of Joseph with its resulting anguish would now begin. While the righteous might seek tranquility, the Holy One, Blessed is He, according to the *Rashi* that we quoted above, denies it to them.

The question is: "Why?" Does Hashem somehow object to a righteous person's having some benefit from this world as well as the next?

In terms of the application of this question to our case, we could answer as follows: Already from the time that he was in his mother's womb, Jacob had been involved in an ongoing, constant struggle with Esau: וַיִּתְרֹצְצוּ הַבָּנִים בְּקִרְבָּהּ, *And the children agitated within her* (25:22).

All of his strength had been invested in this endeavor.

Now, though, he sees that he has finally achieved a modicum of peace with his brother. Perhaps he can begin to live in relative tranquility, free to concentrate on development of his own self. But, then, קָפַץ עָלָיו רוֹגְזוֹ שֶׁל יוֹסֵף, *the ordeal of Joseph sprung upon him.*

Why?

Perhaps it was in order to teach us the lesson that as long as there is no peace between the brothers (as symbolized by the episode of Joseph), meaning no peace among the Jews themselves, then the very existence of the Jewish people is still imperiled. It would simply not be possible for Jacob to relax from his mission.

Of course, the hatred and attacks of the nations also pose a serious threat to our people. But, we may trust that Hashem will protect us from their succeeding in their efforts to drive us off our Holy Land.

However, when it comes to the internal threat, meaning the fraternal jealousy, hatred, and division that mark the relations between ourselves, we have no such promise. In fact, it is the underlying cause for our exile.

The final *galus* is sometimes referred to as being personified by Jacob. As we know, the Second Temple was destroyed not due to the Roman forces (rooted in Edom), but rather due to *sinas chinam,* causeless hatred, rooted in the way that we brothers (as alluded to in the story of Joseph) relate to each other.

This, then, is an answer to our question as to why peace with Esau (Edom) would not suffice. Peace with our enemies is certainly important, but it does not obviate the need to secure peace among the brothers — an end to the petty hatreds, jealousies, and disunity among ourselves.

וַיַּחַלְמוּ חֲלוֹם שְׁנֵיהֶם
The two of them dreamt a dream (40:5).

וַיְסַפֵּר שַׂר הַמַּשְׁקִים אֶת חֲלֹמוֹ לְיוֹסֵף וַיֹּאמֶר לוֹ בַּחֲלוֹמִי וְהִנֵּה גֶפֶן לְפָנָי:
וּבַגֶּפֶן שְׁלֹשָׁה שָׂרִיגִם וְהִיא כְפֹרַחַת עָלְתָה נִצָּהּ הִבְשִׁילוּ אַשְׁכְּלֹתֶיהָ עֲנָבִים:
וְכוֹס פַּרְעֹה בְּיָדִי וָאֶקַּח אֶת הָעֲנָבִים וָאֶשְׂחַט אֹתָם אֶל כּוֹס פַּרְעֹה וָאֶתֵּן
אֶת הַכּוֹס עַל כַּף פַּרְעֹה.

Then the Chamberlain of the Cupbearers recounted his dream to Joseph and said to him, "In my dream — behold! there was a grapevine in front of me! On the grapevine were three tendrils; and it was as though it budded — its blossoms bloomed and its clusters ripened into grapes. And Pharaoh's cup was in my hand and I took the grapes, pressed them into Pharaoh's cup, and I placed the cup on Pharaoh's palm" (40:9-11).

וַיֹּאמֶר לוֹ יוֹסֵף זֶה פִּתְרֹנוֹ שְׁלֹשֶׁת הַשָּׂרִגִים שְׁלֹשֶׁת יָמִים הֵם ... וְנָתַתָּ
כוֹס פַּרְעֹה בְּיָדוֹ כַּמִּשְׁפָּט הָרִאשׁוֹן אֲשֶׁר הָיִיתָ מַשְׁקֵהוּ.

Joseph said to him, "This is its interpretation: The three tendrils are three days. ... and you will place Pharaoh's cup in his hand as was the former practice when you were his cupbearer" (40:12,13).

וַיַּרְא שַׂר הָאֹפִים כִּי טוֹב פָּתָר וַיֹּאמֶר אֶל יוֹסֵף אַף אֲנִי בַּחֲלוֹמִי וְהִנֵּה שְׁלֹשָׁה סַלֵּי חֹרִי עַל רֹאשִׁי. וּבַסַּל הָעֶלְיוֹן מִכֹּל מַאֲכַל פַּרְעֹה מַעֲשֵׂה אֹפֶה וְהָעוֹף אֹכֵל אֹתָם מִן הַסַּל מֵעַל רֹאשִׁי.

The Chamberlain of the Bakers saw that he interpreted well, so he said to Joseph, "I too! In my dream — behold! three wicker baskets were on my head. And in the uppermost basket were all kinds of Pharaoh's food — baker's handiwork — and the birds were eating them from the basket above my head" (40:16,17).

וַיַּעַן יוֹסֵף וַיֹּאמֶר זֶה פִּתְרֹנוֹ שְׁלֹשֶׁת הַסַּלִּים שְׁלֹשֶׁת יָמִים הֵם. בְּעוֹד שְׁלֹשֶׁת יָמִים יִשָּׂא פַרְעֹה אֶת רֹאשְׁךָ מֵעָלֶיךָ ...

Joseph responded and said, "This is its interpretation: The three baskets are three days. In three days Pharaoh will lift your head from you ... " (40:18,19).

This dream recounted to Joseph by the Officer (Chamberlain) of the Cupbearers includes certain aspects that seem to not quite parallel Joseph's solution. This stands in contrast to the dream recounted by the Officer (Chamberlain) of the Bakers.

The Officer of the Bakers' dream was of three baskets that were on his head. The three baskets represented three days. The detail of their being on his head indicated that he would be beheaded.

The solution to the the Officer of the Cupbearers' dream was that there would be three days and that he would place a single cup into Pharaoh's hand. If that was the solution, then shouldn't the dream have been of the Officer having three cups in his hand, one of the cups being given to Pharaoh?

Instead, there is a grapevine; it has three branches, and the grapes are then squeezed into a single cup which was sitting in the Officer of the Cupbearers' hand. He then takes the cup and places it into Pharaoh's palm.

Pharaoh's behavior toward them is also quite puzzling. According to *Rashi's* understanding, Pharaoh counted them among the menial servants rather than immediately restoring them to their executive positions. (This stands in contradistinction to the plain meaning of the words. יִשָּׂא פַרְעֹה אֶת רֹאשֶׁךָ וַהֲשִׁיבְךָ עַל כַּנֶּךָ (40:13) would seem to be saying that they were, in fact, restored to their administrative roles, followed by the Officer of the Bakers then being hanged. *Rashi* seems to have understood the phrase as meaning that they would be "counted" — rather than "appointed." Therefore, upon counting the other servants, he remembered these two also and decided to reinstate the Officer of the Cupbearers but hang the Officer of the Bakers.)

Furthermore, why was it that the Officer of the Cupbearers was so disturbed by his dream? On the contrary, he should have been pleased! After all, he saw that Pharaoh would restore him to his former position!

The answer could be, as is written in the commentaries of *Malbim* and the *Netziv*, that the officers were not the actual offenders here. Rather, it was the servant who poured the drinks and the one who baked the bread. Still, Pharaoh's anger was directed at their superiors, holding the officers accountable for the actions of their staff.

The head cupbearer accepted responsibility, acknowledging that he was accountable for the actions of his subordinates and that he would have to suffer the consequences. The head baker, however, did not see it that way and felt that his incarceration was unjustifiable.

Each one's dream was consistent with his attitude. Because the head cupbearer considered himself as having failed in his role of chamberlain, he envisioned himself as a servant, the one who holds the cup, takes the grapes, presses them, and then places the cup into his master's palm. Every step in the process was laid out in front of him. This would explain his reaction: To him, it was as if he had been demoted.

Joseph's interpretation was that the dream was showing him how he would make amends for his crime. For three days, despite his high status, he would personally do all of the menial tasks, and do so without complaining that they were beneath his station. He would thereby rectify his error and Pharaoh would re-elevate him and restore him to his former position.

The head baker, however, would not acknowledge his culpability. He therefore saw three wicker baskets upon his head, the uppermost holding all kinds of baked goods. But, he would not be doing any baking. He could not see himself as anything but the "head" of the bakers, and not as the actual baker. He would therefore not be the one removing the items from the basket on his head. That honor would go to the birds. After all, he saw the actual work as beneath his dignity.

On Pharaoh's birthday, a day that would normally feature granting of amnesty, he decided to see whether these two "executives" could really be counted among his faithful servants, taking personal responsibility for the fly that was found in his drink and the pebble that was found in the bread. Would they take the place of the servants or would they maintain their "executive" posture?

The Officer of the Cupbearers humbly put the cup into Pharaoh's hand himself, while the Officer of the Bakers stayed aloof. Since he did not conduct himself as a "servant," he was hanged.

וְלֹא זָכַר שַׂר הַמַּשְׁקִים אֶת יוֹסֵף וַיִּשְׁכָּחֵהוּ

Yet the Chamberlain of the Cupbearers did not remember Joseph, but he forgot him (40:23).

וַיְהִי מִקֵּץ שְׁנָתַיִם יָמִים

It happened at the end of two years to the day (41:1).

Even after carefully studying the words of the commentators and of our Rabbis, it is still not very clear to me why it is that the *Chumash* details so many specifics regarding the dreams and their interpretations. Abraham was thrown into a fiery furnace and Jacob warred with Shechem, but it was left to the Oral Torah to relate the details. Why wasn't the same done here? Let the *Chumash* simply say that there were some dreams and Joseph interpreted them, thereby achieving great recognition, high position, and fulfillment of what he had prophesied earlier. The particulars could have been filled in by the Oral Tradition. Why did they merit being put into the Written Torah?

Let us propose that the significance of these details is that they reveal important aspects of our interaction with the nations, both past and future.

Let me explain. Pharaoh was a dictator, ruling with unquestioned authority. While the population was totally subordinate to his system of law, he, personally, was beyond any checks or balances, beholden to no one. In fact, he cultivated an image of being possessed with powers that were not only total, but even godly.

Society was hierarchical. There were the privileged, those fortunate enough to have close ties to Pharaoh. Then there were the priests. The bottom stratum belonged to the majority, in effect, the servants of servants. The class structure was clearly defined, with no one having any expectation of improving his status.

Upon this scene came Joseph. He would be a catalyst, one who would potentially upset this entire system. The "laws" which kept the people subjugated would be questioned, the potential to improve their station could become not only a possibility, but a reality.

The challenge to the status quo would sometimes be made openly and sometimes occur in a roundabout fashion.

Everyone was taken with Joseph's righteousness, honesty, and capabilities — made all the more remarkable by the fact that he had begun his "career" as a slave. Perspectives would now change, both as to the way that the masters would see their servants and as to the way that the servants would see themselves. Neither the masters nor the servants could continue viewing a servant as little more than a field animal or prisoner. Joseph demonstrated by personal example that servants were human, possessed of talent and intelligence — qualities that could be put to use. It was neither logical nor expedient for anyone to deny their humanity.

Upon receipt of (false) reports of Joseph's audacious attempt to seduce his master's wife, loud alarms went off throughout the land: Masters must now be in fear of their newly emboldened servants, rather than the other way around.

וַיְהִי אַחַר הַדְּבָרִים הָאֵלֶּה, *And it happened after those things ...* (40:1), "those things" referring to the incident of Joseph and Potiphar's wife. חָטְאוּ מַשְׁקֵה מֶלֶךְ מִצְרַיִם וְהָאֹפֶה לַאֲדֹנֵיהֶם לְמֶלֶךְ מִצְרָיִם, *... that the cupbearer of the king of Egypt and the baker transgressed against their master* (continuation of 40:1). According to some, the reference here is to nothing less than an act of outright rebellion — an attempt on Pharaoh's life. The plan was to place poison into the food and drink of their master, the king of Egypt.

Take note of the words of the verse: the act was to be committed not against Pharaoh, but *against their master, the king of Egypt.* The king was losing his grip on power and the servants were ready to revolt.

וַיִּתֵּן אֹתָם בְּמִשְׁמַר ... מְקוֹם אֲשֶׁר יוֹסֵף אָסוּר שָׁם, *And he placed them in the ward ... the place where Joseph was confined* (40:3). They, too, would be not ordinary inmates, but political prisoners. The significance of their being in the same place as Joseph was that from them,

Joseph would learn of the groundswell of resentment against the king's authority.

～～～

וַיַּחַלְמוּ חֲלוֹם שְׁנֵיהֶם ...
The two of them dreamt a dream (40:5).

וְהִנֵּה גֶּפֶן לְפָנָי. וּבַגֶּפֶן שְׁלשָׁה שָׂרִיגִם וְהִיא כְפֹרַחַת עָלְתָה נִצָּהּ הִבְשִׁילוּ אַשְׁכְּלֹתֶיהָ עֲנָבִים.

... there was a grapevine in front of me! On the grapevine were three tendrils; and it was as though it budded — its blossoms bloomed and its clusters ripened into grapes. (40:9-10).

וְכוֹס פַּרְעֹה בְּיָדִי וָאֶקַּח אֶת הָעֲנָבִים וָאֶשְׂחַט אֹתָם אֶל כּוֹס פַּרְעֹה וָאֶתֵּן אֶת הַכּוֹס עַל כַּף פַּרְעֹה.

And Pharaoh's cup was in my hand and I took the grapes, pressed them into Pharaoh's cup, and I placed the cup on Pharaoh's palm" (40:11).

The imagery is of a grapevine, the grapevine having three branches, each representing one of the three classes: the rulers, the wealthy, and the poor. The three branches all stem from one common source, though, *and it was as though it budded — its blossoms bloomed and its clusters ripened into grapes* (40:10). Through their joint effort, the goal was quickly being reached. The grapes were ripe and ready to be made into the wine that was to be presented to Pharaoh.

וְהִנֵּה שְׁלשָׁה סַלֵּי חֹרִי עַל רֹאשִׁי. וּבַסַּל הָעֶלְיוֹן מִכֹּל מַאֲכַל פַּרְעֹה מַעֲשֵׂה אֹפֶה וְהָעוֹף אֹכֵל אֹתָם מִן הַסַּל מֵעַל רֹאשִׁי.

... three wicker baskets were on my head. And in the uppermost basket were all kinds of Pharaoh's food — baker's handiwork — and the birds were eating them from the basket above my head" (40:16,17).

The imagery is of Pharaoh being fearful that his rule would be undermined. The masses (the birds) will come to eat not just from the upper basket, which is the most accessible to them, but will even pick from the one that is closest to Pharaoh's head, meaning that they will go so far as to pluck the crown right off his skull.

וַיַּרְא שַׂר הָאֹפִים כִּי טוֹב פָּתָר

The Chamberlain of the Bakers saw that he had interpreted well (40:16)

What was it that was **טוֹב** about this interpretation? Let us turn to *Bereishis Rabbah*:

"וְכוֹס פַּרְעֹה בְּיָדִי", מִכַּאן קָבְעוּ חֲכָמִים ד' כּוֹסוֹת שֶׁל לֵילֵי פֶּסַח

"And Pharaoh's cup was in my hand" — *This is the source for the Sages' legislating four cups for Pesach night.*

What was *good* was that the four times that *cup* is mentioned allude to *geulah*. The Chamberlain of the Bakers' dream was interpreted to be *not* for good, an allusion to cruel domination, to a government that will subjugate its citizenry though physical force and intimidation.

Now, after hearing these two dreams, we can proceed to that of Pharaoh.

He saw seven lean cows swallowing seven fat ones. He was terrified. Was this foreshadowing a popular uprising, where the "lean" underclass would "swallow up" the fat and privileged ruling class?

Joseph the Righteous, the interpreter of the dream, has plans for improving the nation's lot. He works to improve the national economy, sees to it that plans will be in place to protect the food supply, and that there will be equitable distribution. His decrees are reasonable and fair.

However, he also makes certain to secure his own position, knowing full well that a slave who becomes a ruler will be resented: וְלֹא זָכַר שַׂר הַמַּשְׁקִים אֶת יוֹסֵף וַיִּשְׁכָּחֵהוּ, *Yet the Chamberlain of the Cupbearers did not remember Joseph, and he forgot him.*

Despite all that he has done for them, creating a more equitable society, inspiring them to have their humanity acknowledged, all will be forgotten in the end. The appreciation and recognition will simply not come.

This pattern will continue throughout the course of time. Always, *A new king will arise who knew not Joseph* (*Shemos* 1:8).

This is not to minimize the significance of our being actively involved in the development of fair and just societies. Nor does it mean that we should resign ourselves to being despised.

Rather, we must lead by example, by being just and fair among ourselves, placing God at the center of our existence.

וַיֹּאמֶר יִשְׂרָאֵל לָמָה הֲרֵעֹתֶם לִי לְהַגִּיד לָאִישׁ הַעוֹד לָכֶם אָח

Then Israel (Jacob) said, "Why did you treat me badly, telling the man that you have another brother?" (43:6).

מֵעוֹלָם לֹא הָיָה יַעֲקֹב אָבִינוּ אוֹמֵר דָּבָר שֶׁלְּבַטָּלָה אֶלָּא כַּאן, אָמַר הַקָּדוֹשׁ בָּרוּךְ הוּא אֲנִי עָסוּק לְהַמְלִיךְ אֶת בְּנוֹ בְּמִצְרַיִם, וְהוּא אוֹמֵר לָמָה הֲרֵעֹתֶם לִי ...

Never did Jacob say something in vain — except here. The Holy One, Blessed is He, said, "I am working to make his son into the ruler of Egypt, and he says, 'Why are you treating me badly'! " (Bereishis Rabbah 91 Albeck).

What was it about Jacob's words that deserved reproach? How was he to know that Joseph was still alive and a ruler in Egypt? After all, Jacob was under the impression that Joseph had been killed by a wild animal!

Yet, according to the Midrash quoted above, Hashem considered his question, "*Why did you treat me badly*," to have been in vain!

One could possibly argue that it is one thing for Jacob to wonder about the worst having happened to his son immediately upon seeing the bloody coat, but twenty-two years after the fact, perhaps Hashem would expect Jacob to have contemplated His ways more thoughtfully and trusted that everything was for the good.

However, we could instead view the Midrash as singing Jacob's praises.

When it says that he had never spoken a word in vain other than in this instance, the Midrash is also saying that this incident was an anomaly, inconsistent with what is seen everywhere else. In all other instances, the words of our forefathers were Torah, even if they were expressing a misreading of the prophecy's subtle message.

———

וַיַּכִּירָהּ וַיֹּאמֶר כְּתֹנֶת בְּנִי חַיָּה רָעָה אֲכָלָתְהוּ טָרֹף טֹרַף יוֹסֵף

He recognized it and said, "My son's tunic!
An evil beast devoured him!
Joseph has surely been torn to bits!" (37:33).

Actually, the "wild animal" who had "devoured Joseph" was Potiphar's wife, who had grabbed Joseph's garment. Jacob had misinterpreted the message. The metaphor had been missed, but he was still reacting to what he was shown. Yet, it was only in our case that he was taken to task for having spoken "vain words."

In our instance, though, he had done more, characterizing a situation as being "bad" where, in fact, there was nothing bad about it.

It's stunning to imagine to how high a standard he was being held. Look at the situation: He was mourning (what he thought was) the loss of Joseph, he has just received word of Simeon's imprisonment

— and now they are coming to take away Benjamin! He reacts by saying that things are bad. And for this, he is given reproach!

Why? Because Jacob's consistent standard had been that of Torah, truth, and Divine Inspiration.

When, however, this standard could not be met, when there was no way to say that his words were correct on some level, even based on the physical reality that had been presented to him (as with the bloody coat), he was reproached.

Jacob's words, when they could not be judged as correct according to the highest level of truth, would have to be considered falsity. This was despite the fact that his reaction might have been perfectly understandable for someone else.

Ultimately, this was a tribute to his *emes.*

הָבֵא אֶת הָאֲנָשִׁים הַבָּיְתָה וּטְבֹחַ טֶבַח וְהָכֵן כִּי אִתִּי יֹאכְלוּ הָאֲנָשִׁים בַּצָּהֳרָיִם

Bring the men into the house. Have meat slaughtered and prepare it, for with me will these men dine at noon (43:16).

Rearrange the letters of וְהָכֵן, combine them with the last letter of the word that precedes it in this verse, טְבַח, and you could spell the word, חֲנוּכָּה, *Chanukah.* The same word, וְהָכֵן , also alludes to Joseph's having observed the Shabbos: וְהָיָה בַּיּוֹם הַשִּׁשִּׁי וְהֵכִינוּ, *on the sixth day when they prepare* [the manna] ... (*Shemos* 16:5) .

What connections could we draw between שַׁבָּת and חֲנוּכָּה?

Chanukah's primary miracle was that of the oil, as explained in *Maseches Shabbos* 21b in response to the question, מַאי חֲנוּכָּה, *In commemoration of which miracle was this holiday established?* (*Rashi*).

While it is certainly true that the military aspect was quite re-markable and miraculous, its occurrence would not, in and of itself, have justified the institution of a new holiday, to be celebrated yearly from that point onward. The phenomenon of the many being routed by the few was not something unprecedented, even among the na-tions. Only within the context of the miracle of the oil could its true significance be appreciated.

There was only one day's worth of pure oil, yet it lasted for eight. The Greeks had contaminated practically the entire supply of ritually pure oil. Their actions symbolized their intention of contaminating all that was holy and pure to the Jewish nation. They confused our minds, distracted our thoughts, and disrupted our collective ability to learn Torah. It almost seemed that there would not be the where-withal to kindle the lights symbolizing our connection to the pure traditions of Torah from Sinai.

It was not until after the few Jews to remain resolute in their devo-tion to Torah had rekindled the Torah's flame throughout the Land, that the Rabbis saw fit to dedicate a new holiday to commemorate the military victory.

As in the case of the military victory, the spiritual triumph also demonstrated the possibility of a minority's devotion to holiness prevailing over the majority. The few could potentially redirect the many — a bit of light dispels much darkness.

And that is the basis of Chanukah.

It is also the basis of the Sabbath.

Shabbos is one day among seven. There are six days of work and one of rest. Which set would be granted the greatest holiness? The unit of six or the unit of one? That which is most numerous?

Of course, the extra measure of holiness was given to the single day of rest. The larger group will not necessarily be the one that will predominate and be the most influential.

This was demonstrated through Chanukah and through the choosing of the Sabbath.

So too, it is demonstrated through the concept of Shabbos being the sign between the Jewish people and their God: Hashem sanctifies us through the Shabbos because we, too, are numerically fewer than all other nations.

Ultimately, though, our numeric insignificance is not indicative of our potential for making the difference.

As in the miracle of Chanukah.

וַיִּגַּשׁ אֵלָיו יְהוּדָה וַיֹּאמֶר ...
Then Judah approached him and said ... (44:18).

The verse relates that Judah approached Joseph and that he then spoke to him. Why didn't the Torah simply state that Judah spoke to Joseph without mentioning that he first approached him? Every word written in the Torah is there for a purpose; what purpose is served by telling us of something that is so seemingly insignificant?

In fact, there is great significance to our being told that Judah "approached," as seen in other sources.

Midrash Rabbah teaches that the word וַיִּגַּשׁ, *approached*, is indicative of three things: an act of war, an action of appeasement, and prayer. A certain *sefer* explains that the three הַגָּשׁוֹת are similar: Just as departure for war demands preparation, both physical and emotional, so too with mollification and with prayer.

I might add that, in anticipation of battle, it is obvious that one must know his enemy well — what strengths should be avoided and which vulnerabilities could be exploited. Lacking proper reconnaissance, one will fail.

So too, with prayer — only here, the reconnaissance is turned inward. What are my strengths? Where are my weaknesses? What kind of relationship do I have with my Maker? Only after careful consideration of one's inner self, and proper emotional composure, might one begin pouring out his heart to his Creator.

When it comes to successfully winning over another individual in an attempt to mollify him, the process of discovery is not dissimilar. What type of person is he? What makes him tick? What moves him? How will I penetrate his feelings and make my appeal successful?

All of the above — prayer, warfare, and appeasement — demand coming closer. Judah's approaching Joseph was not incidental. Rather, it was essential.

He needed to reach Joseph's innermost self, to appeal to that which was closest to Joseph. Therefore, he had to approach. He recognized Joseph's strong feelings for his father. After all, Joseph had repeatedly inquired about Jacob's welfare. Even as he sent his brothers off, he told them to go in peace to their father.

Judah could now see where Joseph's soft spot would be. So, he told him that Benjamin's failure to return would cause untold grief to Jacob.

Joseph's heart was touched. Judah's forethought in "approaching" was successful.

And Joseph revealed himself to his brothers.

... יְדַבֶּר נָא עַבְדְּךָ ...
... *may your servant speak* ... (44:18).

Judah reiterates to Joseph what had previously transpired between them. Nothing is added; it's basically a repetition of what had been said once before. There must be some lesson here.

Otherwise, why would the Torah find it necessary to include these words a second time?

This is a question that is asked by *Ramban* to verse 19, and I refer you to his response.

Allow me, though, to suggest a different approach.

The verse in *Parashas Kedoshim* (*Vayikra* 19:17) says:

לֹא תִשְׂנָא אֶת אָחִיךָ בִּלְבָבֶךָ הוֹכֵחַ תּוֹכִיחַ אֶת עֲמִיתֶךָ וְלֹא תִשָּׂא עָלָיו חֵטְא.

You shall not hate your brother in your heart; you shall reprove your fellow and do not bear a sin because of him.

One way of understanding this injunction is that it is telling us that should we have some sort of grievance with another Jew, we should allow him to know how we feel. Rather than suppress these feelings, carrying them around within ourselves, eventually leading to our seething with resentment, we should express our displeasure — constructively, of course. Otherwise, these feelings could lead to endless quarreling, even bloodshed, God forbid.

In fact, this would seem to have been an issue that was present in the story of Joseph and his brothers:

וַיִּרְאוּ אֶחָיו כִּי אֹתוֹ אָהַב אֲבִיהֶם מִכָּל אֶחָיו וַיִּשְׂנְאוּ אֹתוֹ וְלֹא יָכְלוּ דַּבְּרוֹ לְשָׁלֹם,
His brothers saw that it was he whom their father loved most of all his brothers, so they hated him; and they were not able to speak to him peaceably (37:4).

They could not speak to him peaceably, so they did not speak to him at all. They never expressed their anger toward him. Eventually, the ill-will built up to the extent that they would act with cruelty, selling him to slavery in Egypt, deaf to his pleas.

Recognizing the toll that his brothers' pent-up feelings had taken many years before, Joseph would now attempt to show them the proper approach. He became the catalyst for this new mode of behavior, whereby they would speak again of the difficulties of the past, not allowing the wounds to fester.

Instead, the past hatreds would be uprooted, ultimately to foster brotherly love.

וְאֶת יְהוּדָה שָׁלַח לְפָנָיו אֶל יוֹסֵף לְהוֹרֹת לְפָנָיו גֹּשְׁנָה

He sent Judah ahead of him to Joseph, to prepare ahead of him in Goshen (46:28).

The Hebrew spellings of the words גֹּשְׁנָה (*to Goshen*) and מָשִׁיחַ (*Mashiach*) have the same numerical value — 358. And, it is not incidental that the residence of the Jewish people in Egypt was called גֹּשֶׁן. *Goshen* stems from the word הַגָּשָׁה, which means *to draw close*, as we see in the verses, וַיִּגַּשׁ אֵלָיו יְהוּדָה, *Then Judah approached* (44:18), and וַיֹּאמֶר יוֹסֵף אֶל אֶחָיו גְּשׁוּ נָא אֵלַי וַיִּגָּשׁוּ וַיֹּאמֶר אֲנִי יוֹסֵף אֲחִיכֶם, *Then Joseph said to his brothers, "Come close to me, if you please," and they came close. And he said, "I am Joseph, your brother"* (45:4).

Joseph reveals his identity only after they have drawn close to him. Only then could the extent of their mutual affection and brotherhood become manifest.

Similarly, when all the Jewish people see themselves as brothers, approaching one another amicably — not cautiously or warily, from a distance — then will we also bring closer the *geulah*, the period of redemption.

And then there is the alternative: וַיִּרְאוּ אֹתוֹ מֵרָחֹק וּבְטֶרֶם יִקְרַב אֲלֵיהֶם וַיִּתְנַכְּלוּ אֹתוֹ לַהֲמִיתוֹ, *They saw him from afar; and when he had not yet approached them, they conspired toward him to kill him* (37:18).

When they saw him from afar, when he had not yet approached them, that is when they conspired to kill him.

וַיְחִי יַעֲקֹב בְּאֶרֶץ מִצְרַיִם

Jacob lived in the land of Egypt (47:28).

רש"י: וַיְחִי יַעֲקֹב – לָמָּה פָּרָשָׁה זוּ סְתוּמָה

RASHI: JACOB LIVED — *Why is this passage "closed"?*

Based on a Midrash, *Rashi* asks why, despite this being the beginning of a new passage, it is "closed," that is, not set off with the usual number of spaces that would mark its being distinct from the passage that precedes it.

Rashi offers two answers; I would like to offer yet another as to why this appears as a "closed" *parashah*.

Life can be unpredictable and mysterious, a "closed" book, its final chapters hidden from those in its midst. Man, who is "formed out of clay" (to paraphrase Job), is left to wonder when his end will come to pass; and, when he is in distress, from which corner his deliverance will present itself. Good might spring from situations that appear to be absolutely bad, and vice versa.

Nor does man know at what time or from where his true salvation will come.

וַיְחִי יַעֲקֹב בְּאֶרֶץ מִצְרַיִם, *Jacob lived in the land of Egypt.* Did Jacob ever dream th at these years in Egypt would be his best? Did he even imagine that he would see the face of Joseph again? And, that Joseph would have remained as righteous as before — and here in Egypt no less?

There were many such surprises. At the end of the day, there's very good reason why the Hebrew word for "world" is עוֹלָם, which shares its root meaning with הֶעֱלֵם , *concealment.* That is its name and so it will be forever, לְעוֹלָם.

טימות

וְאֵלֶּה שְׁמוֹת בְּנֵי יִשְׂרָאֵל הַבָּאִים מִצְרָיְמָה
אֵת יַעֲקֹב אִישׁ וּבֵיתוֹ בָּאוּ

And these are the names of the Children of Israel
who were coming to Egypt; with Jacob, each man
and his household came (1:1).

he Book of *Shemos* is the book of גְּאוּלָה, *redemption.*

Let me explain:

The word גְּאוּלָה is related to the word הַגְעָלָה, *purging.* Both refer to taking one thing out from another, similar to the actualization of a given item, that is, transforming it from its potential state to its actual.

This parallels the relationship between the Book of *Bereishis* and that of *Shemos.*

Again, let me explain.

The period of the *Avos,* as described in *Sefer Bereishis,* saw the future history of the Jewish people being set in motion, albeit in potential. This potential would then be actualized through their children, as described in *Sefer Shemos*.

וְאֵלֶּה שְׁמוֹת בְּנֵי יִשְׂרָאֵל ... אֵת יַעֲקֹב אִישׁ וּבֵיתוֹ בָּאוּ, *And these are the names of the Children of Israel who were coming to Egypt; with Jacob, each man and his household came.* They were originally called "Jacob and his household." But now they are known by an independent, proper name — בְּנֵי יִשְׂרָאֵל, *the Children of Israel.*

Earlier, they had been subordinate to Jacob, hidden and nameless. Now they emerge, fully named — their hidden potential ready to be actualized.

<hr/>

וְאֵלֶּה שְׁמוֹת בְּנֵי יִשְׂרָאֵל הַבָּאִים מִצְרָיְמָה אֵת יַעֲקֹב אִישׁ וּבֵיתוֹ בָּאוּ

And these are the names of the Children of Israel who were coming to Egypt; with Jacob, each man and his household came (1:1).

This verse contains two inconsistencies of language. The first involves the term used when referring to the Jewish people and the second concerns the change of tense when describing their passage.

Allow me to elaborate.

The Jews are called Children of *Israel* at the beginning of the verse, but then referred to as part of the household of Jacob at the conclusion of the same verse. And, in the first part of the verse they are described as "*coming*," in the present tense; but the latter part of the verse says that they "*came*," past tense.

What accounts for these discrepancies, and are they, in some way, related?

Certain members of the first wave of immigration were at the level of *Bnei Yisrael*. They never allowed themselves to become accustomed to the life of Egypt. They never came to terms with the *galus*. Each and every day they felt as if they were coming anew to some strange, foreign land.

Others, however, reacted quite differently. These were no longer *Israel*, but the household of Jacob. The consisted largely of the sons and daughters of the first group, and acclimated to their surroundings much more quickly. While not exactly accepting of their situation, the suffering closed their hearts; they coped by learning not to feel the *galus* so much anymore. Surely, their initial reaction was that they had come to a strange, foreign land. But, that became the reaction of their past; in their ongoing day-to-day life, they no longer felt the *galus* so acutely.

There is another aspect of this verse of which I would like to take note: Why does it say that they were *coming* to Egypt? Wouldn't it have been more appropriate to have written that they were *descending*? After all, weren't they traveling from Eretz Yisrael? *Any* place would be considered a descent from the Holy Land. Certainly Egypt!

Of course, there is no question that the trip from Eretz Yisrael to Egypt constitutes a spiritual descent from the place of supreme holiness to one that is among the most lowly.

However, the Jewish people were arriving with Jacob. The very presence of one as holy as he was enough to mitigate the effect of the transition from a place of great holiness to a place devoid of it. Spiritually linked with Jacob, the Jewish people need not necessarily decline, even as they move on to Egypt.

וְאֵלֶּה שְׁמוֹת בְּנֵי יִשְׂרָאֵל
And these are the names
of the Children of Israel (1:1).

*R*ashi comments that although Hashem counted them when they were still alive, He recounted them after their death to make known how precious they are to Him.

Most people in the world at large will affect society only during the course of their own lifetimes, if at all. Certainly, those who do merit to have an impact are often forgotten once they are dead and gone. As King Solomon stated: אֵין זִכְרוֹן לָרִאשֹׁנִים וְגַם לָאַחֲרֹנִים שֶׁיִּהְיוּ לֹא יִהְיֶה לָהֶם זִכָּרוֹן עִם שֶׁיִּהְיוּ לָאַחֲרֹנָה, *As there is no recollection of the former ones, so too, of the latter ones that are yet to be, there will be no recollection among those of a still later time* (Koheles 1:11).

In contrast, the impact (*names,* as in this verse) of members of the Jewish people extends long after their departure from this world. Their life is eternal. They implant holiness, faith, and fear of God — attributes that will never be destroyed.

Just as seeds are concealed beneath the ground, only to sprout forth with fruit, so will the traits of holiness implanted by the righteous live on, continuing to bear fruit, forever.

וַיָּקָם מֶלֶךְ חָדָשׁ עַל מִצְרָיִם אֲשֶׁר לֹא יָדַע אֶת יוֹסֵף
A new king arose over Egypt,
who did not know of Joseph (1:8).

*T*his was מִדָּה כְּנֶגֶד מִדָּה, *one measure corresponding to another.* Joseph had done his best to try and prevent his people from assimilating into the surrounding culture. He designated a specific place for them to live — Goshen, and, in order to remove any possible hesitancy the Jews might have about becoming circumcised, went so far as to decree that even the Egyptians should undergo the procedure.

Hashem's Name never left Joseph's mouth, nor did his father's image cease from appearing before his eyes. Joseph further demonstrated his distaste for Egypt by commanding the Jewish people not to leave his bones behind when they would eventually leave the country.

Despite Joseph's efforts, however, the Jews rejected his wishes — at least according to one possible understanding of the verse that precedes ours, וַתִּמָּלֵא הָאָרֶץ אֹתָם, *and the land became filled with them* (1:7). According to this reading, rather than heed Joseph's warnings, they had begun to assimilate into the surrounding culture.

The Jews had chosen not to emulate Joseph. They had "forgotten" him.

Therefore, מִדָּה כְּנֶגֶד מִדָּה, a new king arose, one who, likewise, did not "know" Joseph, but had forgotten him.

וַתִּירֶאןָ הַמְיַלְּדֹת אֶת הָאֱלֹהִים וְלֹא עָשׂוּ
כַּאֲשֶׁר דִּבֶּר אֲלֵיהֶן מֶלֶךְ מִצְרָיִם וַתְּחַיֶּיןָ אֶת הַיְלָדִים
*But the midwives feared God and they did not
do as the king of Egypt spoke to them,
and they caused the boys to live (1:17).*

The *sefer Yavin Shemuah* infers from the wording of this verse that the Egyptians had been denying the Jewish male children food and water. Once Pharaoh decreed that all the boys be killed, however, the midwives began to feed them!

This interpretation seems to illustrate an important lesson. Hashem created certain opposites in the world, and for every negative there is something positive. We can learn from this that when faced with situations or periods in history that are marked by overwhelming cruelty — perhaps *especially* at those times — we must give increased attention to performing good deeds and acts of kindness, so as not to be sucked in by the depravity that is rampant.

Pharaoh had ordered that the males be killed, and it was then that the midwives began to sustain them with food. Not only did they ignore Pharaoh's edict, but they increased their level of care, providing the previously neglected children with nutrition. The greater the negativity that they saw, the more they increased their response — more good deeds.

וַיֵּיטֶב אֱלֹהִים לַמְיַלְּדֹת, *God benefited the midwives* (1:20). He saw to it that they would be able to perform *more good* than they had previously, that they would be able to act in a kinder manner than before.

Hashem increased their opportunities to do goodness — at a time of increasing evil.

And so must we.

וַיַּעַשׂ לָהֶם בָּתִּים
He made for them houses (1:21).

"וַיְהִי כִּי יָרְאוּ הַמְיַלְּדֹת וגו' ", רַב וְלֵוִי, חַד אָמַר בָּתֵּי כְהוּנָה וּבָתֵּי לְוִיָּה, וְחַד אָמַר בָּתֵּי מַלְכוּת, בָּתֵּי כְהוּנָה וּלְוִיָּה מִמֹּשֶׁה וְאַהֲרֹן, בָּתֵּי מַלְכוּת מִמִּרְיָם, לְפִי שֶׁדָּוִד בָּא מִמִּרְיָם.

"And it was because the midwives feared God that He made them houses." Rav and Levi agreed that the word "houses" here is a reference to the midwives' reward, but disagreed as to what type of "houses" they were being rewarded with. One said that it meant dynasties

of Kohanim and Leviim; one said that it (additionally) meant dynasties of royalty. "Houses of Kohanim and Leviim" — from Moses and Aaron. "Houses of Royalty" — from Miriam, as David came from Miriam (Shemos Rabbah 1:17).

This Midrash would seem to be based on a prior Midrash which identifies the midwife pair as either Jochebed and Elisheba (her daughter-in-law, wife of Aaron) or Jochebed and Miriam (her daughter). The first pairing is a precursor to Houses of Kohanim and Leviim, through Aaron and Moses. The other pairing indicates a future reward of Houses of Royalty, with David ultimately being born from the line of Miriam.

What underlies these two opinions?

The first, which emphasizes that there will be a reward of future Kohanim and Leviim, shows the link between the reason for their reward (their *fear* [*yirah*] of Heaven) and the reward itself — Kohanim and Leviim, whose defining characteristic is service, *avodah*. These midwives would be progenitors of *ovdei Hashem*, stemming from their actions of *yirah*, as fulfillment of *ivdu es Hashem b'yirah*, "Serve Hashem with fear and awe."

As for the other opinion, that which links the pair with *malchus*, it is testimony to their own regal posture of not allowing themselves to be intimidated by Pharaoh, unlike mere servants, who would have immediately capitulated to his every desire.

David's future kingdom would emerge not from those who had acted as slaves, but rather from those who had acted as future kings.

וַיְצַו פַּרְעֹה לְכָל עַמּוֹ לֵאמֹר כָּל הַבֵּן הַיִּלּוֹד
הַיְאֹרָה תַּשְׁלִיכֻהוּ וְכָל הַבַּת תְּחַיּוּן

Pharaoh commanded his entire people,
saying, "Every son that will be born —
into the River you shall throw him!
And every daughter you shall keep alive" (1:22).

רש"י: לְכָל עַמּוֹ – אַף עֲלֵיהֶם גָּזַר

RASHI: TO HIS ENTIRE PEOPLE — *that their newborn*
infants be cast into the Nile.

---

*A*ccording to *Rashi*, the Egyptians were being ordered to
kill even their own sons.

Wasn't this risky? Wasn't Pharaoh concerned about internal opposition, perhaps even the beginnings of a rebellion? Why
was he willing to take such a chance?

It seems to me that Pharaoh was making a cold calculation, choosing a path that would actually be serving his own long-term interests. In fact, he did have cause to be concerned about a possible
rebellion — but for a different reason, as a reaction to the potential
for mass shortages of food, due to the tremendously high number of
children being born.

This was a problem that had to be addressed!

First, he thought he could stem the tide by having his people persecute and oppress the Jews. Hashem thwarted that plan and saw
to it that the Jews would continue multiplying and become even
more numerous.

Plan Number 2 was to go beyond mere persecution and advance
to outright murder, having the midwives kill the Jewish children as
they were being born. That, too, did not work out as planned.

Plan Number 3 was to have the Egyptians kill off their very own newborns. That would be the best plan of all for solving the food-supply problems!

Targum Onkelos translates וַיָּקָם מֶלֶךְ חָדָשׁ עַל מִצְרָיִם אֲשֶׁר לֹא יָדַע אֶת יוֹסֵף as דְּלָא מְקַיֵּם גְּזֵרַת יוֹסֵף, *a king who did not carry out Joseph's decrees.* Perhaps, this reading could be understood as being consistent with what we have just suggested, namely that he did not follow Joseph's advice to prepare for times of famine by storing sufficient quantities of food.

To continue with this thought, as to Pharaoh's urging the murder of his own people's sons as a way of staving off food shortages, let us also suggest that it might put verse 1:10 into new perspective. Pharaoh urges his people toward war, using the phrase, וְהָיָה כִּי תִקְרֶאנָה מִלְחָמָה, normally translated, *and it may be that if a war will occur.*

The word וְהָיָה is sometimes understood as a term that indicates joy. But, why would Pharaoh be happy at the prospect of war?

Simple. Wars bring casualties. Lots of them.

Less mouths to feed.

וַתִּפְתַּח וַתִּרְאֵהוּ אֶת הַיֶּלֶד וְהִנֵּה נַעַר בֹּכֶה וַתַּחְמֹל עָלָיו וַתֹּאמֶר מִיַּלְדֵי הָעִבְרִים זֶה

She opened it and saw him, the boy, and behold! a youth was crying. She took pity on him and said, "This is one of the Hebrew boys" (2:6).

I noticed that one of the latter-day commentators questions why it is that the Torah did not first mention that this was a Hebrew child, and only afterward tell us that Pharaoh's daughter took pity on him.

Wasn't the child's Jewish identity the most relevant aspect of the story being related here?

Well, perhaps it is not.

Rather, the reversal of the expected order comes to teach us an important lesson.

Upon seeing someone who is greatly distressed and sorely in need, our first reaction should be to feel his pain, to take pity on him and reach out, hoping that there will, in fact, be something that we can do for him.

All of this before the cold calculations begin: Is it feasible? Realistic? Is it really within our capability to make a difference for this person? Do we have the resources? Is this the type of person to whom we could justifiably dedicate the level of resources that would actually be needed?

Witness what it was that Bithyah, Pharaoh's daughter, did here. She took pity on this child, before ever having identified him, seeing which group it was to which he belonged, or considering what the consequences might be of wanting to help such a child.

It turned out that he was not one of her own people; rather, he was a Jew. But this was not of immediate importance; she had wanted to help without regard for analyses as to the risks.

In fact, this too was the *middah* of the child whose life she was now about to save.

... Moses grew up and went out to his brethren and observed their burdens (2:11). Moses was "with them" in their pain. *And he saw an Egyptian man striking a Hebrew man of his brethren.* He rose up immediately, without thought as to personal danger. He felt that he must put an end to this injustice. When faced with the possibility of having to forfeit his own life, it certainly could be argued that there really was no absolute obligation on Moses' part to do this. He was putting himself into a situation of *pikuach nefesh* rather than walk away from witnessing the beating of his fellow.

But, he was already "with them" in their pain.

Pharaoh's daughter had made a similar decision. She could have reconsidered her initial impulse to act. After all, this was a Hebrew child and by saving him she would be violating her own father's decree. Still, she was determined to do so in a way that would pose the least danger to herself. But, that calculation came only later, after she had already committed herself to taking action.

The idea we have just suggested can be developed a bit further. We find that when the Torah uses the expression *chessed v'emes*, the word *chessed* always precedes the word *emes*.

The order of the words reflects the ideal approach. One's first thought should be to want to help, to feel compassion and have a desire to perform *chessed*.

Only afterward should a person look at the situation rationally, logically, with *emes*. Both traits are essential and must be used in conjunction with each other.

But, if one *begins* with *emes*, it is more likely that he will never get to the *chessed*. There are always too many reasons why it might be best not to get involved, or to believe that one wouldn't be able to make much of a difference in the face of the overwhelming need.

However, if that were to happen, not only would the *chessed* not be actualized, but there would also be no *emes*. Neither *chessed* nor *emes*.

Let us proceed first with *chessed* and only afterward with *emes*.

That way, we are most likely to live our lives with both.

וַיֹּאמֶר מֹשֶׁה אָסֻרָה נָּא וְאֶרְאֶה
אֶת הַמַּרְאֶה הַגָּדֹל הַזֶּה מַדּוּעַ לֹא יִבְעַר הַסְּנֶה

*Moses thought, "I will turn aside now
and look at this great sight —
why will the bush not be burned?"* (3:3).

The question being asked here seems quite simple and obvious, something that would be unremarkable even if it were asked by a small child. It is even less remarkable when asked by a great wise man. Why does the Torah bother to tell us about it? What possible significance is there to our knowing that Moses asked why the bush was not being consumed by the fire?

Let the Torah skip this detail and immediately proceed to what seems most important — that God called out to him from the midst of the fire and spoke to him.

I believe that the Torah's inclusion of this question teaches us an important fundamental of our faith.

Allow me to explain.

We are all familiar with Rav Elchanan Wasserman's famous approach as to why it is that many otherwise brilliant thinkers fail to recognize what seems most obvious to anyone who takes a clear look around him and sees the wonders of our universe, namely that it is all the work of a Living God. Rav Elchanan tells us that it is because they are blinded, incapable of seeing certain things in a clear light.

Their blindness stems not from a bodily defect, but from a spiritual one — their ongoing attachment to desires for physical indulgence.

Their rejection of God, therefore, is based not on rational thought and careful, objective analysis, but instead is a result of their being slaves to their passions. These passions blind the thought process, compelling it to avoid coming to any conclusions that would threaten their chosen lifestyle.

The Torah therefore warns us not to be led astray by our heart's passions. Rather, we must become masters of our physical drives.

Only then can we hope to have an open mind and clearly see how God's hand is behind all of Creation. Were it not for the *yetzer hara's* pull on a man's thoughts, there would be no heresy, for denial of God is inherently irrational.

Were man to free himself of these bonds, belief would then come easily and naturally, without the prodigious effort and struggle that seem so commonplace for many.

Only a drunkard would imagine that life's purpose is nothing more than the pursuit of more and more liquor. Yet, that is precisely what he thinks, due to his enslavement to alcohol. Were he to be cured of his addiction, though, he would immediately realize how great was his error.

Similarly, true rational thought would lead one to recognize that his true purpose is to advance the goals of the One Who created him. Having acknowledged that Creation was purposeful and that God must therefore have certain expectations of man, it would follow logically that He must have made available to us a way of knowing what it is that He wants.

This would seem to be an extremely compelling argument for *Torah min HaShamayim*, that Torah is from Heaven.

All of us, from the most naive and unschooled to the most sophisticated and highly educated, are commanded to believe in God. It would therefore follow that the process of achieving faith would not be dependent upon highly complex arguments or exposure to a unique, extraordinary experience of the spirit.

Rather, it is accessible to all — but only to those who allow themselves to be receptive. And, that can occur only if someone truly wishes to know — and is willing to accept — certain simple truths.

And that is the lesson that is learned from the Torah's inclusion of the episode described in our verse.

Were it left to our own imagination, we might have thought that

Moses' "seeing" of Hashem must have been preceded by profound analysis, exhaustive questioning, and subtleties of nuance that are beyond the capabilities of mere mortals like ourselves. We might have thought that only a Man of G-d, like Moses, could possibly grasp these great truths.

Of course, Moses was the greatest prophet and, obviously, he did indeed attain levels of intellectual and spiritual insight that are beyond anything we could possibly imagine.

However, what we see here is that Hashem reveals Himself in the wake of Moses' having made a very simple observation and having posed a very unsophisticated question.

This was a question that any man could have asked. It followed an observation that any man could have made.

And that is precisely why it is here.

To show us that these truths are really quite simple.

If we would only open up our eyes and be receptive to what is right here before us.

A further thought, also brought to mind by the question asked by Moses:

The nations of the world often consider the continued existence of the Jewish people to be a thorn in their sides. Similarly, our situation might be considered analogous to that of a bush on fire.

Our enemies have repeatedly sought to annihilate us, to eradicate us from this world. Our brothers and sisters throughout history have literally been set afire, in the course of the Spanish Inquisition, during pogroms, and in concentration camps. Yet, the Jewish people have continued to flourish.

Meanwhile, great empires have come and gone. And we are still here.

Our continued existence and national resurgence in the Land of Israel represent an astounding, living miracle, testimony to the hand of God.

It is a miracle that even the nations could not fail to acknowledge.

Yet, sadly, we see that many of our own brethren have somehow failed to take notice. They seem to not be following the ways of the Living God and appear to be quite distant from Torah.

It is not that they have openly and willingly rejected the Torah. How could they? They don't even know what it is. Without benefit of a Jewish education, and positive exposure in the home and community to Jews who are living a pure, Torah lifestyle, how could they even know what it is that they are missing?

For that lack of knowledge, they can hardly be held accountable.

Still, though, we have to wonder. And to dream.

If only they would ask the question whose answer seems so obvious. A question that does not demand any great level of prior knowledge — and which could bring them to see certain simple truths:

How is it that the bush has not been consumed?

How is it that the Jewish people are still alive?

What could possibly account for this astounding phenomenon?

וַיְדַבֵּר אֱלֹהִים אֶל מֹשֶׁה וַיֹּאמֶר אֵלָיו אֲנִי ה'
**God spoke to Moses and said to him,
"I am Hashem" (6:2).**

רש"י : **וַיְדַבֵּר אֱלֹהִים אֶל מֹשֶׁה** – דִּבֵּר אִתּוֹ מִשְׁפָּט עַל שֶׁהִקְשָׁה לְדַבֵּר
וְלוֹמַר (ה:כב) "לָמָה הֲרֵעֹתָה לָעָם הַזֶּה".

RASHI: AND GOD SPOKE TO MOSES — *He spoke to
[Moses] with words of rebuke for speaking harshly and
saying, "Why have you harmed this people?"*

---

ashi's interpretation of this verse is that Hashem is rebuking Moses for the manner in which he had earlier spoken
to Him, "*My Lord, why have You harmed this people, why
have You sent me? From the time I came to Pha-
raoh to speak in Your Name he harmed this people, but You did not
rescue Your people*" (5:22, 23).

The verse containing Hashem's response to Moses starts with the Name אֱלֹהִים rather than the Name 'ה. The name אֱלֹהִים alludes to the fact that the words are words of reproof. But it is not clear exactly what it was that made Hashem angry.

My understanding of *Rashi* is that Hashem is rebuking Moses, leader of the Jewish people, rather than Moses, private citizen.

The leader and savior of his people represents Hashem. As long as he is acting in that role, Moses is forbidden to express thoughts that would seem to indicate a questioning of God's actions.

All the pain welling up in his heart over the suffering of his people would have to stay inside of Moses, the leader.

According to my suggested interpretation of this verse, let us take note of the phrase that immediately follows, וַיֹּאמֶר אֵלָיו אֲנִי ה', *He said to him, "I am Hashem."*

Rashi explains: With this declaration of His Name to Moses, God wishes to say, *"I am faithful to pay a good reward to those who walk before Me."*

The words *vayomer eilav* might be understood as God speaking to Moses in a more personal sense, as Moses the man who saw his brothers' sorrow and cried for their well-being. Thus, *Ani Hashem* is Hashem as Merciful Father.

It is as if He is telling Moses, "In your role as private individual, of course it is My desire that you feel mercifully toward the Jewish people. However, when filling your public role as leader of the Jews, you are acting in My stead and are permitted only to act within the parameters that I have given you."

You may neither diminish nor may you add. Your role is to be My agent. Nothing more and nothing less.

Thus, while I value your greatness as an individual, as long as you are acting as My representative, it is wholly inappropriate for you to publicly wonder as to My ways.

וַיְדַבֵּר ה' אֶל מֹשֶׁה וְאֶל אַהֲרֹן וַיְצַוֵּם אֶל בְּנֵי יִשְׂרָאֵל
וְאֶל פַּרְעֹה מֶלֶךְ מִצְרָיִם לְהוֹצִיא אֶת בְּנֵי יִשְׂרָאֵל מֵאֶרֶץ מִצְרָיִם

Hashem spoke to Moses and Aaron and
commanded them regarding the Children of Israel
and regarding Pharaoh, king of Egypt, to take the
Children of Israel out of the land of Egypt (6:13).

What is Hashem telling them here? According to the *Ohr HaChaim*, He is responding to Moses' concerns that neither Pharaoh nor the Jewish people will heed what he has to say. "Don't worry," says Hashem, "I have appointed you to be their ruler."

How has this addressed Moses' concern? Why would Moses simply telling this to them suddenly guarantee that they will accept his authority? Wouldn't there be a need for something more than mere words here? Perhaps, Moses would actually require a healthy dose of supernatural powers.

Also, since it was Hashem's goal that the Jewish people listen to Moses and Aaron, why didn't He command *the people themselves* to listen rather than commanding Moses to *tell* them to listen? Wouldn't His commanding them directly have been more effective?

It is like the story of the chassid who excitedly informed his Rebbe of the dream he had just dreamt — that he, the chassid, would now be the new Rebbe. "Well," said the Rebbe, "as long as you're the only one having the dream, it's not going to do you very much good. Had it been my chassidim who had been having that dream, rather than just yourself, you would be in a lot better position right now."

So, what is the explanation?

Perhaps, it is as follows: God is telling Moses: In order for the people to listen, it will be up to *you* to make yourself into a king. To the extent that you will be successful at this, to that degree will they listen.

And, how was this to occur?

Note the verses that immediately follow, beginning with: *These were the heads of their fathers' houses* ... These people (i.e., the Children of Israel) are descendants of the *Avos*; the heart and soul of the holy *Avos* dwells within them. They are royalty: kings, the sons of kings; believers, offspring of believers.

Look! See their lineage!

You, Moses, help them to recognize what they really are!

Help them to believe in themselves. And, once you have succeeded, once you have successfully helped them to recognize their own royal heritage, then you, too, will be a king.

That is, once you have helped the people to see who they are themselves, namely sons of kings, then they will be able to also accept you as their king.

And then they will be ready to listen.

בֹּא

וַיֹּאמֶר ה׳ אֶל מֹשֶׁה בֹּא אֶל פַּרְעֹה
כִּי אֲנִי הִכְבַּדְתִּי אֶת לִבּוֹ וְאֶת לֵב עֲבָדָיו

Hashem said to Moses, "Come to Pharaoh,
for I have made his heart and the heart
of his servants stubborn" (10:1).

Our verse has Hashem telling Moses to "Come to Pharaoh,"
but does not explain the purpose of this "coming." *Rashi*
says that it was in order to warn him. But, the warning does
not come until verse 10:3. We are left with the question as to why
our *pasuk* should be so enigmatic, its meaning becoming apparent
only several verses later.

It would seem that the verse would read more clearly if the words,
"and you should say to him (Pharaoh)," had been inserted right after
the phrase, "Come to Pharaoh." In that way, it would read, *Come to*
Pharaoh and say to him, *"I have made his heart and the heart of his*
servants stubborn so that I can put these signs of Mine in his midst;

and so that you may relate in the ears of your son and your son's son that I made a mockery of Egypt, and My signs that I placed among them — so you may know that I am Hashem."

Let me suggest a reason as to why the phrase, "and say to him," was omitted.

In every generation, the wicked son asks, "What is this *service* to you?" It is the service, the *avodah*, with which he has difficulty. He has no objection to the abstract ideals that make up our philosophy and outlook, but his discomfort begins when the talk ends and the obligations and details of day-to-day Divine service begin.

He can very well relate to the beauty and symbolism of the Seder: The *chametz* represents pride, the evil inclination, laziness, etc. The matzah is symbolic of the positive traits: alacrity, humility, simplicity, peace.

At his ideal Seder, he would eloquently speak of the lofty ideas hidden behind each of the rituals and the great ideals they embody. Yet, he would be prepared to simultaneously consume both *chametz* and matzah.

He would speak of God's mercy — and skip the unpleasant details of being obligated to roast, prepare, and offer the *korban pesach*. When he says, "What is this *avodah* to you," he is saying, "Why would an enlightened and refined person possibly want anything to do with something as primitive as this? Why not stick to discussions of ethical ideals?"

So, how does this relate to *Parashas Bo*?

Parashas Bo is where the Torah first delineates the 613 obligatory commandments. It begins with: *Come to Pharaoh* [and say to him], *"I have made his heart and the heart of his servants stubborn so that I can put these signs of Mine in his midst; and so that you may relate in the ears of your son and your son's son that I made a mockery of Egypt, and My signs that I placed among them — so you may know that I am Hashem."*

Read this way, the verses state that the multiple signs will be used so that *Pharaoh* will "*know that I am Hashem."*

Why?

Wouldn't one sign have been enough? If his goal was merely to impress upon Pharaoh the fact that He exists, and to compel him to liberate the Jewish people, it would certainly seem that the bringing of a single plague upon Egypt would have been more than sufficient.

Even that one sign would have proven to Pharaoh that Hashem watches over everything and that He is capable of accomplishing whatever He chooses.

So why were there ten plagues? And, why did He "harden" Pharaoh's heart to the idea of releasing the Jewish people?

The verse itself gives us the answer, "... *so that I can put these signs of Mine in his midst.*"

Apparently, a change of heart is something that Pharaoh could not be expected to achieve very easily. It would demand an ingrained, profound understanding of a totally new worldview.

One plague followed another. Miracle after miracle. All, so that Pharaoh would "know" that God is One.

External knowledge will go no further than provide an intellectual awareness, and is therefore inadequate in this case. Rather, what is needed is a process through which the ideas will become etched upon one's innermost self. Even the words of Moses, as told to Pharaoh by Aaron, would not suffice.

With the Jewish people, it is only the mitzvos, which are to be done constantly, that will achieve the goal of affecting the heart. For Pharaoh, the ten *makkos* were his *osos,* signs; they were his *tefillin.*

It was, therefore, with great foresight that the Torah omitted the words, "*and say to him,*" because, through this omission, we learn that mere words are simply not enough. Sometimes, when the task is to inculcate something within a person's very being, words are so inadequate that they are almost worthless.

Rather, what is needed are *osos,* signs — that are seen, felt, and experienced through a person's physical senses. Only then will it be possible for a person to internalize the true way, the way of Hashem.

And that is why, in order to remember *Yetzias Mitzrayim*, we do more than talk. Our goal is to transmit the message of there being one God Who rules over everything. Words will not suffice. We have matzah, *maror*, the *korban pesach*, *tefillin,* and sanctification of the firstborn. These mitzvos concretize the message that is spoken about in the words. And, given the spiritual level of the Jewish people, these mitzvos are appropriate for inculcating these ideas.

Pharaoh, however, needed much more than symbolic remembrances. He needed *makkos.*

Ten of them.

Hard ones.

Each one essential. This was the only way to impress upon someone like him that *Hashem Echad u'Shemo Echad.*

Mere words would not have been enough.

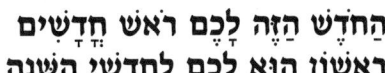

הַחֹדֶשׁ הַזֶּה לָכֶם רֹאשׁ חֳדָשִׁים רִאשׁוֹן הוּא לָכֶם לְחָדְשֵׁי הַשָּׁנָה

This month shall be for you the beginning of the months; it shall be for you the first of the months of the year (12:2).

The *sefer Derosh Av* quotes the following as a Midrash:

At the time that God said, "This month shall be for you …," the ministering angels questioned Him: "Why did You decree on Adam, כִּי בְּיוֹם אֲכָלְךָ מִמֶּנּוּ מוֹת תָּמוּת, 'On the day you eat of [the Tree of Knowledge], you will surely die?'" (Bereishis 2:17).

God responded that, in the future, a son will come from Yishai who will say: רִגְזוּ וְאַל תֶּחֱטָאוּ אִמְרוּ בִלְבַבְכֶם עַל מִשְׁכַּבְכֶם וְדֹמּוּ סֶלָה, *"Tremble and sin not; reflect in your hearts while on your beds and be utterly silent, selah"* (Tehillim 4:5).

Three things are mentioned here: *Parashas HaChodesh,* the death of Adam HaRishon, and a *pasuk* said by David, king of Israel. What connection do these have to one another?

Allow me to suggest an answer.

When Hashem wanted to liberate the Jews from Egypt the heavenly prosecutor protested, saying that there is no justice: The Jews are no better than the Egyptians; both worship idols. How could the Jews deserve redemption?

There was silence.

And then, God Himself responded: הַחֹדֶשׁ הַזֶּה לָכֶם, *This month shall be for you.*

Yes, it's true. The Jewish people have faltered and worshiped idols. But, they also have within them the spirit of renewal; they are capable of immediate change: with the greatest of alacrity, they can shake the dust of idol worship off themselves and remake themselves anew.

They worshiped sheep, just as the Egyptians did. But, witness their greatness: Moses will command them: מִשְׁכוּ וּקְחוּ לָכֶם צֹאן לְמִשְׁפְּחֹתֵיכֶם וְשַׁחֲטוּ הַפָּסַח, *Draw forth or buy for yourselves one of the flock for your families, and slaughter the pesach-offering (Shemos* 12:21). Pull yourselves away from idol worship; take the very same species that you had worshiped until now and offer it instead to the one true God.

And, how will they react? They will respond immediately and enthusiastically: They will offer the animal with the greatest of holiness and purity, as if they had never had anything to do with the idolatrous worship of this very same species. They will put that loathsome past behind them, as if it never were.

And so it was.

And through this merit, they would be redeemed from Egypt. They will be as if they had become a new creation. They will be as if the ones who had been worshiping idols had been someone other than themselves.

With all of the above in mind, let us proceed to answer our original question: What association is there between *Parashas HaChodesh,* the death of Adam HaRishon, and a *pasuk* said by David, king of Israel?

Given man's ability for self-renewal and disassociation from his past, of becoming a new creation, as if the past had never happened, the ministering angels could then ask why God had decreed that Adam HaRishon would die as a result of his sin. Why wouldn't he be given the opportunity to reject his past sin — and walk away clean?

"A son will be born from Yishai," answered Hashem, "who will provide the answer to this question."

And what is this answer? It is as we have learned in the Gemara (*Berachos* 5a):

אָמַר רַבִּי לֵוִי בַּר חָמָא אָמַר רַבִּי שִׁמְעוֹן בֶּן לָקִישׁ: לְעוֹלָם יַרְגִּיז
אָדָם יֵצֶר טוֹב עַל יֵצֶר הָרַע, שֶׁנֶּאֱמַר, "רִגְזוּ וְאַל תֶּחֱטָאוּ". אִם נִצְּחוֹ
– מוּטָב, וְאִם לָאו – יַעֲסוֹק בַּתּוֹרָה, שֶׁנֶּאֱמַר: "אִמְרוּ בִלְבַבְכֶם";
אִם נִצְּחוֹ – מוּטָב, וְאִם לָאו – יִקְרָא קְרִיאַת שְׁמַע, שֶׁנֶּאֱמַר: "עַל
מִשְׁכַּבְכֶם"; אִם נִצְּחוֹ – מוּטָב, וְאִם לָאו – יִזְכּוֹר לוֹ יוֹם הַמִּיתָה,
שֶׁנֶּאֱמַר: "וְדֹמּוּ סֶלָה".

R' Levi bar Chama said in the name of R' Shimon ben Lakish: A person should constantly agitate his good inclination to fight against his evil inclination, as it is stated, "Tremble (be agitated) and sin not." If he vanquishes it, fine. But, if not, he should engage in Torah study, as it is stated in that verse, "reflect in your hearts." If he vanquishes it, fine. But, if not, he should recite the Shema, as it is stated in that verse, "on your beds." If he vanquishes it, fine. But, if not, he should remind himself of the day of death, as it is stated at the end of that verse, "and be utterly silent, selah."

The remembrance of one's mortality, the image of one's own return to dust, is man's strongest weapon in overcoming his evil inclination. Nothing will come of his desires; they only lead to a time when he will be compelled to give a personal accounting.

Therefore, let him ponder the humiliation!

Thought of in this way, death becomes a positive. Thoughts of it looming in the future provide a most effective deterrent to sin. Man will be properly motivated to resist temptation. He will be less likely to transgress the will of his Creator. And, should he slip into momentary failure, anticipation of a time of final accounting will deter him from allowing the weakness to become entrenched. Fear of death will prevent the ephemeral transgression from becoming a permanent fixture of his personality.

That is certainly important. For, once the ephemeral becomes the permanent, repentance — personal renewal, like that of the moon — becomes a practical impossibility.

We will now see the significance of the final part of our puzzle, the juxtaposition of King David with the proceeding two elements: *Parashas HaChodesh* and Adam HaRishon at his time of death.

King David and Adam HaRishon were linked by a powerful bond: Adam had donated 70 years of life to this son of Yishai.

Perhaps he did so as an act of ultimate repentance in the face of death. Through the giving up of these 70 years in order to provide life for another human being, it was as if he were creating a *beriah chadashah*, a new creation. The catalyst that effected this noble deed was Adam's anticipation of death. Perhaps, had Hashem not warned him about the possibility of dying, he might not have made this decision.

This decision, then, amounted to an act of repentance, ultimately resulting in his personal renewal. The interdependencies have now become more apparent: *Parashas HaChodesh* (renewal), the death of Adam HaRishon (repentance as a recognition of one's mortality), and David (the "new creation").

וַיְהִי בְּשַׁלַּח פַּרְעֹה אֶת הָעָם וְלֹא נָחָם אֱלֹהִים
דֶּרֶךְ אֶרֶץ פְּלִשְׁתִּים כִּי קָרוֹב הוּא כִּי אָמַר אֱלֹהִים
פֶּן יִנָּחֵם הָעָם בִּרְאֹתָם מִלְחָמָה וְשָׁבוּ מִצְרָיְמָה

It happened when Pharaoh sent out the people
that God did not lead them by way of the land of
the Philistines, because it was near, for God said,
"Perhaps the people will reconsider when they see
a war, and they will return to Egypt" (13:17).

They were led through the Wilderness for many years so that they would become accustomed to trust in Him and believe that He sustains mankind, and to come to the realization that there is nothing that is beyond His ability.

This is what is meant by וְלֹא נָחָם אֱלֹהִים דֶּרֶךְ אֶרֶץ פְּלִשְׁתִּים, *God did not lead them derech eretz Pelishtim:* Hashem did not lead them by the way of *"derech eretz,"* meaning, He did not lead them in the way of the natural world. כִּי קָרוֹב הוּא, *ki karov hu,* because it was still too *close* to their having left Egypt.

Because they were still *close* to the time they had left Egypt, their faith in God had not yet penetrated their essence. They had not yet learned to rely upon Hashem, no matter what.

It therefore became essential that they be witness to great miracles, including the Splitting of the Sea. This event demonstrated to them that even when surrounded by hostile forces, even when the cold steel of the sword's blade is close to their necks, they have no reason to despair. Hashem would be there for them.

They would need a period of transition, forty years' worth of experience with Hashem under harsh circumstances, to help them develop this deep faith.

═══════

וַיַּרְא יִשְׂרָאֵל אֶת הַיָּד הַגְּדֹלָה אֲשֶׁר עָשָׂה ה' בְּמִצְרַיִם
וַיִּירְאוּ הָעָם אֶת ה' וַיַּאֲמִינוּ בַּה' וּבְמֹשֶׁה עַבְדּוֹ

Israel saw the great hand that Hashem had inflicted upon Egypt, and the people revered Hashem and they had faith in Hashem and in Moses His servant (14:31).

This verse immediately precedes the *Shiras HaYam*, and it comes to tell us what it was that inspired them to this great height of spiritual expression. It was the fact that they had now seen the *yad hagedolah*, the great hand. What is the significance of the word, *"yad"*? It alludes to the ability to see everything as a whole, as a complete picture, not as "fingers" but as a "hand." For the Jewish people, the past, the present, and the future now came into focus as a single, unified image.

Prior to this, in Egypt, what the Egyptians had seen was "merely" the *etzba* (the finger), but not the *yad*. What this means is that while they bore witness to many great miracles, they could appreciate them only for their immediate impact. They recognized the greatness of what was occurring at that moment, but were not able to take the broader view and see God's plan in its entirety.

Bnei Yisrael, however, could now perceive what the Egyptians could not.

The Jewish people declared, "*Zeh Keili v'anvayhu*, This is my God and I will build Him a Sanctuary" (regarding the present); *"Elokei avi v'aromemenhu*, the God of my father and I will exalt Him" (regarding the past); and *"Hashem yimloch l'olam va'ed*, Hashem shall reign for all eternity" (regarding the future). Everything was one, all due to Hashem's *yad hagedolah*, through the direct intervention of the Master of the World, all because of his *middah* of Goodness which he lavished upon them.

The *pasuk* continues, וַיִּירְאוּ הָעָם אֶת ה', meaning that they merited to achieve *yiras Shamayim*.

And then, וַיַּאֲמִינוּ בַּה', meaning that they merited to achieve faith and trust in Hashem: They leaped into the sea.

וַיִּשְׁמַע יִתְרוֹ ...
And Yisro heard ... (18:1).

*A*nd Yisro heard .... What did he hear? According to *Rashi*, he heard of the Splitting of the Sea and the war with Amalek. But, hadn't the entire world heard? Don't *Bnei Yisrael* say, in their song immediately after the Splitting of the Sea — *Peoples heard, they were agitated ... (15:14)*? Why, then, is it so remarkable that Yisro heard as well, so remarkable that we need an explicit verse to tell us so?

One answer I would suggest is that there is hearing and there is hearing. In other words, there are those whose "hearing" is primarily intellectual, unfiltered by emotion. And, there are others whose "hearing" is primarily emotional, not filtered by rational analysis. For the former, their failure to internalize what they "hear" often causes it to pass in one ear and out the other. The latter, while initially moved by what they have heard, fail to put it in proper perspective.

שָׁמְעוּ עַמִּים יִרְגָּזוּן, *Peoples heard and were agitated*, but that's about all. The great leaders shook and were frightened. Eventually, however, it was forgotten, no lasting impression having been made, no changes.

The lone individual to have truly taken the *shemuah* to heart was Yisro. This was because, only in his case, did it shake his heart, his mind, and his soul.

There is a Midrash that says that both Yisro and Amalek were advisers to Pharaoh in Egypt, the ancient civilization most renowned for its wisdom. As their leader, Pharaoh doubtless effused culture and wisdom and valued it in others, particularly in his trusted advisers. Yisro, perhaps, believed that culture and wisdom would be the basis for improving the world. Yet, he would soon witness how a ruler celebrated for these seemingly admirable qualities could act like a wild animal, vicious and unmerciful, ready to destroy an entire nation.

Yisro decided to flee. Rather than being a cure for the world's problems, it was now evident to him that man-generated wisdom would only increase human misery. He turned to the wisdom of what he took to be a higher power — that of idolatry. He was soon to realize that idolatry as well was rooted in human conception: The gods were understood to be jealous of one another, they fought with one another, and had to be appeased; they lacked mercy, they were vengeful.

Yisro investigated one type of idolatry after another. And then he met Moses! His son-in-law tutored him in the ways of Hashem, unique among gods, One Who truly benefited mankind, Who was merciful, patient, and just. Hashem gave man choice and offered reward to those who follow Him, and punishment to those who reject His ways. There was justice in the world; Hashem reciprocated in accordance with man's deeds.

Yisro heard all of this and was intrigued. But, where was the evidence? Didn't the political situation seem quite the opposite, with an evil ruler persecuting an innocent nation?

But then Yisro saw what Hashem had done, freeing His people from Pharaoh's domination and punishing the Egyptians in the most spectacular way — and, precisely measure for measure. Yisro decided to join the Jewish nation.

When can we say that someone has truly "heard"? When he is prepared to reexamine his previously held beliefs, alter the direction of his life, and accept the consequences of his new realization. This can occur only when one "hears" with every one of his faculties.

וַיִּשְׁמַע יִתְרוֹ — He heard with his intellect,

כֹּהֵן מִדְיָן — using the spiritual resources of his past,

חֹתֵן מֹשֶׁה — using the wisdom of Torah, taught to him by Moses.

Amalek and Bilaam heard as well, but did not change their ways. They heard something with their intellects that they were not prepared to incorporate into their deeds.

Just as Yisro learned to "listen," Amalek learned to resist. He would be remembered for turning his neck.

וְאֵלֶּה הַמִּשְׁפָּטִים אֲשֶׁר תָּשִׂים לִפְנֵיהֶם

And these are the judgments
that you shall place before them (21:1).

רַשִׁ"י. **וְאֵלֶּה הַמִּשְׁפָּטִים** – כָּל מָקוֹם שֶׁנֶּאֱמַר אֵלֶּה פָּסַל אֶת
הָרִאשׁוֹנִים, וְאֵלֶּה מוֹסִיף עַל הָרִאשׁוֹנִים, מָה הָרִאשׁוֹנִים מִסִּינַי,
אַף אֵלּוּ מִסִּינַי. וְלָמָּה נִסְמְכָה פָּרָשַׁת דִּינִין לְפָרָשַׁת מִזְבֵּחַ, לוֹמַר לְךָ
שֶׁתָּשִׂים סַנְהֶדְרִין אֵצֶל הַמִּקְדָּשׁ [הַמִּזְבֵּחַ].

RASHI: AND THESE ARE THE JUDGMENTS — ... *just
as those which have been stated previously (the Ten
Commandments) are from Sinai, so, too, are these from
Sinai. And why was the section that deals with judicial
cases juxtaposed with the passage that deals with the
Altar? To tell you that you should place the Sanhedrin
adjacent to the Beis HaMikdash.*

By way of clarification, let us quote *Tehillim* (147:19-20): מַגִּיד דְּבָרָיו לְיַעֲקֹב חֻקָּיו וּמִשְׁפָּטָיו לְיִשְׂרָאֵל. לֹא עָשָׂה כֵן לְכָל גּוֹי וּמִשְׁפָּטִים בַּל יְדָעוּם הַלְלוּ יָהּ, *He relates His Word to Jacob, His statutes and judgments to Israel. He did not do so for any other nation; such judgments — they know them not. Halleluyah!*

Service of God as we understand it is totally different from the way it is understood by the nations, even when they happen to be serving the same God that we serve, i.e., the *Borei Olam*. Their concept of worship limits itself to prayer, expressions of faith, demonstrations of subservience and subjugation. Their focus is on theology.

Our way, however, puts the focus on "Life." We call it *Toras Chaim*. Its reach extends to all areas of practical living, providing the guidelines for how each of us should relate to the other. When a man conducts his business affairs with honesty and integrity, is careful not to harm anyone else's person or property — and rightfully accepts responsibility for damages that he might have caused someone else — he is thereby performing an act of Divine worship, as if he had offered a sacrifice to God.

The Torah and its mitzvos were given to shape man. When man steals and robs, it is as if he denies the existence of God Himself.

The first of the Ten Commandments is *Anochi;* the last is *Lo Sachmod*. One is inseparable from the other.

This difference between ourselves and the nations is what is expressed in the verse:

מַגִּיד דְּבָרָיו לְיַעֲקֹב חֻקָּיו וּמִשְׁפָּטָיו לְיִשְׂרָאֵל. Hashem revealed Himself only to *Klal Yisrael,* who would then tell the nations of the seven mitzvos that obligate them. Regarding the *mishpatim,* however, בַּל יְדָעוּם, *they know them not.* Not at all.

This means that we don't share this wisdom with them.

It then turns out that their civil system, unlike ours, is to be based solely upon convention, expedience, and pragmatism. It is not Holy. And, it has no connection to the Holy.

Their intention in following their laws is only that they should be in sync with their various governmental bodies and legislative directives. They do not associate any of this with God, the King of the Universe.

For us, however, it is all one Torah, from the first of the Ten Commandments, *Anochi,* to the last, *Lo Sachmod,* which corresponds to the category of Torah laws that are know as *mishpatim.*

It now becomes much more apparent why *Chazal,* as quoted by *Rashi* above, pointed out that the Sanhedrin sits near the *Mikdash:* to demonstrate that the laws which govern conduct between man and his fellow are just as much a part of Divine worship as is the offering of sacrifices.

We now have a new perspective as to why a Jew is not allowed to have his legal dispute with another Jew heard by a secular court, even where, in theory, they are applying Jewish law. Similarly, we can better understand the issue of nonreliance upon witnesses who are not fully observant of Torah, even though they might be otherwise trustworthy.

When either the court or the witnesses do not view themselves as doing Hashem's work and participating in a holy endeavor, they are not truly involved in *mishpatim.* It is not just a matter of the outcome being different (perhaps it would not be), but that their allegiances and intentions are somewhere else.

This will help explain why one who goes to their courts for judgment is considered as if he had engaged in idol worship. In a sense, he is turning his back on the Torah, cheapening its value, and paying homage to this foreign approach.

Another word used for judges of the Sanhedrin is *"Elohim."* The reason now becomes apparent: When they judge correctly according to Torah Law, they are serving *Elokim,* crowning the world with His Torah.

Similarly, we see from the juxtaposition of the *pasuk* (*Devarim* 16:18): שֹׁפְטִים וְשֹׁטְרִים תִּתֶּן לְךָ בְּכָל שְׁעָרֶיךָ, *Judges and officers shall you ap-*

point in all your cities, with the one that follows several *pesukim* later
(v. 21): לֹא תִטַּע לְךָ אֲשֵׁרָה כָּל עֵץ אֵצֶל מִזְבַּח ה' אֱלֹהֶיךָ, *You shall not plant for*
yourselves an idolatrous tree — any tree — near the Altar of Hashem,
that "whoever appoints a judge who is not qualified, it is as if he had
planted an idolatrous tree in Israel" (*Avodah Zarah* 52a). By distorting
Torah judgment, the *dayan* has, in effect, desecrated the *avodah.*

━━━━━━

וַיִּשְׁכֹּן כְּבוֹד ה' עַל הַר סִינַי וַיְכַסֵּהוּ הֶעָנָן שֵׁשֶׁת יָמִים.
וַיִּקְרָא אֶל מֹשֶׁה בַּיּוֹם הַשְּׁבִיעִי מִתּוֹךְ הֶעָנָן.
וּמַרְאֵה כְּבוֹד ה' כְּאֵשׁ אֹכֶלֶת בְּרֹאשׁ הָהָר לְעֵינֵי
בְּנֵי יִשְׂרָאֵל. וַיָּבֹא מֹשֶׁה בְּתוֹךְ הֶעָנָן וַיַּעַל אֶל הָהָר
וַיְהִי מֹשֶׁה בָּהָר אַרְבָּעִים יוֹם וְאַרְבָּעִים לָיְלָה

The glory of Hashem rested upon Mount Sinai,
and the cloud covered it for a six-day period.
He called to Moses on the seventh day from the
midst of the cloud. The appearance of the glory
of Hashem was like a consuming fire on the
mountaintop before the eyes of the Children of
Israel. Moses arrived in the midst of the cloud and
ascended the mountain, and Moses was on the
mountain for forty days and forty nights (24:16-18).

רש"י: **וַיְכַסֵּהוּ הֶעָנָן** – רַבּוֹתֵינוּ חוֹלְקִין בַּדָּבָר. יֵשׁ מֵהֶם אוֹמְרִים אֵלּוּ
שִׁשָּׁה יָמִים שֶׁמֵּרֹאשׁ חֹדֶשׁ עַד עֲצֶרֶת יוֹם מַתַּן תּוֹרָה.
וַיִּקְרָא אֶל מֹשֶׁה בַּיּוֹם הַשְּׁבִיעִי – לוֹמַר עֲשֶׂרֶת הַדִּבְּרוֹת, וּמֹשֶׁה
וְכָל יִשְׂרָאֵל עוֹמְדִים, אֶלָּא שֶׁחָלַק הַכָּתוּב כָּבוֹד לְמֹשֶׁה, וְיֵשׁ אוֹמְרִים
וַיְכַסֵּהוּ הֶעָנָן לְמֹשֶׁה שִׁשָּׁה יָמִים לְאַחַר עֲשֶׂרֶת הַדִּבְּרוֹת, וְהֵם הָיוּ
בִּתְחִלַּת אַרְבָּעִים יוֹם שֶׁעָלָה מֹשֶׁה לְקַבֵּל הַלּוּחוֹת, וְלִמְּדָךָ, שֶׁכָּל הַנִּכְנָס
לְמַחֲנֵה שְׁכִינָה טָעוּן פְּרִישָׁה שִׁשָּׁה יָמִים:

RASHI: AND THE CLOUD COVERED IT — *Our Rabbis argue about the matter. There are those among them who say that these days of the covering by the cloud are the six days from the first of the month of Sivan until Shavuos, the day of the giving of the Torah.*

He called to Moses on the seventh day — to say the Ten Commandments. Actually, Moses and all of Israel were standing and heard the Ten Commandments, not Moses alone as the verse seems to imply; but Scripture accords honor to Moses by singling him out among all of Israel. And there are those who say that the cloud covered Moses for a six-day period after the giving of the Ten Commandments. The six days were at the beginning of the forty days that Moses ascended to receive the Tablets. This fact teaches that whoever enters the Camp of the Shechinah requires prior separation for six days.

*R*ashi comments that the Sages differ as to which "six days" are being referred to. Some say these were the first six days of Sivan, when Moses and the people were preparing to receive the Ten Commandments. According to this interpretation, God called to the entire nation, but only Moses is mentioned, as a tribute to his greatness.

The other view is that the six days in question are at the beginning of Moses' forty-day sojourn on Mount Sinai. This teaches that before someone can enter God's own precinct, as it were, he must seclude himself for six days.

Both interpretations emphasize that one cannot simply leap from *chol* to *kodesh*. Rather, it is essential that there be a period of transition as one approaches the moment of receiving the Torah or entering before the Divine Presence.

The reason is quite obvious: We wish to avoid the inevitable pitfall of peering at this new situation through the filter of familiar, recent experience. In doing so, we would wind up diminishing the power of this new moment, as we try to squeeze it into the realm with which we are most comfortable.

We must therefore separate from what we were before, take our time, step back, and then focus upon the steps toward the holy that we are about to take.

Rambam, in *Hilchos Yesodei HaTorah* 2:2, expresses this as follows:

וְהֵיאַךְ הִיא הַדֶּרֶךְ לְאַהֲבָתוֹ וְיִרְאָתוֹ? בְּשָׁעָה שֶׁיִּתְבּוֹנֵן הָאָדָם בְּמַעֲשָׂיו וּבְרוּאָיו הַנִּפְלָאִים הַגְּדוֹלִים וְיִרְאֶה מֵהֶן חָכְמָתוֹ שֶׁאֵין לָהּ עֵרֶךְ וְלֹא קֵץ מִיָּד הוּא אוֹהֵב וּמְשַׁבֵּחַ וּמְפָאֵר וּמִתְאַוֶּה תַּאֲוָה גְדוֹלָה לֵידַע הַשֵּׁם הַגָּדוֹל, כְּמוֹ שֶׁאָמַר דָּוִד: "צָמְאָה נַפְשִׁי לֵאלֹהִים לְאֵל חָי", וּכְשֶׁמְּחַשֵּׁב בַּדְּבָרִים הָאֵלּוּ עַצְמָן מִיָּד הוּא נִרְתָּע לַאֲחוֹרָיו וְיִפְחַד וְיוֹדֵעַ שֶׁהוּא בְּרִיָּה קְטַנָּה שְׁפָלָה אֲפֵלָה עוֹמֵד בְּדַעַת קַלָּה מְעוּטָה לִפְנֵי תְמִים דֵּעוֹת, כְּמוֹ שֶׁאָמַר דָּוִד "כִּי אֶרְאֶה שָׁמֶיךָ מַעֲשֵׂה אֶצְבְּעוֹתֶיךָ ... מָה אֱנוֹשׁ כִּי תִזְכְּרֶנּוּ".

What is the path toward loving and fearing Him? When one contemplates His deeds and wondrous and great creations — and sees from them His incomparable wisdom, which is endless and beyond measure, he will immediately love, praise, and yearn with the most powerful of yearnings to know His Great Name. This is reminiscent of what David said, צָמְאָה נַפְשִׁי לֵאלֹהִים לְאֵל חָי, *My soul thirsts for Elokim, the Living God (Tehillim 42:3).*

And, when meditating upon these matters, he will immediately draw backward with fear and awe — and realize what a tiny and insignificant creature he is, who, despite his feeble understanding, is standing before the the One with complete wisdom. As was said by David, "When I behold Your heavens, the work of Your fingers, the moon and the stars that You have set in place, [I think], 'What is frail man that You should remember him?'"

This idea can be further developed by looking at the following Gemara, which appears in *Shabbos* 14a:

הָאוֹחֵז סֵפֶר תּוֹרָה עָרוֹם, נִקְבָּר עָרוֹם. עָרוֹם סַלְקָא דַּעְתָּךְ? אֶלָּא אָמַר רַבִּי זֵירָא: עָרוֹם בְּלֹא מִצְוֹת. בְּלֹא מִצְוֹת סַלְקָא דַּעְתָּךְ? אֶלָּא אֵימָא: עָרוֹם בְּלֹא אוֹתָהּ מִצְוָה.

... One who holds a Sefer Torah while naked — will be buried naked. Literally naked, you mean to say? Rather, R' Zeira said, "Naked without mitzvos." Literally without mitzvos? Rather, say, "Naked without this particular mitzvah."

The Gemara seems to be saying that treating a mitzvah with proper honor is absolutely essential; in its absence the mitzvah simply has not occurred.

We can now look back again at the idea of the six days of separation. Perhaps it was in order to allow Moses to properly honor the mitzvah of Talmud Torah and prepare for his encounter with Hashem.

כְּכֹל אֲשֶׁר אֲנִי מַרְאֶה אוֹתְךָ אֵת תַּבְנִית הַמִּשְׁכָּן
וְאֵת תַּבְנִית כָּל כֵּלָיו וְכֵן תַּעֲשׂוּ.
וְעָשׂוּ אֲרוֹן עֲצֵי שִׁטִּים

*Like everything that I show you, the form
of the Tabernacle and the form of all its vessels,
and so shall you do. They shall make
an Ark of acacia wood (25:9).*

"וְעָשׂוּ אֲרוֹן עֲצֵי שִׁטִּים", מַה כְּתִיב לְמַעְלָה "וְיִקְחוּ לִי תְּרוּמָה"
מִיָּד "וְעָשׂוּ אֲרוֹן עֲצֵי שִׁטִּים", מָה הַתּוֹרָה קָדְמָה לַכֹּל, כַּךְ בְּמַעֲשֵׂה
הַמִּשְׁכָּן הִקְדִּים אֶת הָאָרוֹן לְכָל הַכֵּלִים, מָה הָאוֹר קָדַם לְכָל מַעֲשֵׂה
בְרֵאשִׁית דִּכְתִיב (בְּרֵאשִׁית א:ג) "וַיֹּאמֶר אֱלֹהִים יְהִי אוֹר" וְאַף
בַּמִּשְׁכָּן בַּתּוֹרָה שֶׁנִּקְרֵאת אוֹר דִּכְתִיב "כִּי נֵר מִצְוָה וְתוֹרָה אוֹר",
קָדְמוּ מַעֲשִׂיָה לְכָל הַכֵּלִים.

THEY SHALL MAKE AN ARK OF ACACIA WOOD
— What is the significance of the phrase, וְיִקְחוּ לִי תְּרוּמָה

appearing first, followed by the phrase, וְעָשׂוּ אֲרוֹן עֲצֵי שִׁטִּים? Just as the Torah came before everything else, so too with the building of the Mishkan, the command of building the Aron preceded that of all the other vessels. Just as the creation of light preceded the rest of Creation, as the pasuk says (Bereishis 1:3), "... and Elokim said, 'Let there be Light,'" so too with the Mishkan. The Torah is referred to as "light," as it says, "A mitzvah is a candle and the Torah is light." Therefore the making of the Aron preceded that of all the other vessels (Shemos Rabbah 34).

This Midrash points out the primacy of *limud haTorah* and stresses that it must precede everything else. It was certainly laudatory that the first Jews who came to the States invested in building beautiful houses of worship. However, it would seem to me that they should rather have placed a higher priority on building yeshivos, as *limud haTorah* should be the community foundation. One must certainly wonder as to how many souls were lost to our people due to this mistaken priority.

The *Cherubim*, with their childlike appearance, also remind us that we must place the educational needs of our young people at the very forefront, ahead of all else.

וְהָיוּ הַכְּרֻבִים פֹּרְשֵׂי כְנָפַיִם לְמַעְלָה סֹכְכִים בְּכַנְפֵיהֶם
עַל הַכַּפֹּרֶת וּפְנֵיהֶם אִישׁ אֶל אָחִיו אֶל הַכַּפֹּרֶת יִהְיוּ פְּנֵי הַכְּרֻבִים

***The Cherubim shall be with wings spread
upward, sheltering the cover with their wings
with their faces toward one another; toward the
cover shall be the faces of the Cherubim (25:20).***

Ben Zoma says: Which is the *pasuk* that best exemplifies
the essence of the entire Torah? שְׁמַע יִשְׂרָאֵל (*Deuteronomy*
6:4). Ben Namas says: ...וְאָהַבְתָּ לְרֵעֲךָ כָּמוֹךָ, *And you shall
love your fellow as yourself* (*Vayikra* 19:18). Shimon ben Pazzi says:
אֶת הַכֶּבֶשׂ הָאֶחָד תַּעֲשֶׂה בַבֹּקֶר וְאֵת הַכֶּבֶשׂ הַשֵּׁנִי תַּעֲשֶׂה בֵּין הָעַרְבָּיִם, *One sheep
you shall prepare in the morning and the second sheep you shall pre-
pare at twilight* (*Shemos* 29:39).

One of the Rabbis declared that the law is like Shimon ben Pazzi,
based upon the verse which says: כְּכֹל אֲשֶׁר אֲנִי מַרְאֶה אוֹתְךָ אֵת תַּבְנִית
הַמִּשְׁכָּן וְאֵת תַּבְנִית כָּל כֵּלָיו וְכֵן תַּעֲשׂוּ, *Like everything that I show you, the
form of the Tabernacle and the form of all its vessels, and so you shall
do* (25:9).

How is it that this verse was decisive in proving that the halachah
is in accordance with Shimon ben Pazzi, who said that the verse that
best encapsulates the essence of Torah is, *One sheep you shall prepare
in the morning and the second sheep you shall prepare at twilight*?

Let us try to understand something about the intentions behind
each of the opinions expressed in this dispute. It would appear that
Ben Zoma would say that the primary service of God is "Fear of
Heaven" and "Acceptance of the Heavenly Yoke." Only upon attain-
ing "Fear of God" can one begin to acquire the other parts of Torah.
Ben Namas, on the other hand, would say that the primary theme of
Torah is love between man and his fellow.

Shimon ben Pazzi holds that both of the above aspects are essential, and that achieving "Fear of Heaven" is a necessary prerequisite

to acquiring the trait of "love between man and his fellow."

We can now understand what he meant by quoting the verse about preparing one sheep in the morning and another in the evening. If you notice, you will see that even though the verse refers to a *second* sheep, the one that is previous to it is not called *first*, but *one*. The distinction between the words "one" and "first" is highly significant. The word *one*, of course, suggests an allusion to the "*One*" of the world, Hashem. Affirmation of His being "*One*" is expressed through *Shema Yisrael*, the *Krias Shema*.

"Faith and Fear of Heaven" are best developed during one's youth and into his young adulthood, at a stage of life when achieving the level of וְאָהַבְתָּ לְרֵעֲךָ כָּמוֹךָ will be relatively difficult.

Youth and young adulthood are the stage of life when one is most involved in pursuit of his ambitions, both personal and professional. Generally, one becomes so preoccupied with the "self" that it is very difficult for him to focus also on the needs of others. He is able, however, to strive to develop an increased sense of "Fear of Heaven."

When he reaches middle age, however, his ambition has somewhat subsided, and he can better focus on bringing the "second sacrifice" — developing his sense of love between himself and his fellow. The *yiras Shamayim* that he worked on beforehand will serve as a catalyst to move him in this direction.

Of all the attributes a Jew must work at developing, that of וְאָהַבְתָּ לְרֵעֲךָ כָּמוֹךָ is the most difficult to attain. In a sense, it is the culmination of all the other traits toward which one must work.

It is therefore similar to the *korban tamid*, which culminates the day's sacrificial order, offered *bein ha'arbayim*, at twilight.

The *mashal* continues as we reexamine the *pasuk* that is quoted: אֵת תַּבְנִית הַמִּשְׁכָּן וְאֵת תַּבְנִית כָּל כֵּלָיו וְכֵן תַּעֲשׂוּ, *the form of the Tabernacle and the form of all its vessels, and so shall you do.* Among the commandments referred to is that of shaping the childlike *cherubin*, hinting at the responsibility we have toward shaping the next generation.

The Torah says that their wings should spread *upward*, and their faces should be toward one another. This suggests the idea of one man looking toward his brother — in other words, וְאָהַבְתָּ לְרֵעֲךָ.

The connection to the *pasuk* now becomes more obvious.

Purity of faith and *kabbalas ol Malchus Shamayim* are the first traits to cultivate. Then, as one matures, imbued with these traits, he is prepared to look directly at his fellow Jew, straight at his *face*, and love him and truly care about him, without any hint of dissension or discord.

It is now apparent why the halachah is like Shimon ben Pazzi.

עָשִׂיתָ מְנֹרַת זָהָב טָהוֹר מִקְשָׁה תֵּיעָשֶׂה הַמְּנוֹרָה
יְרֵכָהּ וְקָנָהּ גְּבִיעֶיהָ כַּפְתֹּרֶיהָ וּפְרָחֶיהָ מִמֶּנָּה יִהְיוּ

You shall make a Menorah of pure gold, hammered out shall the Menorah be made, its base, its shaft, its cups, its knobs, and its blossoms shall be [hammered] from it (25:31).

רש"י: תֵּיעָשֶׂה הַמְּנוֹרָה – מֵאֵלֶיהָ, לְפִי שֶׁהָיָה מֹשֶׁה מִתְקַשֶּׁה בָּהּ, אָמַר לוֹ הקב"ה הַשְׁלֵךְ אֶת הַכִּכָּר לָאוּר וְהִיא נַעֲשֵׂית מֵאֵלֶיהָ, לְכַךְ לֹא נִכְתַּב תַּעֲשֶׂה.

RASHI: SHALL THE MENORAH BE MADE — *On its own. Because Moses was perplexed by the way in which it was supposed to be made, the Holy One, Blessed is He, said to him, "Throw the block of gold into the fire, and it will be made by itself." This is why "You shall make" is not written.*

ashi, quoting a Midrash, tells us that Moses had such difficulty understanding how the Menorah should be made, that Hashem performed a miracle and the Menorah was fashioned by itself. What was it about the making of this particular vessel that presented Moses with so great a challenge?

The Menorah, with its seven branches emanating from a single stem and formed in its entirety from a single block of gold, is symbolic of the wisdom of Torah as well as the seven wisdoms of the world, all of which emanate from a single source. The Menorah alluded to the fact that there is no distinction between the wisdom of Torah and that of science (nature). Everything emerges from Torah, for the sake of Torah.

And that was Moses' problem: How can a mortal man, who is physical and material, possibly grasp such a profound level of unity and wholeness, and fashion this Menorah, which is illuminated by the pure light of Torah?

God told him, according to *Rashi, Throw the block of gold into the fire, and it will be made by itself.*

And how would this response resolve Moses' concerns?

The Torah is compared to fire: 'הֲלוֹא כֹה דְּבָרִי כָּאֵשׁ נְאֻם ה, *Behold, My word is like fire, the word of Hashem* (*Yirmiyahu* 23:29). Fire destroys physical substances, while also incorporating them into its flame. The more physical material that is added to the fire, the larger it becomes.

This can be seen as a metaphor for man's relationship with Torah, for it, too, is like a flame that engulfs the individual, purifies him, and makes him, in a sense, a candle to Hashem. In the process he grows, just as a fire grows when it is fed with fuel.

וְאֵלֶּה הַבְּגָדִים אֲשֶׁר יַעֲשׂוּ חֹשֶׁן וְאֵפוֹד וּמְעִיל
וּכְתֹנֶת תַּשְׁבֵּץ מִצְנֶפֶת וְאַבְנֵט

These are the garments that they shall make:
a Breastplate, and an Ephod, and a Robe,
and a Tunic of checkered texture, a Turban
and a Sash (28:4).

Am Yisrael's inherent mercy is unique; spilling of blood in their midst is practically unheard of. While this is certainly a good thing, occasionally, however, it can occasionally lead to a misplaced sense of mercy. Potentially, this could cause them to "cover" for a murderer rather than punish him. This is alluded to in *Devarim* 13:9,10: לֹא תֹאבֶה לוֹ וְלֹא תִשְׁמַע אֵלָיו וְלֹא תָחוֹס עֵינְךָ עָלָיו וְלֹא תַחְמֹל וְלֹא תְכַסֶּה עָלָיו. כִּי הָרֹג תַּהַרְגֶנּוּ יָדְךָ תִּהְיֶה בּוֹ בָרִאשׁוֹנָה לַהֲמִיתוֹ וְיַד כָּל הָעָם בָּאַחֲ־ רֹנָה. *Do not be favorably inclined toward him, and do not listen to him; and do not view him compassionately, and do not take pity and do not cover for him. For you must surely execute him. Let your hand strike* *him first to execute him, and the hand of the entire people afterward.*

The Gemara (*Arachin* 16a) teaches that just as offerings atone, so do the priestly vestments. Each garment, along with its appropriate teaching, is discussed by this Gemara:

כְּתֹנֶת מְכַפֶּרֶת עַל שְׁפִיכוּת דָּמִים דִּכְתִיב "וַיִּשְׁחֲטוּ שְׂעִיר עִזִּים וַיִּטְבְּלוּ אֶת הַכֻּתֹּנֶת בַּדָּם" (בְּרֵאשִׁית לז:לא), *The Kutoness atones for the spilling of blood, as the verse says* (regarding Yosef): *"And they slaughtered a goat, and dipped the coat in the blood."*

In order to conceal the truth of what they had done, Yosef's brothers took his *kutoness* (tunic) and dipped it in the blood of a goat they had slaughtered. The Gemara links this episode with the function of the *Kutoness* worn by the Kohen in the *Beis HaMikdash*:

The Kohanim are expected to "uncover" the *nega* found in the *machaneh* and לְהוֹצִיא (to banish, to cause to be revealed) the one who spills blood from the midst of *Machaneh Yisrael*.

מִכְנָסַיִם מְכַפְּרִים עַל גִּלּוּי עֲרָיוֹת, דִּכְתִיב "וַעֲשֵׂה לָהֶם מִכְנְסֵי בָד לְכַסּוֹת בְּשַׂר עֶרְוָה" (שמות כח:מב), *The trousers atone for immorality, as it is written: "You shall make for them linen trousers to cover the flesh of nakedness"* (28:42).

Wild abandon, foolishness, and lightheartedness draw a person toward עֶרְוָה. Modesty, however, acts as a shield.

מִצְנֶפֶת מְכַפֶּרֶת עַל גַּסֵּי הָרוּחַ, כִּדְרַבִּי חֲנִינָא, דְּאָ"ר חֲנִינָא: יָבֹא דָּבָר שֶׁבְּגוֹבַהּ וִיכַפֵּר עַל מַעֲשֵׂה גוֹבַהּ, *The turban (Mitznefes) atones for those who are arrogant. The source for this is as R' Chanina has said: Let something that is worn high on the head come and atone for acts of haughtiness.*

Often, people are led to error, sometimes even to sin, when their approach to the spiritual is improper. Perhaps their approach to matters of Torah is coarse, vulgar, and lacking sensitivity to the reality that they are dealing with that which is lofty and mighty. That which is holy calls for subtlety, not the crass immediacy of day-to-day involvement with the physical.

Think for a moment. Note that the blessing for *Kedushah* (אַתָּה קָדוֹשׁ) precedes the one for *daas* (אַתָּה חוֹנֵן לְאָדָם דַּעַת). This latter blessing precedes the one for Torah and *teshuvah* (–הֲשִׁיבֵנוּ אָבִינוּ לְתוֹרָתָךְ, וְקָר בָּנוּ מַלְכֵּנוּ לַעֲבוֹדָתָךְ, וְהַחֲזִירֵנוּ בִּתְשׁוּבָה שְׁלֵמָה לְפָנֶיךָ). Similarly the blessing of יוֹצֵר אוֹר, which includes *Kedushah* (קָדוֹשׁ, קָדוֹשׁ, קָדוֹשׁ), precedes the blessing of אַהֲבָה רַבָּה, which is the one for Torah.

One could say that even the way the Kohen steps toward the Altar to do his *avodah* is an integral aspect of the *avodah*, meaning that even the walking must be done with an appropriate state of mind and with awe. As Shlomo HaMelech writes in *Koheles* (4:17, 5:1): שְׁמֹר רַגְלְךָ כַּאֲשֶׁר תֵּלֵךְ אֶל בֵּית הָאֱלֹהִים וְקָרוֹב לִשְׁמֹעַ מִתֵּת הַכְּסִילִים זָבַח כִּי אֵינָם יוֹדְעִים לַעֲשׂוֹת רָע. אַל תְּבַהֵל עַל פִּיךָ וְלִבְּךָ אַל יְמַהֵר לְהוֹצִיא דָבָר לִפְנֵי הָאֱלֹהִים כִּי הָאֱלֹהִים בַּשָּׁמַיִם וְאַתָּה עַל הָאָרֶץ עַל כֵּן יִהְיוּ דְבָרֶיךָ מְעַטִּים, *Guard your foot when you go to the House of God; better to draw near and hearken than to offer the sacrifices of fools, for they do not consider that they do evil. Be not rash with your mouth, and let not your heart be hasty to utter a word before God; for God is in heaven and you are on earth, so let your words be few.*

When the verse says, *better to draw near and hearken than to offer the sacrifices of fools*, one meaning is that your coming to the *Mikdash* should be in order to listen, to learn — rather than to give (i.e., לִשְׁמֹעַ, and not לָתֵת).

One might say that the turban (*Mitznefes*) comes to cover the head, to subordinate it, so that the Kohen's mind and spirit do not "burst forth" inappropriately.

אַבְנֵט מְכַפֵּר עַל הִרְהוּר הַלֵּב, *The belt atones for improper thoughts of the heart.*

Hirhur is associated with the heart, and this makes full sense. The heart supplies the body with blood. It is a pump, pushing the life force through the arteries to each and every limb.

What is it that motivates man, "pushing" him to action? His thoughts and impulses.

It starts with an idea that must then be implemented. This requires strength and persistence. One must steel himself, or using an idiom of *lashon hakodesh*, לַחֲגוֹר עַצְמוֹ בְּאַבְנֵט, *to gird oneself with a belt*. Similarly, we say in the *berachah* אוֹזֵר יִשְׂרָאֵל בִּגְבוּרָה, *Who girds Israel with strength*.

The *Avneit* symbolizes the strength and effort required in order to allow one's ideas, one's musings, one's *hirhurim hatovim*, good thoughts, to materialize. Wrapped around one's midsection, it serves not only as a physical separation, but as a symbolic reminder to separate ourselves from improper thoughts. It is worn so that the heart does not see one's *ervah*.

חוֹשֶׁן מְכַפֵּר עַל הַדִּינִין, דִּכְתִיב "וְעָשִׂיתָ חֹשֶׁן מִשְׁפָּט ..." , *The Choshen atones for miscarriages of justice, as it is written: "You shall make a Choshen of judgment"* (28:15).

Rashi states that the *Choshen* atones for קִלְקוּל הַדִּין, *miscarriage of justice*.

Some commentators associate the word חֹשֶׁן with the words נַחֵשׁ and חוֹצֵן, this latter term referring to its functioning as a shield or protection against קִלְקוּל הַדִּין.

Let us try to understand what this means.

What are some of the factors that might lead to קִלְקוּל הַדִּין, *judicial miscarriage*? For one, the deliberations might have been marked by a lack of precision and thoroughness — both with regard to the facts of the case and the relevant law. How could this have happened? Perhaps the power of נַחֵשׁ within the judges has blinded them or caused them to be irresponsible or lazy. Maybe they failed to take the time, use the mental energy, and display the type of caution required of anyone who genuinely wishes to get to the truth of a matter. In other words, they had been seduced by the נָחָשׁ within.

How thorough must one be when acting as a judge? One must be so familiar with both the relevant facts and the case law that they are ingrained within him, as a result of his having gone over them again and again. In *lashon hakodesh*, this is known as שִׁינוּן, reminiscent of the verse in *Devarim* 6:7: וְשִׁנַּנְתָּם לְבָנֶיךָ, *and you shall teach them thoroughly to your children*. *Rashi* comments there:

וְשִׁנַּנְתָּם – לְשׁוֹן חִדּוּד הוּא, שֶׁיִּהְיוּ מְחוּדָּדִים בְּפִיךָ, שֶׁאִם יִשְׁאָלְךָ אָדָם דָּבָר לֹא תְהֵא צָרִיךְ לְגַמְגֵּם בּוֹ, אֶלָּא אֱמוֹר לוֹ מִיָּד:

V'SHINANTAM — *This word expresses sharpness. It implies that [the words of the Torah] should be "sharp" in your mouth, so that if someone asks you a matter of Torah, you will be capable of responding clearly, without hesitation.*

We see as well that the process of *talmud Torah* is also referred to by the word וּשְׁמַרְתֶּם. The *Sifra* to *Parashas Emor* comments: וַעֲשִׂיתֶם זוֹ הַמַּעֲשֶׂה, *"and you shall do,"* this refers to deeds. וּשְׁמַרְתֶּם זוֹ מִשְׁנָה, *"and you shall guard,"* this refers to learning. Also, similar language is used in *Devarim* 4:9 to warn us against forgetting the Giving of the Torah: רַק הִשָּׁמֶר לְךָ וּשְׁמֹר נַפְשְׁךָ מְאֹד פֶּן תִּשְׁכַּח אֶת הַדְּבָרִים אֲשֶׁר רָאוּ עֵינֶיךָ ..., *Only beware for yourself and greatly beware for your soul, lest you forget the things that your eyes have beheld.*

This, then, is one of the ways to understand חֹשֶׁן— it means חוֹצֵן, a *protection*, a שְׁמִירָה, to guard against the forgetting of one's Torah.

In order that there not be קִלְקוּל הַדִּין, *miscarriage of justice*.

אֵפוֹד מְכַפֵּר עַל עֲבוֹדָה זָרָה, דִּכְתִיב "וְאֵין אֵפוֹד וּתְרָפִים", *The Ephod atones for idolatry, as it is written:... "And neither Ephod nor teraphim" (Hoshea 3:4).*

Why would one reject the "Living God" in favor of idolatry? One factor could be that the person is enmeshed in physicality and materialism to the extent that he can no longer envision himself as even a moderately spiritual being. That which is totally spiritual is beyond his "grasp." He cannot relate to a God Who, "sees but cannot be seen." He must therefore either fashion for himself a god that can be seen or worship heavenly bodies.

Another reason for choosing idolatry could be that he no longer wishes to share the burden of being part of the Jewish people. This is reminiscent of the Midrash that says that Esau renounced his portion in Eretz Yisrael in order to avoid being part of *Klal Yisrael's* subjugation in Egypt. Even today there are those who share that mentality, choosing the path of assimilation, attempting to thereby distance themselves from their people's travails.

כי תשא

... אַךְ אֶת שַׁבְּתֹתַי תִּשְׁמֹרוּ כִּי אוֹת הִוא
בֵּינִי וּבֵינֵיכֶם לְדֹרֹתֵיכֶם לָדַעַת כִּי אֲנִי ה' מְקַדִּשְׁכֶם

Just observe my Shabbasos, for it is a sign
between Me and you for your generations, to know
that I am Hashem Who sanctifies you (31:13).

רש״י: **אַךְ אֶת שַׁבְּתֹתַי תִּשְׁמֹרוּ** – אַף עַל פִּי שֶׁתִּהְיוּ רְדוּפִין וּזְרִיזִין
בִּזְרִיזוּת מְלָאכָה שַׁבָּת אַל תִּדָּחֶה מִפָּנֶיהָ. כָּל אַכִין וְרַקִּין מִעוּטִין,
לְמַעֵט שַׁבָּת מִמְּלֶאכֶת הַמִּשְׁכָּן.

RASHI: JUST OBSERVE MY SHABBASOS — *Although*
you will be eager and enthusiastic in the enthusiasm of
the work, let not Shabbos be pushed aside before it. All
appearances of the words אַךְ *and* רַק *in the Torah are*
exclusions. In this case, אַךְ *serves to exclude Shabbos from*
the work of the Mishkan.

---

he verse refers to שַׁבְּתֹתַי, *Shabbasos*, in the plural, as if to allude that there are many forms of "Shabbos," various things from which one should refrain, ultimately leading to the building of various kinds of *Mishkans*. There is a "Shabbos from saying that which is unseemly"; by dong so one is *mekadesh* his mouth. There is a "Shabbos from eating that which he should not"; by doing so one is sanctifying his throat. When he does not allow his mind to entertain improper thoughts, he is thereby sanctifying his head.

The verse says that one should keep His *Shabbasos* כִּי אֲנִי ה' מְקַדִּשְׁכֶם, *because I am Hashem Who sanctifies you*. Shabbos represents holiness, separation from materialism and worldly matters. It is a force that separates us from all that contaminates. In that sense, there are many *Shabbasos*.

The day of Shabbos has, however, a special status, for it is the period during which Hashem rested from His *melachah*.

תָּנֵי ר"ש בֶּן יוֹחַאי אָמְרָה שַׁבָּת לִפְנֵי הקב"ה רבש"ע לְכוּלָּן יֵשׁ בֶּן זוּג, וְלִי אֵין בֶּן זוּג, א"ל הקב"ה כְּנֶסֶת יִשְׂרָאֵל הִיא בֶּן זוּגֵךְ, וְכֵיוָן שֶׁעָמְדוּ יִשְׂרָאֵל לִפְנֵי הַר סִינַי אָמַר לָהֶם הקב"ה זִכְרוּ הַדָּבָר שֶׁאָמַרְתִּי לַשַּׁבָּת כְּנֶסֶת יִשְׂרָאֵל הִיא בֶּן זוּגֵךְ הַיְינוּ דִּבּוּר (שְׁמוֹת כ) "זָכוֹר אֶת יוֹם הַשַּׁבָּת לְקַדְּשׁוֹ".

Rabbi Shimon bar Yochai taught: The Shabbos came before HaKadosh Baruch Hu and said, "Master of the Universe: Everyone has a partner, but I do not." HaKadosh Baruch Hu said, "Knesses Yisrael is your partner." When Yisrael stood before Mount Sinai, HaKadosh Baruch Hu said to them, "Remember the Shabbos to keep it holy" (Bereishis Rabbah, Vilna ed., parashah II).

Each day had a partner, but Shabbos did not. Each day, defined by its *melachah*, had its complement, meaning another day of creative worldly activity to help actualize its potential. Shabbos, however, was bereft.

Its potential could not be actualized through a weekday. Only the *Bnei Yisrael* could achieve that for Shabbos. And that is why we were commanded (31:16): וְשָׁמְרוּ בְנֵי יִשְׂרָאֵל אֶת הַשַּׁבָּת לַעֲשׂוֹת אֶת הַשַּׁבָּת לְדֹרֹתָם בְּרִית עוֹלָם, *The Children of Israel shall observe the Sabbath, to make the Sabbath an eternal covenant for their generations.*

וַיֹּאמֶר מֹשֶׁה אֶל בְּנֵי יִשְׂרָאֵל רְאוּ קָרָא ה'
בְּשֵׁם בְּצַלְאֵל בֶּן אוּרִי בֶּן חוּר לְמַטֵּה יְהוּדָה.

Moses said to the Children of Israel, "See,
Hashem has proclaimed by name, Betzalel
son of Uri son of Hur, of the tribe of Judah" (35:30).

O
n this verse, *Midrash Tanchuma* makes several points. One may not don a garment of *kilayim* (a mixture of wool and linen) even if ninety-nine garments interpose between his flesh and the forbidden garment.

The Midrash states further that when a person performs a good deed, he creates a protecting angel and he merits the privilege of performing more good deeds.

How are all these elements connected to the choice of Betzalel?

Whenever a person performs a good deed, he acquires a "good name" for himself — and that good reputation is very precious. This is indicated by the choice of Betzalel to build the Tabernacle and comprehend the profound mystical secrets that were needed for this awesome spiritual accomplishment. Our verse states that Hashem proclaimed Betzalel *by name,* implying that his name, i.e., his good reputation, was an essential factor in his choice.

The Midrash is teaching us that because of his "good name" he was able to construct a "dwelling place" for Hashem. Even though he had *zechus avos,* in that he was the son of Hur, who was killed when trying to stop the nation from building the *eigel,* it was ultimately through his own name that Betzalel merited building the *Mishkan.*

How does a person develop "a good name," asks the Tanna? Initially, it is by being one who distances himself from evil, that is, he guards himself from committing transgressions. Afterward, he will merit to do good.

What is the great evil from which a man must keep his distance? It is the evil that hides within the gray area of what is technically permissible, due to the Torah's never having specifically said that such a thing is forbidden — despite its being the antithesis of what the Torah wants of a Jew. He is warned not to become a נָבָל בִּרְשׁוּת הַתּוֹרָה, one who is despicable, with the Torah's "permission," so to speak.

And that is the meaning of the Midrash's comparison to *kilayim.* What is *kilayim*? It is a mixture of two things that are each independently permitted. Despite that, when combined, they result in something that carries a very serious transgression. How much should a person distance himself from this combination of "permitted" things, says the Midrash? Not even the ninety-nine layers of non-*kilayim* garments that lie between oneself and the *kilayim* sitting upon his back would protect him from the spiritual damage, says the Midrash. What this means, in a sense, is that even if there is technically a complete "*heter*" for some matter, and one could even say that it will not directly lead to anything *assur,*" nevertheless, if one knows "deep down" that certain not-so-nice things will happen indirectly, "somewhere down the road," then one absolutely may not do it!

It is only certain individuals who are able to anticipate and are clearly aware of the traces of *issur* that potentially cling to every technical *heter*. Regarding such people, one can truly say that they are genuinely careful in performing the mitzvos, and all of their deeds are truly a רֵיחַ נִיחוֹחַ, a "pleasant aroma" before Hashem.

And that is the type of person, the Betzalel, who is uniquely qualified to build the Tabernacle of Hashem.

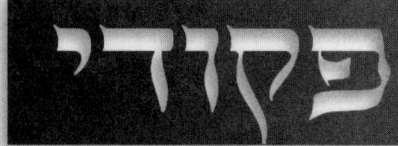

וַיְהִי בַחֹדֶשׁ הָרִאשׁוֹן בַּשָּׁנָה הַשֵּׁנִית
בְּאֶחָד לַחֹדֶשׁ הוּקַם הַמִּשְׁכָּן

It was in the first month of the second year
on the first of the month that
the Tabernacle was erected (40:17).

The wording of our verse, which says הוּקַם הַמִּשְׁכָּן, in the passive voice, would seem to indicate that the *Mishkan* was raised up on its own. The very next verse, however, says וַיָּקֶם מֹשֶׁה אֶת הַמִּשְׁכָּן, *Moses erected the Mishkan,* which seems to indicate that it was Moses who raised it up. This paradox is addressed by *Rashi* in 39:33:

רש"י: וַיָּבִיאוּ אֶת הַמִּשְׁכָּן וגו' שֶׁלֹּא הָיוּ יְכוֹלִין לַהֲקִימוֹ, וּלְפִי שֶׁלֹּא
עָשָׂה מֹשֶׁה שׁוּם מְלָאכָה בַּמִּשְׁכָּן, הִנִּיחַ לוֹ הַקָּדוֹשׁ בָּרוּךְ הוּא הֲקָמָתוֹ,
שֶׁלֹּא הָיָה יָכוֹל לַהֲקִימוֹ שׁוּם אָדָם מֵחֲמַת כּוֹבֶד הַקְּרָשִׁים, שֶׁאֵין כֹּחַ
בְּאָדָם לְזָקְפָן, וּמֹשֶׁה הֶעֱמִידוֹ. אָמַר מֹשֶׁה לִפְנֵי הַקָּדוֹשׁ בָּרוּךְ הוּא:

אֵיךְ אֶפְשָׁר הֲקָמָתוֹ עַל יְדֵי אָדָם, אָמַר לוֹ: עֲסוֹק אַתָּה בְּיָדְךָ וְנִרְאֶה כְּמַקִּימוֹ, וְהוּא נִזְקַף וְקָם מֵאֵלָיו, וְזֶהוּ שֶׁנֶּאֱמַר (שְׁמוֹת מ:יז) "הוּקַם הַמִּשְׁכָּן," הוּקַם מֵאֵלָיו. מִדְרָשׁ רַבִּי תַּנְחוּמָא.

> **RASHI: AND THEY BROUGHT THE MISHKAN ETC.,** —
> *because they were not able to erect it. Because Moses had not done any of the melachah for the Mishkan, Hashem left the raising of the Mishkan for him. No man was able to set it up due to the great weight of the beams; they were too heavy for a normal man. However, Moses raised them up. Moses said before HaKadosh Baruch Hu, "How can the Mishkan's erection be accomplished by man?" HaKadosh Baruch Hu said to him, "Try doing it with your own hands and it will appear as if you are doing the raising, but it will rise upright and stand by itself." This is what is what is referred to in the verse (40:17) which says* הוּקַם הַמִּשְׁכָּן, *meaning* הוּקַם מֵאֵלָיו, *it was raised up on its own. This is a Midrash of R' Tanchuma.*

I would like to present a different approach, based upon a Midrash which appears in several places, among them *Yalkut Shimoni.* I would like to address the aspect of why the raising of the *Mishkan* was accomplished only through a miracle:

Yalkut Shimoni (*Pekudei* 417) teaches that once the separate parts of the Tabernacle were ready, only Moses was able to erect it — and even he needed miraculous assistance.

I find it hard to understand why it was so difficult to raise up the *Mishkan.* After all, the sockets were prepared and ready to have the boards placed within them. The curtains that served as a tent over the *Mishkan* could then follow.

Wouldn't it seem that the placing together of the components should be a lot more simple than the creation of the *Mishkan's* vessels? If they were able to accomplish the complex task of sewing, weaving, and constructing the various *keilim* needed for the *Mishkan*, why wouldn't they be able to assemble the pieces? Even Moses required miraculous intervention, as our verse says, הוּקַם הַמִּשְׁכָּן, meaning that it occurred through a miracle.

An answer to our question might be found by applying *Maharal's* classic interpretation of the phrase (*Devarim* 20:19): כִּי הָאָדָם עֵץ הַשָּׂדֶה, *Is the tree of the field a man?* He writes that the "roots" of man are to be found within his head, which is the part of him closest to the heavens. This is in contradistinction to a tree, whose roots are at its bottommost part, facing the ground. Man, with his "roots" facing the heavens, therefore walks upright, drawn toward his source of nourishment, just as the tree is drawn down, earthward, toward its source of food.

Let us now try to apply that thought to the building of the *Mishkan*. Perhaps, even more so than man's, the *Mishkan's* "roots" are in the heavens, not in the ground below. If so, it must be built not according to "earthbound" concepts, but rather with foundations that suit something heavenly.

One might suggest that it was for this reason that when Moses assembled the *Mishkan*, he seems to have begun with the Curtains that served as a tent over the *Mishkan,* and only afterward placed down the sockets (which are at the bottom). While at first glance this might seem illogical and impractical, it would conform with the idea of the *Mishkan's* foundations residing "above" rather than "below."

Similarly, this would illustrate why the *Mishkan* had to be assembled through miracles rather than through the mundane processes through which other buildings' components are joined. For Hashem wished to demonstrate, through Moses, that this building's support was from "above," not from "below." In fact, no support from "below" was needed at all.

The *Chachamim*, mentioned by the *Yalkut Shimoni*, who tried unsuccessfully to raise the *Mishkan* had started from below, from the sockets up. But, Moses, being the *Ish HaElokim,* was able, through the help of Hashem, to miraculously work from the top down.

Why was this so important? Because it shows that it was not the *Mishkan* that was being supported, but rather that the *Mishkan* was providing support to those below. But, why was Moses needed at all, then? Because the true foundations of the *Mishkan* are *emunah, yiras Shamayim,* and *zehirus* regarding each and every detail of halachah. It therefore had to be built through a man. And not just any man.

It had to be built through Moses, about whom it could be said that, for him, great *yiras Shamayim* was but a small thing.

Let us develop this thought a bit further.

Man's connection to the *Mishkan* was through the *shekalim.* But, who is supporting whom? It can be said about the *Mishkan,* like we say about the Torah (*Mishlei* 3:18): עֵץ חַיִּים הִיא לַמַּחֲזִיקִים בָּהּ וְתֹמְכֶיהָ מְאֻשָּׁר, *It is a "tree of life" to those who grasp it; and its supporters are praiseworthy.* By donating to our contemporary *Mishkans,* that is, the *batei kennesios, talmudei Torah,* and yeshivos, we connect ourselves to eternity.

When speaking of the half-*shekels* that were to be donated to the *Mishkan, Rashi* brings a Midrash that describes Hashem showing Moses a coin made of fire. This alluded to the idea that fire, depending upon how it is used, can be constructive, as when it warms things — or, it can be destructive and burn things. So too, with money that is given to our contemporary institutions of *kodesh.*

Let me explain.

There are those who generously support schools and synagogues, but delude themselves into believing that the institution's entire existence depends on themselves and upon what they choose to give. And they feel that, in recognition of the institution's dependence on their contributions, they should be allowed to dictate its policies — all according to their own ideas as to how the institution should be run. In fact, they feel that the spiritual leaders can be bypassed. As far as they are concerned, there is no real need for the "Moses."

When that happens, the *shekalim* they have donated become coins of fire that incinerate the *kodesh* and desecrate its purpose. This happens because they have dared to go too close. If, however, they allow themselves to stand at a distance, in awe of the holiness, acknowledging the limits of their own perspective and deferring to the *talmidei chachamim*, then their coins of fire will not incinerate, but will add more warmth. And, these coins will not only add more warmth to their *Mishkan,* but will add more light to their own lives.

To sum up, in the Midrash that we originally brought, the *Chachamim* thought that the foundation of the *Mishkan* would be the sockets that rested on the ground. Hence, they were unsuccessful in erecting it. Moses, however, understood that the support would be from above. Therefore, he began with the roof of the *Mishkan* itself. That is why the verse says first וַיָּקֶם מֹשֶׁה אֶת הַמִּשְׁכָּן. And, only afterward does it say that he placed down the sockets.

ויקרא

וַיִּקְרָא אֶל מֹשֶׁה וַיְדַבֵּר ה' אֵלָיו מֵאֹהֶל מוֹעֵד לֵאמֹר

He called to Moses, and Hashem spoke to him
from the Tent of Meeting, saying (1:1).

Many reasons have been given to explain why God commanded us to bring *korbanos*. *Rambam*, in his *Moreh Nevuchim*, writes that they help to cure the Jewish people of the effects they experienced from having been exposed to the surrounding cultures' false beliefs in idol worship. Notwithstanding *Rambam*'s viewing *korbanos* in a historical context, we still pray daily for the opportunity to begin offering *korbanos* once again, in a rebuilt *Beis HaMikdash*.

I would therefore like to discuss the meaning of *korbanos* for our own times.

It is interesting to note the sequence in which the various types of *korbanos* were presented to Moses, as it does not seem to follow the order we would have expected. Moses is first told of the voluntary offering, the *olas nedavah*. He is then commanded regarding the *shelamim*. Then comes the sin-offering, which is brought due to a sin committed *b'shegagah*, without intent. Next is the *korban asham*, brought for a sin committed willfully.

At first glance, this order seems somewhat puzzling. One would have thought it more logical to begin with the *korbanos* that are obligations. And then, only afterward, it would have been appropriate to discuss the *korbanos* that are voluntary. In other words, we should have been told first about what we must do *min hadin*, according to the law. And then, only then, once we have learned about fulfilling obligations, would it be time to discuss what we could do *lifnim mishuras hadin* — that is, those things that we may do voluntarily.

After all, shouldn't a man first be concerned with paying his debts, and only afterward with the giving of gifts?

The explanation, in my opinion, is that the Torah is addressing one who wishes to save himself from one day committing the sin of theft and having to bring a *korban asham*. The way to do that is to set one's goal much higher; that is, to seek to climb the ladder that stretches from the ground toward the heavens. One must strive to go beyond the letter of the law. One must strive to be like the *olah*, totally dedicated to Hashem.

Only then will one be assured of never coming to do his fellow harm, never causing him even the slightest financial loss, and being completely distant from evil. *Sof maaseh b'machshavah techillah*, whatever one does in the end was preceded by a certain thought. And why is an *olah* brought? What leads to the necessity of bringing an *olah*? It is an improper thought.

One must constantly reflect, "When will my deeds ever reach those of my ancestors?" Whatever is accomplished in the end, the main thing is to aspire to climb the ladder that stretches toward the heavens. Even if one does not quite reach the highest rung, *HaKadosh Baruch Hu* will count it for him as if he had reached the very heavens. The main thing is that he be far from the earth.

When a Jew wishes to take the yoke of heaven upon himself, he must shut his eyes and not give any thought to this world. He must yearn to dedicate himself totally to Hashem and to help spread His glory upon every corner of the planet. He should not focus on anything other than Hashem and His Torah.

Let us return to our initial question. Why was Moses told about the voluntary offerings before the obligatory ones? It was in order to demonstrate that one's first priority should be to improve and elevate himself so that he will not sin and be required to seek atonement through obligatory offerings. Rather than seeking cures for spiritual deficiencies, a Jew should focus on personal growth in *avodas Hashem*, service of God, that will save him from unintentional sins. One who is grateful for what God gives him will not become a common thief, who must seek atonement.

אֵשׁ תָּמִיד תּוּקַד עַל הַמִּזְבֵּחַ לֹא תִכְבֶּה

Fire shall be kept continually
upon the Altar; it shall not go out (6:6).

lthough, in the standard calculation of the Jewish day, daytime follows evening, in the calculation of the *Mikdash* it is the reverse: evening follows day. The way of the physical world is that the symbolic evening precedes the symbolic day. For instance, before man can see what will become of his labor, he must first "sit in darkness," not knowing whether the seed he planted will ever bear fruit. This unease over having to "sit in darkness," of not knowing when — and if — he will see tangible results from his efforts, places a great burden on man. Even Jacob our forefather asked Hashem: וְנָתַן לִי לֶחֶם לֶאֱכֹל וּבֶגֶד לִלְבֹּשׁ, *Give me bread to eat and clothes to wear.* And sometimes, when one physically has the bread, he will often feel unsure as to whether he will actually get to consume it.

Feelings of insecurity about one's physical well-being can impoverish the spirit. It can truly be said that, in the physical realm, an inevitable "evening" seems to always precede the "day."

However, when it comes to entering the realm of the *Shechinah,* just the opposite occurs: One is filled with security as to the future. Even when hearing a distant cry originating from his own neighborhood, he tells himself that the home it is coming from could not be his own. His trust is so great that the "day" overpowers the "evenings" of his life. Even when things look bleak, he tells himself that a bright new day is just around the corner. אַשְׁרֵי הַגֶּבֶר אֲשֶׁר שָׂם ה' מִבְטַחוֹ, *Fortunate is the man who has made Hashem his trust.* This is alluded to by our opening verse. The illuminating fire of the spirit burns constantly on the altar of our mind and heart.

זֹאת הַחַיָּה אֲשֶׁר תֹּאכְלוּ מִכָּל הַבְּהֵמָה אֲשֶׁר עַל הָאָרֶץ
This is the animal that you may eat, from among all the animals that are upon the earth (11:2).

*T*he first commandment given to Adam HaRishon had to do with eating (*Bereishis* 2:17): -מֵעֵץ הַדַּעַת טוֹב וָרָע לֹא תֹאכַל מִמֶּ־ נּוּ כִּי בְּיוֹם אֲכָלְךָ מִמֶּנּוּ מוֹת תָּמוּת, *But of the Tree of Knowledge of Good and Bad, you must not eat thereof; for on the day you eat of it, you shall surely die.* Similarly, the first thing Aaron and his sons were commanded to tell the Jewish people concerned eating: זֹאת הַחַיָּה אֲשֶׁר תֹּאכְלוּ מִכָּל הַבְּהֵמָה אֲשֶׁר עַל הָאָרֶץ.

What could be the reason for this being the focus of the very first mitzvah in both these cases?

We say daily, as part of our prayers, מְכַלְכֵּל חַיִּים בְּחֶסֶד; מְחַיֶּה מֵתִים בְּרַחֲמִים רַבִּים, *Who sustains the living with kindness, resuscitates the dead with abundant mercy.* The words מְכַלְכֵּל, *sustains,* and מְחַיֶּה, *resuscitates,* allude to the resurrection of the soul. Death is not a one-time, sudden event. Rather, it can take different forms and be ongoing, even lasting throughout the period of one's life.

Let me explain.

From the very beginning, Hashem told us, *"... on the day you eat of it, you shall surely die."* This could be understood as referring to many deaths — one that repeats itself over the course of every day, hour, and second. Every day that a sinner is alive is considered like one more day of being dead, of a life lacking any real life — as long as it is one additional day when he does not repent. Of course, from the sinner's perspective, at least in terms of his physical self, all of this will be undetectable. He will see no dramatic changes. However, in terms of his spirit, there will be a decline, one that will gradually creep up on him.

In the realm of the physical, the effect that food can have is nothing short of miraculous. It gives strength to the weakened body and restores the weakened spirit as well. It is not for nothing that the imagery of being "fed" appears throughout *Tanach* and *Chazal*.

Once one has been "fed," what is he supposed to do with his new-found energy? Toward what will he direct it? In general, energy can be used for constructive purposes as well as for destructive ones. It can be used for fighting and blind warfare, and it can be used to benefit mankind. It is totally neutral. It can fuel the *yetzer hatov,* as well as the *yetzer hara.*

It is for this reason that we must dedicate ourselves to Torah, for Torah and service of Hashem implant within us the right priorities, directing us to devote our energies to what is proper. Otherwise, lacking dedication to Torah, one would direct his energy solely toward the physical, on a course that will bring him farther and farther from the life that would truly nourish his spirit. He will eat for the same reason that animals eat, and direct his energy to the same types of things that the animal does.

אִשָּׁה כִּי תַזְרִיעַ וְיָלְדָה זָכָר וְטָמְאָה שִׁבְעַת יָמִים
כִּימֵי נִדַּת דְּוֹתָהּ תִּטְמָא

If a woman conceives and gives birth to a male,
she shall be unclean for seven days;
as [in] the days of her menstrual flow,
she shall be unclean (12:2).

When first created, is man טָמֵא, *unclean,* or is he טָהוֹר, *pure?* Is it his essential nature to be honest and good, or is it the opposite? In commenting on *Bereishis* 8:21, כִּי יֵצֶר לֵב הָאָדָם רַע מִנְּעָרָיו, ... *for the imagery of man's heart is evil from his youth, Midrash Tehillim* expands on the word מִנְּעָרָיו. It says: מִשֶּׁנִּנְעָר מִמְּעֵי אִמּוֹ (i.e., at the time man is "shaken," (מִשֶּׁנִּנְעָר)) from the womb, he is רַע, *evil*). One could understand this to mean that he was evil even when first created. Or, one could learn the opposite, that the Midrash demonstrates that he was not evil when created; he becomes so only upon emerging from the womb. In either event, it would seem from this source that he is evil at least from birth.

However, I wonder how one would reconcile this with the Midrash that says that the fetus, inside the womb, is taught the entirety of Torah. Fresh from this experience, he then emerges. He is like gold that lies embedded within other elements; in order to extract the gold, it must be separated from the dross that surrounds it. Even while hidden, however, the gold is still there, ready to be revealed. So, too, with man's goodness. No matter what one sees on the surface, the essential goodness lies within. After enough struggle, it will emerge. Therefore, one should never give up on someone or think him unworthy of being judged favorably.

Upon giving birth, a woman becomes טָמֵא, *unclean*, as indicated by our verse. However, one should not say that, because a person is born in *tumah*, his very essence is *tamei* as well, as if he were a vessel formed through impurity. One might think that such a vessel would never have the potential to become *tahor*, that the gold within could never emerge from the surrounding impurity.

Rather, one should base his approach to this issue on the *Malbim's* commentary to the verse (*Iyov* 36:3): אֶשָּׂא דֵעִי לְמֵרָחוֹק וּלְפֹעֲלִי אֶתֵּן צֶדֶק (literally, *I will take up my knowledge from afar, and to my Maker I will ascribe righteousness*). *Malbim* writes of how the *nefesh*, the soul, placed within the body has come from a "faraway" place, the heavens (far away from the physical world), and its essence (meaning the essence of man as well) is therefore entirely pure.

The soul must therefore struggle to shed the impurities of the physical body. An allusion to this is found in the idea of circumcision: on the eighth day man must rid himself of his *orlah*. This, perhaps, can be seen as a rectification of the state of *tumah* from which man is born. (See *Vayikra Rabbah* 14:2.)

זֹאת תִּהְיֶה תּוֹרַת הַמְּצֹרָע בְּיוֹם טָהֳרָתוֹ וְהוּבָא אֶל הַכֹּהֵן
This shall be the law of the metzora
on the day of his purification:
He shall be brought to the Kohen (14:1).

אָמַר רֵישׁ לָקִישׁ, מַאי דִכְתִיב: "זֹאת תִּהְיֶה תּוֹרַת הַמְּצוֹרָע"? זֹאת
תִּהְיֶה תּוֹרָתוֹ שֶׁל מוֹצִיא שֵׁם רַע (ערכין טו).

Reish Lakish said: What is the meaning of that which is
written, "This shall be the law of the metzora"? It means:
This shall be the law of the motzi shem ra [defamer]
(Arachin 15b).

s quoted above, *Chazal* associate *tzaraas* with the prohibition of *motzi shem ra*. I would like to explore this in
depth by pointing out certain unusual aspects of *tzaraas*
and of *motzi shem ra*.

Perhaps the most-often quoted verse in *Tanach* as regards this *issur* (prohibition) is *Mishlei* 18:21: מָוֶת וְחַיִּים בְּיַד לָשׁוֹן, *Death and life are in the hand* (i.e., power) *of the tongue*. Its wording is somewhat curious: Why מָוֶת וְחַיִּים בְּיַד לָשׁוֹן rather than מָוֶת וְחַיִּים בְּלָשׁוֹן? The word בְּיַד seems out of place.

It is interesting to note that some of the laws of the impurity of *tzaraas* are strikingly different than those of other *tumos*. Most notably, they are dependent upon the Kohen's making a statement. Even where one's house or person definitely shows the signs of *tzaraas*, lacking the Kohen's pronouncement, everything is still considered *tahor*. The opposite is true as well: Even when all signs of the *tzaraas* have completely disappeared, the house and the person remain *tamei* until the Kohen has declared them *tahor*.

Another curious aspect is the Torah's insistence that the witness not say, נֶגַע נִרְאָה לִי, *I have seen a nega* (an affliction). Rather, he must say, כְּנֶגַע נִרְאָה לִי, *It seems to me that I have seen a nega;* but he should not say that he is certain of it.

Let us have a look at both these anomalies.

The purification process prescribed by the Torah for the *metzora* includes the use of cedar wood and hyssop. *Rashi*, in his comments to the words *crimson wool and hyssop* in *Vayikra* 14:4, says: What is the remedy for one who is guilty of malicious talk or haughtiness? He should lower himself from his arrogance like a worm (תּוֹלַעַת) and like hyssop. He is explaining that the hyssop, an herb which does not grow tall, is used because it symbolizes that the *metzora's* cure comes from "lowering" himself from his pride.

By apparently saying that the source of the *metzora's* affliction was his excessive pride, is this Aggadic interpretation reconcilable with the earlier one cited, which says that *tzaraas* stems from speaking evil against one's fellow? I think so.

In fact, excessive, unjustified pride lies at the very heart of the sin of *motzi shem ra*. The most common defense for *motzi shem ra* is,

"But, I was only saying the truth!" In fact, one might even go so far as to declare, "Not only was it not an *aveirah,* but in fact it was a mitzvah!" How could this be? It is because of excessive pride. A person looks at a situation involving someone else, bends over backward to interpret it in the most negative possible light, and then convinces himself that his perception of the events is flawless.

Not only does the speaker fail to consider that his understanding of events might be wrong, but he proceeds to speak with not a care as to the damage that his words will cause his fellow. He is so self-centered, so wrapped up in himself, that he cannot even imagine what it would be like to walk in his fellow's shoes, to have to live down the damage caused by the slanderous words. Once again, this is nothing but pure *gaavah,* pride.

It is not only words that can damage the reputation of one's fellow. The job can be done equally well with a well-timed public waving of the hand, showing one and all your contempt for another person. Even though not a single word was spoken, the public humiliation is no less effective and cutting.

And that is why the verse says specifically that *Death and life are in "the hand of" the tongue.* Sometimes it is the tongue that does the damage, and sometimes it is the well-timed gesture of contempt, the flip of the *hand.*

It all comes down to the same thing: We are not permitted to lose our humility. We must conquer the foolish pride that leads us to confuse highly subjective perceptions with objective, established fact. We must not think that it is up to us to judge others and make pronouncements as to what they deserve, what they have coming to them. Lacking that kind of humility, we will often be tempted to become involved in defaming others.

And there's one more thing, something that not only causes great damage, but stands in the path of any possibility of limiting the damage: When, even after we are told that what we said was factually incorrect, we refuse to consider that possibility, we hold onto what we said, and refuse to back down. After all, we say to ourselves, "There's no way I could have been wrong about this."

This is why, when a man sees that there is something wrong with his house, something that looks like *tzaraas,* it is not up to him to "pass judgment." Rather, he must go to the Kohen, the one who is totally dedicated to the service of Hashem and say: כְּנֶגַע נִרְאָה לִי. Not "I am certain that it is a *nega,*" but it is *k'nega,* merely my subjective perception.

And only at this point, upon his conquering of the temptation to be very self-confident about the veracity of his own perception, will he be cured. He must learn that even those things that "everyone says" are *tamei* might very well be *tahor* — notwithstanding the fact that "everyone is saying it." Neither he nor anyone else has the right to make pronouncements as to what or who is *tamei.* That must be left up to the third party whose dedication to following the ways of Hashem is total.

Once he acknowledges this, it will not only mean that he is ready to be cured, but, in fact, this will actually *be* the cure!

וְנָתַן אַהֲרֹן עַל שְׁנֵי הַשְּׂעִירִם גּוֹרָלוֹת
גּוֹרָל אֶחָד לַה' וְגוֹרָל אֶחָד לַעֲזָאזֵל

***And Aaron shall place lots
on the two goats: one lot "for Hashem"
and one "for Azazel" (16:8).***

T
he matter of the two goats, with one carrying the transgressions of the Jewish people and being sent to *Azazel,* is truly
a wonder!

Rav Samson Raphael Hirsch writes that the fact that the two goats,
each destined for a different fate, must be identical as to their appearance, height, and monetary value teaches something about the
nature of free choice. Should it be one's desire, he can overcome his
material drives and devote himself to Hashem. And, just as easily, he
can turn his back on Hashem and devote his energies to the call of
his *yetzer hara.* In that case, he'll find himself in *Azazel,* unworthy of
participating in civilized society.

And it's all a matter of free, personal choice. One cannot say that the life he chose was an accident of fate, that he was compelled by where and how he was raised, whether or not he had money, or any other external factor. Rav Hirsch says that we see from this verse that the goat whose fate it was to be dedicated to Hashem is no different from the one that wound up going to *Azazel*. In fact, were it not equally suited to have been the one going to *Azazel*, it could have been the one that wound up going to Hashem!

Rav Hirsch's thought is quite beautiful. However, the reason one went to *Azazel* and the other to Hashem had nothing to do with free choice. Rather, it was simply a matter of the draw. Purely external factors accounted for the respective fates of the two goats. There was nothing that the animal could do to wind up going in one direction instead of the other. Wouldn't that, then, show quite the opposite of what Rav Hirsch was trying to teach?

I would like to propose a different approach.

Perhaps the prayers of Yom Kippur can provide us with an insight. One could say that, in relation to the *Torah SheBiksav*, the "Written Torah," of the two goats, the prayers of Yom Kippur serve as the *Torah She'be'al Peh*, the "Oral Torah." Let me explain.

The underlying theme of *Shabbos Shabbason* and Yom Kippur is that all the world's creatures pass before Hashem, to be judged as to who shall live and who shall die. They are judged as to whether they will experience tranquility — or suffering, God forbid. Will their year be one of wealth — or of poverty? And, the individual has no control over his fate of the moment of judgment. His deeds, good and bad, of the previous year have been weighed and evaluated. It is too late for him to change them.

When it comes to the goats, their situation seems to be quite the same. They are identical as to appearance, height, and monetary value. Their fate will be "sealed" when the lots are drawn. The goats have no power to determine whether they will become an offering to Hashem or go to their death in Azazel. This symbolizes the judgment of Yom Kippur, a day of awesome holiness, a day when all creatures pass before Him and none have the power to alter their fate at that moment. If a person has not earned the designation of a *tzaddik,* his fate rests with Hashem's mercy.

This must be internalized down to the very depths of our being. It must fully penetrate our entire thought process. We must live with the absolute recognition that all is in the hands of Heaven. Our fate rests with Him alone.

He sees everything and misses nothing. He will judge us and He is just. He is a God of truth. His justice is never skewed or corrupted. He is righteous and honest.

He is the One Who has given purity and sanctity to this day. And, He is the One Who gives this day the power to atone for us. Even though we have sinned, in His mercy He places our sins upon the head of the goat and disposes of them in Azalzel.

דַּבֵּר אֶל כָּל עֲדַת בְּנֵי יִשְׂרָאֵל וְאָמַרְתָּ אֲלֵהֶם
קְדֹשִׁים תִּהְיוּ כִּי קָדוֹשׁ אֲנִי ה' אֱלֹהֵיכֶם

*Speak to the entire assembly of the Children
of Israel and you shall say to them: "You shall
be holy because I, Hashem, am holy"* (19:2).

רש"י: **דַּבֵּר אֶל כָּל עֲדַת בְּנֵי יִשְׂרָאֵל** – מְלַמֵּד שֶׁנֶּאֶמְרָה פָּרָשָׁה זוֹ
בְּהַקְהֵל, מִפְּנֵי שֶׁרוֹב גּוּפֵי תּוֹרָה תְּלוּיִין בָּהּ.

קְדֹשִׁים תִּהְיוּ – הֱווּ פְרוּשִׁים מִן הָעֲרָיוֹת וּמִן הָעֲבֵירָה, שֶׁכָּל מָקוֹם
שֶׁאַתָּה מוֹצֵא גֶדֶר עֶרְוָה אַתָּה מוֹצֵא קְדוּשָׁה.

Rashi, quoting *Vayikra Rabbah,* says that this *parashah*
was purposefully said to the Jewish people at a time when
they were all gathered together, *b'hakheil,* because most of
the essentials of the Torah depend on it.

If so, why doesn't the verse say so explicitly, or at least emphasize this point? Let it say, for instance, "דַּבֵּר אֶל כָּל הַקָּהָל", *Speak to all the congregation,*" or, "דַּבֵּר אֶל כָּל הָעָם", *Speak to all the people*". Those terms are more general; the noun *eidah,* which is the one used in the verse, occasionally connotes a special segment of the population rather than the entire group. For instance, *Vayikra* 4:13 says, וְאִם כָּל עֲדַת יִשְׂרָאֵל יִשְׁגּוּ, *If the entire assembly of Israel shall err,* and *Rashi* interprets עֲדַת יִשְׂרָאֵל as refering to only one subset, namely the Sanhedrin. It does not refer to the entire congregation. So, why does our *pasuk* say *"Adas Bnei Yisrael"*?

Also, why would the Midrash say that the majority of the essentials of the Torah depend upon these words when only 51 of the Torah's 613 mitzvos appear in this *parashah*?

And, aside from the issue of numbers, exactly what is meant by גּוּפֵי תוֹרָה, *the essentials of the Torah?*

I have one further question, regarding the meaning of קְדֹשִׁים תִּהְיוּ, *You shall be holy.* According to *Rashi,* it means that one should be separated from *arayos* (sins of sexual immorality) and from "*the aveirah.*" What is meant by "*the aveirah*"? According to *Sifsei Chachamim,* it means the *aveirah* of *gilui arayos.* I don't understand. If so, then why say the same thing twice?

I would like to share a few ideas that might provide some answers to these questions.

Let us say that we have two people, neither of whom commits a certain *aveirah.* It is possible that even though neither does the *aveirah,* there are two different reasons for this. One stays away because he is *kadosh;* he is a *parush* (one who is separated) from the *aveirah.* The other, however, is not a *parush,* but he simply would not do this transgression.

This *parashah* includes the following words, in verses 19:35-36: לֹא תַעֲשׂוּ עָוֶל בַּמִּשְׁפָּט בַּמִּדָּה בַּמִּשְׁקָל וּבַמְּשׂוּרָה, *You shall not commit a perversion in justice, in measures of length, weight, or volume.*

The negative commandment is to not cheat our fellow man in all types of weights and measures: liquid weight, dry weight, all types of scales and measuring devices; and regarding all types of goods, everything from real estate to clothing. Whoever has not cheated his fellow in any of the above could be said to have "fulfilled" these negative commandments.

The Torah does not stop, though, with merely telling us to not cheat our fellow man. It continues: מֹאזְנֵי צֶדֶק אַבְנֵי צֶדֶק אֵיפַת צֶדֶק וְהִין צֶדֶק יִהְיֶה לָכֶם, *You shall have correct scales, correct weights, correct dry measures, and correct liquid measures.* In a sense, we are being told that even when we don't happen to be involved in weighing something for purposes of commerce, we still must see to it that there should be no tool in our possession that might somehow be used as a tool of deception.

Of course, what I am saying is not intended as a halachic stricture. There is no halachah requiring that someone who has absolutely nothing to do with commerce has to make sure that his scales are maintained at the highest standard of calibration.

However, I do believe that the Torah is coming to teach us something about the way we should relate to the negative commandments, specifically that we must not only refrain from doing them, but that we should be *parush* (separated) from them.

Please allow me to explain.

Think of someone who is only occasionally involved in commerce but has in his possession a scale that's slightly "off." He's a religious fellow, and when the time comes for him to need the scale for commerce, he will remember to calibrate it properly. But, still, it might not be so good for his *neshamah.*

When the occasion comes for him to weigh out some merchandise on that slightly "off" scale, just think of the *nisayon!* Think of the rationalizations with which he will have to struggle!

Now, compare that to the person whose scales are always in order, properly calibrated at all times, whether or not he is about to use them that day.

He will never have that particular *nisayon.* The difference between the two men is that the second is actually *parush* from the transgression. He has separated himself from it to the extent that temptation will never become an issue for him, for he has seen to it that he will never come to that *nisayon.*

There are other examples.

For instance, judges are commanded to judge fairly. They are told not to rely only on their own impressions. Rather, they must be super careful, and should discuss the issues with other *talmidei chachamim,* even if those others happen to be lesser *talmidei chachamim* than they are. The main thing is to take all possible precautions to distance themselves from the possibility of error.

We see another example of this in the prohibition against *avodah zarah.* Not only do we not engage in actual worship of idols, but we try to keep our distance from all kinds of emptiness and foolishness.

In many places, we are commanded regarding *tzedakah, matnos aniyim, terumos, maaser, leket, shich'chah,* and *pe'ah.* There are degrees as to how these commandments are to be fulfilled, and I am referring to differences of quality, not of quantity. Some do them with *kedushah;* others do them, but are lacking *kedushah.*

What do I mean?

It has to do with their degree of *ahavas habrios.*

One who is filled with *ahavas habrios* will never fail to fulfill these mitzvos and never happen to transgress them. One who is lacking that quality — to say nothing of one who is contemptuous of others — will need to overcome his innate cynicism, callousness, and selfishness each time he is confronted with a situation that demands a response of *tzedakah, matnos aniyim, terumos, maaser, leket, shich'chah,* and *pe'ah.* Yes, he may very well do the mitzvah; after all, he is a *"frummer Yid."* However, it won't come naturally. And, there will be times when it won't come at all.

That's the difference between being a *kadosh* or *parush* in regard to a certain mitzvah and simply being someone who follows the rules.

On the words וְאָהַבְתָּ לְרֵעֲךָ כָּמוֹךָ, *You shall love your fellow as yourself, Rashi,* quoting a Midrash, says: R' Akiva said: This is a great rule in the Torah. One who loves his fellow man will always want what's best for him and will always be ready to give what he can. *Pirkei Avos* 5:21 says: כָּל הַמְזַכֶּה אֶת הָרַבִּים אֵין חֵטְא בָּא עַל יָדוֹ, *Whoever influences the masses to become meritorious shall not be the cause of sin.*

To my mind, this is what is meant by *kedushah.* The mitzvah of *You shall be holy* means to always stay close to the side of merit and distant from sin. And this is also what is meant by being called upon to be *parush.*

Similarly, we can apply this to the mitzvah stated in *Vayikra* 19:33, where the Torah tells us regarding the stranger: וְכִי יָגוּר אִתְּךָ גֵּר בְּאַרְצְכֶם לֹא תוֹנוּ אֹתוֹ, *When a proselyte dwells among you in your land, do not harass him.* We are commanded not to oppress the *ger.* As long as one does not do so, he has not committed this transgression. However, it would seem that Hashem's expectations of us do not end with our simply holding back from taking advantage of those who are most vulnerable. That becomes obvious in the very next *pasuk:* *The proselyte who dwells with you shall be like a native among you, and you shall love him like yourself.*

One might have though that this matter of being *kadosh* or *parush* was limited to the select few among the Jewish people, maybe only the *tzaddikim* of each generation. Perhaps what is being referred to is an "extra measure," way beyond the reach and grasp of the *Klal.*

And that is precisely why this command needed to be said *b'hakheil,* when they were all gathered together. The intent was that we should all see that this applies equally to us all, with no exceptions. When *Rashi* said that most of the essentials of the Torah depend on it, perhaps he was stressing that it applies not only to each and every one of us, but that it applies also to each and every mitzvah. All of the commandments must be done with the utmost level of *kedushah.*

For instance, it's not simply a matter of patting oneself on the back for not having oppressed a *ger* today or for having mailed in a contribution to some organization. Rather, we must maintain the highest level of love for our fellow man at all times, never entertaining the thought of taking advantage of another and constantly sensitive to the plight of our fellow.

One more point: I had originally asked why the verse says דַּבֵּר אֶל כָּל "עֲדַת" בְּנֵי יִשְׂרָאֵל, using the word עֵדָה. I would like to suggest that it is because *kedushah* can be acquired in no other way than through דַּעַת, *wisdom.*

What this means is that only by having a knowledge of the truth and content of a mitzvah can one achieve becoming a *kadosh* with regard to that mitzvah. The word עֵדָה is used because it is related to the words, דֵּעָה and דַּעַת.

And perhaps this is also why *Rashi* states that *Adas Yisrael* in the context of *Vayikra* 4:13 refers to the Sanhedrin. Why? Because what is the Sanhedrin if not those with the highest level of דַּעַת and the ones who are most urgently charged to employ the methods of דַּעַת?

Let's take this even a step further and suggest another twin meaning: קדש/שקד. *Pirkei Avos* 2:19 says, רַבִּי אֶלְעָזָר אוֹמֵר הֱוֵי שָׁקוּד לִלְמוֹד תּוֹרָה, R' Elazar says that one must strive to be שָׁקוּד, *totally immersed and uninterrupted,* in the way he learns Torah. So too with one's attitude toward mitzvos, one must be always ready, always available. In other words, קָדוֹשׁ.

וְלֹא תְחַלְּלוּ אֶת שֵׁם קָדְשִׁי
וְנִקְדַּשְׁתִּי בְּתוֹךְ בְּנֵי יִשְׂרָאֵל אֲנִי ה' מְקַדִּשְׁכֶם

You shall not desecrate
My Holy Name; and I shall be sanctified
among the Children of Israel;
I am Hashem, Who sanctifies you (22:32).

his verse is the source of the commandment to be *me-kadesh Hashem,* to sanctify Hashem, as it says in the *Rambam* (*Yesodei HaTorah* 5:1): All the Jewish people are commanded to sanctify the great and holy Name of Hashem, as it is stated, *I shall be sanctified among the Children of Israel.* That being the case, why wasn't the *pasuk* written using a language of *tzivui,* command? Let it say, for instance, "Sanctify My Name!" Its present form seems to almost be describing a future event — that eventually it will occur that His Name will be sanctified among the Jewish people.

It seems to me that the *pasuk's* wording is actually presenting us with a fundamental insight regarding the nature of *mesirus nefesh* in general and *kiddush Hashem* in particular.

What is *mesirus nefesh*? It is the act of giving over everything — up to and including one's very life. Obviously, this is an extraordinarily high level, one that does not come easily and without a gradual process. It is simply not realistic that an adult would be prepared to give up his life for the sake of the mitzvah of *kiddush Hashem* simply because he found out one day about the existence of such a commandment. Nor could it simply come as a result of a solitary decision.

Rather, it can come only as the logical extension of one's having lived a life dedicated to following the correct path in *taharas hamishpachah* and *kashrus,* honesty and integrity in one's business dealings, care regarding one's speech, and conducting oneself properly both inside the home and outside of it. Does he yearn to draw closer to his Maker? Does he truly regret his sins and seek to atone for them? Do they truly concern him? Does he seek to do *teshuvah*? Is he *mekadesh* his mouth, not allowing falsity or gossip to emerge from within it? Does he do the mitzvos in the right way?

If so, then he has sanctified himself and dedicated all that he has to the service of Hashem. When — and if — the time should ever come that he is faced with the test of literal *mesirus nefesh*, the *kedushah* already within him will direct him toward the proper choice. It would almost come naturally.

That's the meaning of וְנִקְדַּשְׁתִּי בְּתוֹךְ בְּנֵי יִשְׂרָאֵל, *and I shall be sanctified among the Children of Israel.* It will not happen as a result of being commanded, but rather as a natural extension of the way one has lived his life up until this point.

This scenario is vividly portrayed in *Berachos* 61b:

בְּשָׁעָה שֶׁהוֹצִיאוּ אֶת רַבִּי עֲקִיבָא לַהֲרֵיגָה זְמַן קְרִיאַת שְׁמַע הָיָה,
וְהָיוּ סוֹרְקִים אֶת בְּשָׂרוֹ בְּמַסְרֵקוֹת שֶׁל בַּרְזֶל, וְהָיָה מְקַבֵּל עָלָיו עוֹל

מַלְכוּת שָׁמַיִם. אָמְרוּ לוֹ תַּלְמִידָיו: רַבֵּינוּ, עַד כַּאן? אָמַר לָהֶם: כָּל יָמַי
הָיִיתִי מִצְטַעֵר עַל פָּסוּק זֶה "בְּכָל נַפְשְׁךָ" – אֲפִילוּ נוֹטֵל אֶת נִשְׁמָתְךָ,
אָמַרְתִּי: מָתַי יָבֹא לְיָדִי וַאֲקַיְּמֶנּוּ, וְעַכְשָׁיו שֶׁבָּא לְיָדִי לֹא אֲקַיְּמֶנּוּ?

*As they brought R' Akiva out to be killed, it was the time
of Krias Shema, they were raking his flesh with metal
combs — yet he was accepting upon himself the Ol
Malchus Shamayim, the yoke of the Heavenly Kingdom.
His students said to him: "Our master, even to this
extent?" He answered, "All my life I was troubled by this
verse, 'With all your soul' — even if He takes your life. I
thought, 'When will this opportunity be given me so that
I can fulfill it?' And now that the opportunity is here,
should I not fulfill it?"*

Even the *talmidim* were amazed. They asked, "Our teacher, even
to this extent?" Even they, who were well aware of R' Akiva's greatness and holiness, wondered, "Is it truly possible to ignore one's terrible pain and meditate upon accepting upon oneself the *Ol Malchus
Shamayim* at a time like this?"

R' Akiva's answer was that this was not a thought that came to
him only at this point in his life. Rather, it had always been on his
mind. It was the natural continuation of the way he had lived every
moment of his life until then.

וַיְדַבֵּר ה' אֶל מֹשֶׁה בְּהַר סִינַי לֵאמֹר

And Hashem spoke to Moses upon Har Sinai, saying ... (25:1).

רש"י: **דַּבֵּר אֶל כָּל עֲדַת בְּנֵי יִשְׂרָאֵל** – מַה עִנְיַן שְׁמִיטָה אֵצֶל הַר
סִינַי, וַהֲלֹא כָל הַמִּצְוֹת נֶאֶמְרוּ מִסִּינַי, אֶלָּא מַה שְׁמִיטָה נֶאֶמְרוּ
כְּלָלוֹתֶיהָ וּפְרָטוֹתֶיהָ וְדִקְדּוּקֶיהָ מִסִּינַי, אַף כּוּלָן נֶאֶמְרוּ כְּלָלוֹתֵיהֶן
וְדִקְדּוּקֵיהֶן מִסִּינַי, כַּךְ שְׁנוּיָה בְּתוֹרַת כֹּהֲנִים. וְנִרְאֶה לִי שֶׁכַּךְ
פֵּירוּשָׁהּ לְפִי שֶׁלֹּא מָצִינוּ שְׁמִיטַת קַרְקָעוֹת שֶׁנִּשְׁנֵית בְּעַרְבוֹת מוֹאָב
בְּמִשְׁנֵה תּוֹרָה.

According to *Toras Kohanim*, quoted here by *Rashi*, it was not just the general concepts of the mitzvos that were given on Har Sinai, but all their rules and details were given there as well. *Rashi* adds that we see this from the fact that the mitzvah of *shemittah* was not mentioned again in the Plains of Moab.

One could ask: Why is this so significant? Does it really make that much of a difference whether the details were given on Har Sinai as opposed to any other place in the Wilderness? And, as asked by the *Ohr HaChaim*, why is it that Hashem chose to demonstrate this fact through the mitzvah of *shemittah* rather than through some other mitzvah? After all, the Torah could have been written in a way that would demonstrate this fact by using the very first mitzvah of the Torah, or even the very last.

It seems to me that it comes to teach us that we maintained the same level of holiness when hearing the practical details of the mitzvos as we had when hearing of their general principles. In other words, we received the day-to-day details with the same level of holiness that we had when hearing of the concepts.

Why is this so significant?

Think of *Berachos 22a*:

דְּתַנְיָא: וְהוֹדַעְתָּם לְבָנֶיךָ וְלִבְנֵי בָנֶיךָ, וּכְתִיב בַּתְרֵיהּ יוֹם אֲשֶׁר עָמַדְתָּ לִפְנֵי ה' אֱלֹהֶיךָ בְּחוֹרֵב, מַה לְּהַלָּן בְּאֵימָה וּבְיִרְאָה וּבְרֶתֶת וּבְזִיעַ אַף כָּאן בְּאֵימָה וּבְיִרְאָה וּבְרֶתֶת וּבְזִיעַ.

We learned in a Baraisa: "And you shall teach it to your sons and to your grandchildren," and it is written afterward, ... "the day upon which you stood before Hashem, your God, in Chorev." Just as the first [incident] was with fear, awe, trembling, and quaking, so too here should it be with fear, awe, trembling, and quaking.

And, consider *Devarim 26:16* and the *Rashi* there:

הַיּוֹם הַזֶּה ה' אֱלֹהֶיךָ מְצַוְּךָ לַעֲשׂוֹת אֶת הַחֻקִּים הָאֵלֶּה וְאֶת הַמִּשְׁפָּטִים וְשָׁמַרְתָּ וְעָשִׂיתָ אוֹתָם בְּכָל לְבָבְךָ וּבְכָל נַפְשֶׁךָ

This day, Hashem, your God, commands you to perform these statutes and the laws, and you shall observe and perform them with all your heart and with all your soul.

רש"י: הַיּוֹם הַזֶּה ה' אֱלֹהֶיךָ מְצַוְּךָ – בְּכָל יוֹם יִהְיוּ בְעֵינֶיךָ חֲדָשִׁים,
כְּאִלּוּ בּוֹ בַיּוֹם נִצְטַוֵּיתָ עֲלֵיהֶם

RASHI: THIS DAY, HASHEM, YOUR GOD, COMMANDS
YOU — *On each day they shall be new in your eyes, as if
you were commanded regarding them that day.*

And, consider as well *Devarim* 6:6 and its *Rashi*:

וְהָיוּ הַדְּבָרִים הָאֵלֶּה אֲשֶׁר אָנֹכִי מְצַוְּךָ הַיּוֹם עַל לְבָבֶךָ

*And these words that I command you today shall be upon
your heart.*

רש"י: אֲשֶׁר אָנֹכִי מְצַוְּךָ הַיּוֹם – לֹא יִהְיוּ בְעֵינֶיךָ כְּדִיּוֹטַגְמָא יְשָׁנָה שֶׁאֵין
אָדָם סוֹפְנָהּ, אֶלָּא כַּחֲדָשָׁה שֶׁהַכֹּל רָצִין לִקְרָאתָהּ

RASHI: THAT I COMMAND YOU TODAY — *They should
not be in your eyes like an old edict to which a person
does not attach importance, but rather they should be
like a new one, toward which everyone runs.*

Rashi writes, regarding our attitude toward the day-to-day performance of mitzvos, that we should relate to them as if they were
"new" to us, as if we had just been commanded regarding them that
very day. In other words, they should not become "old hat."

This seems somewhat unrealistic. A man has done something
a thousand times — and he's supposed to treat it on the one-
thousand-and-first time as if it were actually the very first?

I saw it written in the name of the Chazon Ish that if each time
one performs a mitzvah, he does so with the intent of fulfilling its

every detail, then each time he performs the mitzvah it will be as if this were his very first time, as if he were just commanded regarding this particular mitzvah.

We have now come to an answer as to why *shemittah* was the mitzvah that made this point most clearly. *Shemittah* occurs only once in seven years. It is exceedingly full of detail. On average, a man could expect to only have ten opportunities in his lifetime for this mitzvah. Each cycle will seem new to him. After all, he had been waiting six years!

Although other mitzvos occur more frequently, some on a routine basis, day in and day out, we are being told to view each opportunity to do them the way we view the mitzvah of *shemittah*. As if we had been waiting six years. And as if we will be waiting another six years before having the opportunity once again.

As the Chazon Ish says, the key is to see the mitzvah as so special, so precious, that we want to take the greatest of care to do it in the most special of ways, with meticulous attention to each of its details.

אִם בְּחֻקֹּתַי תֵּלֵכוּ

If you will follow My decrees (26:3).

ashi comments that "following God's decrees" means that one should toil to understand the Torah. How does *Rashi* see a connection between Torah study and following the Torah's decrees? And why is a law referred to in Hebrew as a "halachah," from the root הלך, *going*? What is the connection between "law" and "going" or "traveling"?

Perhaps we can explain this by referring to verses in *Mishlei* (6:21-23), that describes how much one should dedicate oneself to Torah study:

קָשְׁרֵם עַל לִבְּךָ תָמִיד עָנְדֵם עַל גַּרְגְּרֹתֶיךָ. בְּהִתְהַלֶּכְךָ תַּנְחֶה אֹתָךְ ... כִּי נֵר מִצְוָה וְתוֹרָה אוֹר וְדֶרֶךְ חַיִּים תּוֹכְחוֹת מוּסָר, *Tie them to your heart always; entwine them upon your neck. As you go forth* [i.e., during the course of your life (*Rashi*)], *it will guide you ... For a commandment is a lamp and the Torah is light, and reproving discipline is the way of life.*

The Talmud (*Sotah* 21a) illuminates these verses with a parable. It is like someone who is walking in a forest in the fog of night. He is frightened. He does not know if he is headed in the right direction. He may stumble over unseen obstacles and he may become the prey of animals or bandits, who hunt under cover of darkness. He finds a torch and is no longer afraid of potential obstacles, but he still fears animals and bandits and does not know where he is going. Then, dawn breaks, and the fear of attack recedes, but is he moving in the right direction? Finally he comes to a clearly marked crossroads, and his fears disappear.

The Talmud wonders what is the allusion of the crossroads. Rav Chisda says it alludes to a Torah scholar on the day of his death. Until then he was afraid he might fall into sin, but now he is secure that his scholarship and fear of God are intact (*Rashi*). Rav Nachman says it alludes to a scholar and his fear of sin. Once his scholarship has brought him to the point that he has true fear of God, he can be confident that he will not sin (*Rashi*). Mar Zutra says it is a scholar whose views are accepted by his peers as the correct halachah. Now he is confident that his years of learning have achieved his hoped-for results.

As noted above, the passage in *Mishlei* refers to one's path through life. Like someone walking through a dark forest, he cannot be sure if he is approaching his spiritual goal or if he is heading toward oblivion, as Esau said of himself — without realizing the full implication of his words — "Look, I am on the way to death" (*Bereishis* 25:32).

If a person clings to the Torah and allows it to guide him through his life, if he immerses himself in its study and lets it illuminate his path through the years, it will protect him from the spiritual dangers of the world, and when he is in doubt over which way to turn, it will show him the way.

As the verse in *Mishlei* says, one's devotion to the Torah should be as if one binds it to his heart and entwines it around his neck, meaning that he should yearn to grow in his knowledge and never separate himself from its values. Thus, *Rashi* explains quite correctly that the source of blessing is dedication to the Torah and that such dedication and study is the guiding star that leads one through life to his proper destination.

במדבר

נָשֹׂא אֶת רֹאשׁ בְּנֵי קְהָת מִתּוֹךְ בְּנֵי לֵוִי ...
אֵלֶּה פְקוּדֵי מִשְׁפַּחַת הַקְּהָתִי כָּל הָעֹבֵד בְּאֹהֶל מוֹעֵד ...
וּפְקוּדֵי בְּנֵי גֵרְשׁוֹן לְמִשְׁפְּחוֹתָם וּלְבֵית אֲבֹתָם

Take a census of the sons of Kohath
from among the sons of Levi ... These are
the countings of the Kohathite families,
all who work in the Tent of Meeting ...
The countings of the sons of Gershon
according to their families .... (4:2,37,38).

T he "counting" of the sons of Kohath is listed before that of the sons of Gershon. As Gershon was the *bechor*, shouldn't his family have rightfully been listed first?

Perhaps there was another consideration, far more significant: While Gershon's family was honored with the carrying of the components of the *Ohel Moed*, Kohath's was assigned to carry the Ark, which is the Holy of Holies.

Certainly, there are capabilities one gets through inheritance. And, there are others which arise through one's own effort, through one's striving to mold himself after the "ideal."

The latter can be likened to וָאֶשָּׂא אֶתְכֶם עַל כַּנְפֵי נְשָׁרִים, *I shall carry you upon wings of eagles.*

Whose capabilities are greatest? It is those of the one who seeks to unite with that which is most lofty, meaning one who strives for the highest level of heavenly service.

When he does so, his very effort will lift him. In a sense, it will even carry him. נָשָׂא אָרוֹן אֶת נוֹשְׂאָיו, *The Aron carried those who carried it.*

Perhaps this is why the Torah lists the sons of Kohath first.

כָּל יְמֵי נֶדֶר נִזְרוֹ ... קָדֹשׁ יִהְיֶה ...
**All the days of the vow of his nezirus ...
holy shall he be ... (6:5).**

he *nazir* is referred to as being קָדֹשׁ, *holy;* he has *kedushas haguf,* meaning that his body is holy, as is stated in 6:5: קָדֹשׁ יִהְיֶה גַּדֵּל פֶּרַע שְׂעַר רֹאשׁוֹ, *holy shall he be, the growth of hair on his head shall grow.* Even his head (without its hair) is considered holy, as seen in 6:7: כִּי נֵזֶר אֱלֹהָיו עַל רֹאשׁוֹ, *for the crown of his God is upon his head.* He is not permitted to become contaminated by contact with a corpse, even in order to bury his parents. The Torah gives a reason: לְאָבִיו וּלְאִמּוֹ לְאָחִיו וּלְאַחֹתוֹ לֹא יִטַּמָּא לָהֶם בְּמֹתָם כִּי נֵזֶר אֱלֹהָיו עַל רֹאשׁוֹ, *To his father or to his mother, to his brother or to his sister — he shall not contaminate himself to them upon their death, for the crown of his God is upon his head.*

What does this mean, that *the crown of his God is upon his head?* Why would that be a reason for his not being allowed to become contaminated by contact with a corpse, even for the sake of burying his own father and mother?

Chazal make the following statement regarding the *nazir*:

לֹא יִטַּמָּא לָהֶם בְּמוֹתָם, בְּמוֹתָם אֵין מִטַּמֵּא אֲבָל עוֹמֵד הוּא בְּהֶסְפֵּד וּבְשׁוּרָה: כִּי נֵזֶר אֱלֹהָיו עַל רֹאשׁוֹ, בֵּין שֶׁיֵּשׁ לוֹ שֵׂעָר וּבֵין שֶׁאֵין לוֹ שֵׂעָר (סִפְרֵי בַּמִּדְבָּר פִּיסְקָא כו).

He shall not contaminate himself to them upon their death, but he is permitted to attend the eulogy and to stand in the line of mourners.

The love felt by a mother for her newborn child is beyond measure — as is the pain felt by the child upon the parent's death. Occasions of birth and of death have in common that the intense feelings of love elicited by these two events are unrestrained and unbounded. During the intervening period, though — the lifetime that occurs between the beginning and end of the parental/child relationship — feelings are more complex, more measured.

Why, according to the Torah point of view, should this be? How can we understand this pattern?

Looking at it superficially, one might expect that things should not be this way. After all, as a child develops and grows, he becomes more of a "person." Logically, one might expect that his parents would better relate to offspring who have reached a stage of greater intellectual and personal maturity.

However, one could say quite the opposite as well: that as the child matures, he also becomes more independent, an individual whose connection with his parents becomes less strong. In a sense, he is no longer an extension of his parents' bodies.

The death of a parent or child terminates that state of independence. The deceased is now completely reliant upon his loved one.

The two can now be viewed, once again, as extensions of the other's flesh. Previously suppressed love is now reawakened. And, the remaining relative can now say more easily, "Woe, for what I have lost. Woe, for the part of me that is no longer with me."

When Eve gave birth to Cain, she said,

קָנִיתִי אִישׁ אֶת ה', *I have acquired a man with Hashem.* The bond was not only emotional, but physical as well.

When a man marries a woman, the Torah states that they shall become בָּשָׂר אֶחָד, *one flesh.* Perhaps, just as man and wife become בָּשָׂר אֶחָד, so does the mother with her newborn.

Furthermore, this is why both the birthing mother and the dead become *tamei.* Physical love has burst from its containment. More specifically, a love for the purely physical has burst forth: It is a yearning for a flesh and blood body that is without, so to speak, a *tzelem Elokim.* Or, at least, that love is not focused on the *tzelem Elokim* aspect of the human being. When a death occurs, the soul of the dearly loved relative departs; the mourners grieve over the "body" without a soul. In a similar vein, the love for the newborn babe focuses on the physical, as an extension of the mother's own material self.

[Of course, there is another love as well: that which is purely between two *neshamos,* as in the case of David and Jonathan. וְנֶפֶשׁ יְהוֹנָתָן נִקְשְׁרָה בְּנֶפֶשׁ דָּוִד וַיֶּאֱהָבֵהוּ יְהוֹנָתָן כְּנַפְשׁוֹ, *Jonathan's soul became attached to David's soul, and Jonathan loved him as himself* (I Shmuel 18:1).]

In my humble opinion, this is the meaning of ..., כְּרַחֵם אָב עַל בָּנִים, *As a "father" is merciful toward his children* (Tehillim 103:13). The verse says "father" and not "mother." The mercy of the mother stems from her physical bond with the physical child; the father's comes from his valuing the child's *tzelem Elokim.*

Inordinate attraction to the physical can manifest itself through one's excessive interest in earthly pleasures, or by granting inordinate attention to the purely external aspects of others and oneself (outward appearance, for instance), or being the type of person whose focus is always on what he lacks — rather than what he has. He sees his life as totally empty.

In fact, these personal characteristics are akin to three negative traits, eventual causes of his losing his portion in the World to Come.

Kinnah, jealousy, is the feeling that one's life is empty and he must therefore look to what the other has, to make up for what he believes to be missing in his own life. *Kavod*, seeking honor, is like the obsession with appearance: "How do I look to others?" "How could I make myself even more attractive?" *Ta'avah* is like the inordinate attention given to chasing down the latest physical pleasures.

He who recognizes that his own overemphasis on pursuits of the flesh is wrong — and wishes to take dramatic steps to instead live a life of idealism and closeness to Hashem — is permitted to choose a most radical path to break himself of his bad habits. He can become a *nazir*.

He is forbidden to drink wine, forbidden to cut his hair, and to become contaminated by a corpse. In a sense, he has separated himself from the externality, from the superficial, from the flesh. He no longer tends to his outward appearance. In fact, he neglects it.

Let us recall the Midrash quoted earlier, which stated that the *nazir* is permitted to attend the eulogy. While he may not have physical contact with the deceased, he is permitted to attend the eulogy, where the focus will be on the character and accomplishments of the departed — rather than on his physicality.

Parashas Chayei Sarah tells us: *Abraham came to eulogize Sarah and to cry for her (Bereishis* 23:2). He did this in order to speak of the greatness of her *neshamah,* to tell of the vacuum that the departure of her soul had left behind, so that mankind could learn from her works and from her holiness.

And, also, so that he could cry over the loss of her *guf.*

Perhaps we may see this as an insight into the basis for the *nazir's kedushah*, holiness.

The verse quoted earlier says, כִּי נֵזֶר אֱלֹהָיו עַל רֹאשׁוֹ, *for the crown of his God is upon his head.* In other words, because the *crown* of his God is upon his head, the word of God is the supreme influence on his conduct and he leads his life by following the path shown him by his God. More specifically, it is the path shown him by "אֱלֹהָיו." This Divine Name refers to Hashem's aspect of justice. Hashem is able to judge a man's value clearly, without the distortion of emotion. Similarly, the *nazir* himself doesn't "lose his head" — because his "head" (meaning, his *sechel* and his *chochmah*) is *kadosh to* Hashem, he always maintain control over his desires.

Rashi (to 6:2) asks: Why did the Torah place the passage of the *nazir* adjacent to that of the *sotah*? To teach that whoever sees a *sotah* in her disgrace should take upon himself to abstain from wine, for it can lead one to impropriety.

Come and see how a love strictly derived from attraction to the physical (like that which led the *sotah* astray) can drag a person down to the depths of degradation. The antidote is separation from a life of the flesh and from choices driven solely by physical attraction.

וְזֶה מַעֲשֵׂה הַמְּנֹרָה ... כְּמַרְאֶה אֲשֶׁר הֶרְאָה ה'
אֶת מֹשֶׁה כֵּן עָשָׂה אֶת הַמְּנֹרָה

This is how the Menorah was made ...
according to the image that Hashem
had shown Moses, so did he make
the Menorah (8:4).

רש"י: וְזֶה מַעֲשֵׂה הַמְּנוֹרָה – שֶׁהֶרְאָהוּ הַקָּדוֹשׁ בָּרוּךְ הוּא בְּאֶצְבַּע לְפִי
שֶׁנִּתְקַשָּׁה בָּהּ, לְכַךְ נֶאֱמַר וְזֶה.

RASHI: NOW THIS IS HOW THE MENORAH
WAS MADE — *The Holy One, Blessed is He,*
showed Moses with His finger, as it were, how the
Menorah was to be made, as Moses was having
difficulty with it. This is why the verse says,
"V'zeh, And this."

*T*his can be compared to a case of two neophytes who were given the tools and material to build a house. One, before he even lifted his hammer, first sought out an expert to teach him the necessary skills. Only upon becoming adequately trained did he began to build.

The other decided that he would skip the tutorials and figure things out for himself. It would simply be a matter of trial and error before he would have it down just right.

He saw that he had cut a plank too long. No problem. It's just a matter of sawing it down a bit. (Plank too short? Well, better luck next time.)

Same with the masonry. A block turned out misshapen? Nothing that some added chiseling wouldn't take care of. Still no good? Lift that chisel once again. Isn't that what they're made for?

The block is already beyond salvage? No problem; grab another piece of stone and start all over again.

Eventually, he too had picked up the skills he needed to know and become quite competent, just like the first fellow. Through trial and error, he had taught himself very well. The problem was that he had run out of material with which to build the house.

So is it with our own lives. The time is short, and the work is great. We don't have the luxury of "learning as we go," checking one lifestyle after another ... nor one value system versus another ... until we find something that looks like "a good fit."

Were we to go through life that way, we would be just like fellow Number 2. Except that rather than running out of the building material that had been allocated to us, we would discover that we had run out of something far more precious and irreplaceable.

Life.

We are fortunate that we need not go through this process, for we have the Torah, given to us by Hashem. Through it, He has imparted some of His wisdom. There is no need to experiment or explore as to which system might be the one that holds the greatest truths.

The *pasuk* in *Mishlei* (6:3) states: כִּי נֵר מִצְוָה וְתוֹרָה אוֹר, *for a mitzvah is a lamp and the Torah is light.* The *pasuk* in *Tehillim* (119:105) states: נֵר לְרַגְלִי דְבָרֶךָ וְאוֹר לִנְתִיבָתִי, *Your word is a lamp unto my feet, a light for my path.* *Metzudas David,* commenting on the verse in *Tehillim,* writes: *Just as the candle saves one during the darkness of night from obstacles and from stumbling with one's feet, so do Your words save me from stumbling and transgression.*

This is why Moses and the Jewish people wanted to see the entire image of the Menorah, for it represents the integrated totality of our system for life: the Torah.

No need to experiment.

וַיִּקְרָא מֹשֶׁה לְהוֹשֵׁעַ בֶּן נוּן יְהוֹשֻׁעַ ...

... And Moses called
Hoshea bin Nun, "Joshua" (13:16).

Midrash teaches that when Hashem changed the name "Sarai" to "Sarah," He allocated the displaced *yud* for Joshua's name.

The connection between Joshua and Sarah was hardly incidental. I would like to homiletically suggest that it would not have been possible for Joshua to transfer Eretz Yisrael to the Jewish people without his first having internalized certain *hashkafos,* outlooks and values, of our matriarch Sarah.

In fact, these were *hashkafos* specific to Sarah but not to Abraham.

What I refer to is Sarah's unequivocal and clear belief that Eretz Yisrael is ours ... and that no other individual or nation has any portion in it whatsoever.

Sarah demanded (*Bereishis* 21:10): *Cast out that servant-woman*

Parashas Shelach / 271

and her son, for the son of that servant shall not share in the inheritance with my son, Isaac.

She was saying that neither Ishmael nor his descendants have any portion whatsoever in Eretz Yisrael. Nothing. Not a single *dunam* from one border to the other.

Joshua, who was chosen by Hashem to lead the Jewish people to conquer Eretz Yisrael, received part of his name from Sarah precisely so that he not forget her plea to Abraham: that Ishmael be expelled and not receive any inheritance in the land.

The Torah continues and says that Hashem judged Sarah to be correct. Abraham was told: *All that Sarah tells you, listen to her.*

Just as it was then, so must it be today: Let us be determined to have full faith, just like Sarah, that Eretz Yisrael in its absolute entirety is ours. And ours alone. The descendents of Ishmael have no right to any part of it.

And, when the time comes that Hashem will be pleased with His people, we will have nothing to fear from the nations of the world.

וַיִּקַּח קֹרַח ...

And Korah took ... (16:1).

T he *Chachamim* say that Korah was one of those who carried the Holy Ark. And that he was a *chacham gadol*, a very wise man. He is also described as a *pikei'ach*, a clever man. His mind's eye deceived him, though, when he foresaw the line of great men who would descend from him, including Samuel, whom *Midrash Tanchuma* (quoted by *Rashi*) describes as being the equal of Moses and Aaron.

While his vision as to the greatness of those who would descend from him was quite accurate, he failed to notice what should have been the most salient aspect of this picture: that his descendants would do *teshuvah* and reject his ways. Failing that, they would never have become who they were.

Still, there is no denying that *Chazal* attributed much greatness to Korah himself. His ability to foresee his line of descendants might even be considered a form of *ruach hakodesh*. Without his having attained an extraordinarily high level of personal wholeness, this type of *ruach hakodesh* simply could not have been possible.

We must assume that he was a *tzaddik* and a *yirei Shamayim*, someone who was (at least in certain respects) "head and shoulders" above the rest of the nation.

How, then, could someone so great have the audacity to defy Moses — and to be *choshed* him, to suspect him, no less? And, to entice the nation to join in his rebellion and his slander?

Korah died a *misah meshunah* (a horrible, unnatural death). That's how great his evil was.

What was his failing?

Rashi and the Midrash quoted above offer one answer; I would like to develop an additional thought.

Perhaps one could say that while, on the conscious level, Korah had the qualities of a *tzaddik*, he, like all men, was subconsciously drawn to excessive pride and petty jealousy.

אָמַר רַבִּי שִׁמְעוֹן בֶּן לָקִישׁ: יִצְרוֹ שֶׁל אָדָם מִתְגַּבֵּר עָלָיו בְּכָל יוֹם וּמְבַקֵּשׁ לַהֲמִיתוֹ, שֶׁנֶּאֱמַר "צוֹפֶה רָשָׁע לַצַּדִּיק וּמְבַקֵּשׁ לַהֲמִיתוֹ" (סוּכָּה ה נב:).

Reish Lakish says: Man's yetzer continuously tries to overpower him, trying to kill him, as it says (Tehillim 37:32): "The evil one gazes upon the tzaddik and attempts to kill him" (Succah 52b).

Rav Yisrael Salanter wrote that the "evil one" spoken of in the verse is not some evil individual who tries to trip up a *tzaddik*, but rather is man's own subconscious. When the verse says צוֹפֶה רָשָׁע לַצַּדִּיק , it means that although one could outwardly be a *tzaddik*, within him there is a רָשָׁע. And, as the verse continues, were it not for *HaKadosh Baruch Hu's* help, the individual would not stand a chance of defeating this "רָשָׁע."

Of course, this Divine help is not guaranteed. As it says in the *sefer Halichos Yehudah*, one could lose this assistance upon moving into the category of הַבָּא לִיטַמֵּא פּוֹתְחִין לוֹ, one who wishes to contaminate himself is given the opportunity.

When does one fall out of the category of הַבָּא לְטַהֵר מְסַיְּיעִין לוֹ, one who wishes to purify himself is aided [from Above] and into that of הַבָּא לִיטַמֵּא פּוֹתְחִין לוֹ? One answer would be that this occurs not when one is a *shogeg*, an inadvertent sinner, or is conducting himself in a way that is typical of imperfect man. Rather, it happens only when one's actions place him beyond the pale, beyond the borders of normal acceptability.

In Korah's case, his challenge to the authority of Moses our Teacher demonstrated that he had crossed that line, that the *rasha* that dwelt within him had overpowered and overtaken the *tzaddik* that was without.

How do we guard against this "evil one" within us? One suggestion given by *Chazal* (*Succah* 52b) is: אִם פָּגַע בְּךָ מְנוּוָל זֶה מָשְׁכֵהוּ לְבֵית הַמִּדְרָשׁ, *Should that disgusting one meet up with you, drag him to the Beis HaMidrash!*

One possible explanation for this is the following: When studying Torah, one must carefully examine everything he learns, turning it over and over, so as to be certain that he has looked at all sides fairly and honestly. Is that side correct? Maybe the other way of looking at it makes more sense? Or, maybe I misunderstood — and he is really saying something else?

When one does this, refining and refining until one eliminates as much of the "dross" as one honestly can, he can be called *haba l'taher*, one who wishes to purify himself. In such a situation, *misayin lo*, he is aided from Above.

One must also be honest with oneself and acknowledge that the forces that drew Korah to evil dwell within each of us as well. These are the three *"avos hatumah"* — excessive pride, excessive drive for honor, and petty jealousy.

One must always ask oneself, particularly in one's interactions with his fellow: "Why am I doing what I am about to do? In truth, what is it that is motivating me? Is it pride? Is it honor? Is it jealousy? Am I truly coming from a place of *yiras Shamayim* and acting *l'shem Shamayim*?"

Perhaps one test of whether one is truly acting *l'shem Shamayim* is to see whether one has any doubt whatsoever as to whether what he is doing is correct. If he is totally convinced that it is, and he did not start off with a significant degree of self-doubt, then that might be a sign that his *yetzer hara* has caused him to delude himself.

That was the case with Korah. *Vayikach Korah.* Korah "took." What did he "take"? He took himself.

What does that mean?

Rather than humbly deliberate and question whether his own intentions were truly *l'shem Shamayim*, he convinced himself of a lie, fed to him by the *rasha* that was within: that all was fine and pure.

He had crossed the line beyond which one can no longer say, הַבָּא לְטַהֵר מְסַיְּיעִין לוֹ. There was no more help for him from Above. He had gone over to הַבָּא לִיטַמֵּא פּוֹתְחִין לוֹ.

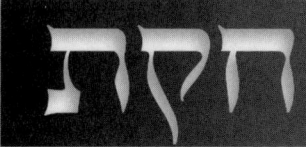

וַיִּקְחוּ אֵלֶיךָ פָרָה אֲדֻמָּה ...
And they shall take to you a red cow ... (19:2).

The *parah adumah* seems, at first glance, to incorporate two opposites. *Rashi* writes that the cow's redness must be "total"; were it to have even two black hairs, it would be invalid. In other words, if it is not absolutely red, it is not fit for use in the process of purification.

This is quite puzzling. For, as we well know, the color red is typically associated with sin and the spilling of blood. As we find in *Yeshayahu* 1:18: אִם יִהְיוּ חֲטָאֵיכֶם כַּשָּׁנִים כַּשֶּׁלֶג יַלְבִּינוּ אִם יַאְדִּימוּ כַתּוֹלָע כַּצֶּמֶר יִהְיוּ, *Though your sins are like scarlet, they shall be as white as snow; though they are red as crimson, they shall be like wool.*

Another of the requirements of the *parah adumah* is: אֲשֶׁר אֵין בָּהּ מוּם, *it must be free of any blemish.* Were it to have a blemish, it is *pasul.* Not fit for purification. Yet, one of its requirements is that it be completely red, which is the very color closely associated with sin itself!

How, then, could it be considered completely free of blemish?

The *pasuk's* continuation, אֲשֶׁר לֹא עָלָה עָלֶיהָ עֹל, *upon which a yoke has not come,* would seem to provide one answer to our question.

We sometimes encounter individuals who seem to possess tremendous strengths, certain talents that far exceed those of most other people. But, how do they apply them? Do they use these gifts for the public good? Or, do they use them solely for self-aggrandizement and for personal advancement — a justification to lord over everyone else?

If the answer is the latter, then we see a great irony: the very talents he was granted become his source of downfall. His misapplication of his special treasure becomes very much like a shiny, beautiful golden ring — prominently placed in the nose of a pig!

How, in *lashon hakodesh,* would we refer to one's obligation to acknowledge personal responsibility for one's fellow men and to empathize with their needs? We say לָשֵׂאת בְּעוֹל עִם הַצִּיבּוּר, *to help carry the burden of one's fellows.*

The verse in *Yeshayahu* 57:15 reads, כִּי כֹה אָמַר רָם וְנִשָּׂא שֹׁכֵן עַד וְקָדוֹשׁ שְׁמוֹ מָרוֹם וְקָדוֹשׁ אֶשְׁכּוֹן וְאֶת דַּכָּא וּשְׁפַל רוּחַ לְהַחֲיוֹת רוּחַ שְׁפָלִים וּלְהַחֲיוֹת לֵב נִדְכָּאִים, *For thus said the exalted and uplifted One, Who abides forever and Whose Name is holy: I dwell on high, in holiness; but I am with the despondent and the lowly of spirit, reviving the spirits of the lowly, reviving the hearts of the despondent. Chazal,* quoted in several places, say that this *pasuk* shows us how Hashem sets an example of how we all must "come down from on high," from pride, aloofness, and from holding ourselves as superior and unconnected to the suffering of our fellow man.

Those who fail to live up to this ideal and have wasted their God-given abilities by using them solely toward advancing their own selves, turning those great gifts into a mere "spade" with which to "dig," would do well to sit in fear of the consequence of what they have done.

Regarding the process through which a *metzora* becomes *tahor* once again, the *pasuk* (*Bamidbar* 19:6) says: וְלָקַח הַכֹּהֵן עֵץ אֶרֶז וְאֵזוֹב וּשְׁנִי תוֹלָעַת וְהִשְׁלִיךְ אֶל תּוֹךְ שְׂרֵפַת הַפָּרָה, *The Kohen shall take cedar wood, hyssop, and crimson thread, and he shall throw [them] into the burning of the cow.*

The specific requirement to use hyssop as a tool for purification is understood by *Rashi* (in *Leviticus* 14:4) as being indicative of what must happen in order for the process to work. Namely, the individual must shift his perspective from haughtiness (one cause of sin) to that of humility, its antidote and the foundation for his atonement. Hyssop is essential, for as a common, lowly bush, it symbolizes the need for humility.

Additionally, I would like to point out that it is not sufficient to use hyssop in any form, but rather it must be an *agudah*, a bundle. Why? Because, I believe, it shows how we must all join into one unit, thereby demonstrating solidarity and empathy with one another. The powerful must unite with the powerless, the vulnerable with the mighty, the successful with the downtrodden.

Most importantly, this means that one may not separate from society, seeing his own fate as being somehow distinct from theirs. Rather, all must bond together to work toward purifying the impurities in our midst, toward driving out inappropriate values and mores, and toward healing the spiritual and material wounds that plague us.

Let us now turn to how this might relate to *parah adumah* and to *tumas meis* (impurity resulting from contact with a dead body).

It is only *mei chatas* (purification water, with ashes from the *parah adumah* being its essential ingredient) that can purify something whose *tumah* status is that of *tumas meis*, the most profound level of *tumah*. I would like to suggest an original thought as to why *tumas meis* is the most extreme level of of *tumah*: The *meis* no longer has any ties to society. He cannot share their burden.

He is at the highest level of *tumah*.

But, is it possible for one at the highest level to connect with that which is way below? Can he who is most highly developed spiritually and intellectually, for instance, relate to those who are relatively unsophisticated and base?

The verse says, וְיִקְחוּ אֵלֶיךָ פָרָה אֲדֻמָּה, which I would like to read as saying that the people should take it to *you*, meaning to go to Moses. From him, from Moses, you will learn the error of your assumptions.

There never was — and never will be — another like Moses. He was greater than all.

Yet, he dedicated all of his talents and and his strengths toward coming *down* to his people, to demonstrate through personal example and through teaching. He was not only the most elevated of all men, but was also the most humble.

One time, though, he became angry with them. Addressing them, he said: שִׁמְעוּ נָא הַמֹּרִים, *Listen now, O rebels.* His punishment? He lost the opportunity to join his people in entering Eretz Yisrael.

Commenting on our verse, *Rashi* writes that the *parah adumah* somehow comes to compensate for the sin of the Golden Calf. At first glance, the association between the two seems unclear.

When normally referring to the sin of the Golden Calf, one thinks of those who played the most active role, meaning those who instigated and actively participated in demanding it and causing it to be made.

Chazal tell us that the active participants were relatively few in number, constituting only a minority.

Perhaps that piece of information provides a key through which to understand why, specifically, it was the mitzvah of *parah adumah* that was the most appropriate vehicle for providing atonement for the sin of the Golden Calf.

Yes, it was a minority that bore direct responsibility for the calf. However, that does not mean that the majority were blameless.

What possible problem was there with the majority, if they were never involved?

Actually, that lack of involvement was, in fact, the basis for their requiring atonement.

How so?

They stood by. They did not interfere. They heard what some of the *tzibbur* was busy with, namely a sin. And they felt that it was none of their business. They felt that whatever this minority was doing had nothing to do with themselves.

They were above it all.

And there's the sin: *They failed to recognize their shared fate with the rest of society.*

They were above it.

They could not lower themselves, לָשֵׂאת בְּעוֹל עִם הַצִּבּוּר.

כָּל מִי שֶׁיֵּשׁ בְּיָדוֹ שְׁלֹשָׁה דְבָרִים הַלָּלוּ הוּא מִתַּלְמִידָיו שֶׁל אַבְרָהָם
אָבִינוּ וּשְׁלֹשָׁה דְבָרִים אֲחֵרִים, הוּא מִתַּלְמִידָיו שֶׁל בִּלְעָם הָרָשָׁע עַיִן
טוֹבָה וְרוּחַ נְמוּכָה וְנֶפֶשׁ שְׁפָלָה מִתַּלְמִידָיו שֶׁל אַבְרָהָם אָבִינוּ עַיִן רָעָה
וְרוּחַ גְּבוֹהָה וְנֶפֶשׁ רְחָבָה מִתַּלְמִידָיו שֶׁל בִּלְעָם הָרָשָׁע ...

He who has the following three things "in his hand"
may be counted among the talmidim of Avraham Avinu.
But, if it's three other things, he is counted among the
talmidim of Balaam the Rasha. Being satisfied with
what one has — and not desiring the wealth of others,
humility, and moderation in marital relations — these
are the traits that count one as among the talmidim of
Avraham Avinu. Ayin ra'ah (the opposite of ayin tovah
— meaning, desiring the wealth of others), excessive
pride, excess in marital relations — these count one as
being among the talmidim of Balaam the Rasha (Pirkei
Avos 5:22).

This Mishnah in *Pirkei Avos* takes three character traits and says that whoever lives up to their highest ideal may be considered "a *talmid* of Avraham Avinu." Whoever embodies their most negative sense is considered "a *talmid* of Balaam the Rasha."

Why were these two personalities set one against the other? One would think that they are two opposites, as different as night is from day. Might it be that, in fact, they have something in common? Might it be that it was specifically because of what they share in common that it was necessary to speak of their differences?

But, what could that be? Is there really something they have in common? The prototypical "*Rasha*" (our Mishnah call him, "Ha*Rasha*") — and Abraham our forefather?

Abraham's mission was to teach the world that there is only One God. I would like to suggest that Balaam did the same; he continued the mission of Abraham. As did Abraham, Balaam set out to teach the nations that there is One God, that He is the Creator, that He formed the world, and that He stands above all creation. And, this was why Balaam merited prophecy. He was to authoritatively tell this great truth to the nations.

One might ask, "But, where in the Torah does one see such a thing? Is there even one verse that suggests this?"

Perhaps, with a bit of imagination, one could see it in the following (23:1): וַיֹּאמֶר בִּלְעָם אֶל בָּלָק בְּנֵה לִי בָזֶה שִׁבְעָה מִזְבְּחֹת וְהָכֵן לִי בָּזֶה שִׁבְעָה פָרִים וְשִׁבְעָה אֵילִים, *Balaam said to Balak, "Build for me here seven altars and prepare for me here seven bulls and seven rams."*

Yes, I realize that there's nothing in this verse that shows what I set out to show you. However, let us use our imagination. Visualize the verse continuing somewhat along the lines of: *... and the altars were built and the korbanos offered to the One God, the One God of the universe.*

Of course, these words don't really appear in the verse. But, it's not unreasonable to project that they form the verse's logical continuation — and that the Torah is giving us the abbreviated version.

Why would I say that?

Let us have a look at what happens several verses later, in 23:4:

> וַיִּקָּר אֱלֹהִים אֶל בִּלְעָם וַיֹּאמֶר אֵלָיו אֶת שִׁבְעַת הַמִּזְבְּחֹת עָרַכְתִּי וָאַעַל
> פָּר וָאַיִל בַּמִּזְבֵּחַ

> *God happened upon Balaam and he said to Him, "I have*
> *prepared the seven altars and brought up a bull and a*
> *ram on each altar."*

Balaam seems to be boasting, as if he had just completed a major accomplishment. And, perhaps there's good reason for his sense of pride: One could imagine that it was no small achievement for him to convince Balak and his ministers to offer *korbanos* to Hashem. After all, by doing so, they would essentially be negating their previous belief system. Once one sacrifices to the One God, and thereby acknowledges Him, there's no room left for the foolishness of whatever one believed before then.

Let's have a look at *Rashi* to the verse just mentioned:

> רש"י: אֶת שִׁבְעַת הַמִּזְבְּחֹת – שִׁבְעָה מִזְבְּחוֹת עָרַכְתִּי אֵין כְּתִיב כַּאן,
> אֶלָּא "אֶת שִׁבְעַת הַמִּזְבְּחוֹת", אָמַר לְפָנָיו אֲבוֹתֵיהֶם שֶׁל אֵלּוּ בָּנוּ לְפָנֶיךָ
> שִׁבְעָה מִזְבְּחוֹת, וַאֲנִי עָרַכְתִּי כְּנֶגֶד כּוּלָן. אַבְרָהָם בָּנָה אַרְבָּעָה ... וְיִצְחָק
> בָּנָה אֶחָד ... וְיַעֲקֹב בָּנָה שְׁתַּיִם ...
>
> וָאַעַל פָּר וָאַיִל בַּמִּזְבֵּחַ – וְאַבְרָהָם לֹא הֶעֱלָה אֶלָּא אַיִל אֶחָד.

Rashi points out that it says אֶת שִׁבְעַת הַמִּזְבְּחֹת, *"the" seven altars*, rather than שִׁבְעָה מִזְבְּחוֹת, *seven altars*. Balaam is calling attention to what he had just done and it is as if he is saying the following, *"Their forefathers built seven altars before You; corresponding to each of them, I have done so as well. Abraham built four ... Isaac built one ... and Jacob built two."*

Let us have a look at the song that was sung when the Jewish people conquered Heshbon, which Sihon had previously taken from Moab (21:29):

אוֹי לְךָ מוֹאָב אָבַדְתָּ עַם כְּמוֹשׁ, *Woe to you, O Moab, you are lost, O people of Chemosh! Rashi* explains that *Woe to you, O Moab* was the curse that led to Moab's defeat, and that *Chemosh* was the Moabites' deity. What this means is that Moab's loss was attributed to their misplaced faith in a false god, rather than in the One God. In a sense, this mocking of their defeat was a lesson in correct belief.

If what I have been saying — that Balaam followed in Abraham's footsteps in spreading faith in One God among the nations and thereby merited to be a prophet — is in fact true, how is it that Balaam remained such a *rasha*? Despite his great mission, his hatred for the Jewish people and his desire to destroy them emerges in the end. He advises Balak to get to the Jews by enticing them into illicit relationships.

The Mishnah reveals where the problem is found: Yes, Balaam's wisdom was highly developed. But, when it came to his personal character, he remained a degenerate. Yes, of course, he had flashes of inspiration, when his wisdom could help him to temporarily overcome the baseness of his character. But, in the end, the personal flaws eventually caused his downfall.

And that is what the Mishnah in *Pirkei Avos* quoted earlier is alluding to. Abraham our forefather worked on himself so that the loftiness of his personal character would match that of his wisdom.

Balaam did not.

When his wisdom failed him and he could no longer rely upon it to control his unchanged essence — that of an egoist and *baal taavah* — his true self emerged.

One cannot fail to notice that, in his wisdom, Balaam was aware of this himself. He prayed (23:10), תָּמֹת נַפְשִׁי מוֹת יְשָׁרִים, *May my soul die the death of the upright.* He wished that in death he would be like the "*yesharim*." And who are these *yesharim?* One opinion states that it refers to the *Avos.*

In his wisdom, he acknowledged his failure: The *Avos* were consistent, they were "straight." They had seen to it that their personal nature would be in line with the nature of their wisdom.

In life, Balaam was not prepared to exercise the requisite discipline. However, perhaps in death, or close to it, sapped of physical and egocentric drives, he thought that he would no longer feel the conflict.

The desires of his soul and that of his body would then be as one.

לָכֵן אֱמֹר הִנְנִי נֹתֵן לוֹ אֶת בְּרִיתִי שָׁלוֹם

Therefore say: Behold! I give him
My covenant of peace (25:12).

he verse says that Phinehas merited God's *"Bris Shalom"*
— His Covenant of Shalom. What exactly does this mean?
What constitutes "His Covenant of Shalom"?

Sheleimus amitis, true perfection, is when one has mastery over
oneself to the extent that he consistently makes decisions intelligent-
ly, unswayed by emotional impulse. This does not mean, however,
that one should disregard his feelings. Rather, he should strike a balance, while not being impulsive.

In a sense, one could learn from Hashem. Even where He wishes
to express אַף, *wrath,* He also has אֶרֶךְ אַפַּיִם. What this means is that
even when Hashem has "wrath," He "exercises patience" as well, not
acting upon His "wrath" until the appropriate time.

We are defining *sheleimus* as the ability to take two seemingly opposites traits and utilize them in tandem.

Phinehas acted with קַנָּאוּת (loosely translated as "jealousy" or "vengeance"), killing a Jewish prince, Zimri, for the sake of defending Hashem's honor. While Zimri's conduct was particularly egregious, the tribe of Simon was blameworthy as well, many of them having sinned through *Ba'al Peor* and then instigating Zimri to act to save their tribe from being punished. Their plan was to disgrace Moses, the greatest of all prophets, and thereby undermine his authority and his ability to mete out their punishment.

The actions of those who took part in this scheme were absolutely appalling — and Phinehas, the great defender of Hashem's honor, certainly must have been outraged. Yet, he prayed that the tribe of Simon be spared. While it was certainly true that many of them had participated in the sins, Phinehas *davened* that the tribe as a whole be spared.

Because of this intervention and through his merit, the plague subsided.

The same person who had such great feelings of disgust at the desecration of God's Name also had the presence of mind, the desire, and the ability to overcome that passion and to pray that the innocents not be destroyed.

This is the mark of *sheleimus*.

In return, he was given a *Bris Shalom*.

For, the root of the Hebrew word "*shalom*" is "*shaleim*."

One further thought: Regarding Phinehas, *Chazal* say that certain aspects of this episode were engineered in a way that would ultimately allow Phinehas to receive his reward.

This is curious. Don't we say, שְׂכַר מִצְוָה בְּהַאי עָלְמָא לֵיכָּא, *Reward for mitzvos is not given in this world?*

One way of responding would be to suggest that man does not receive his complete reward in this world (שְׂכָרוֹ הַשָּׁלֵם) because man is himself lacking *sheleimus*. Were he to receive reward in this world, perhaps he would be unable to handle it; by nature, he lacks the proper vessel with which to receive a שָׂכָר שָׁלֵם. Similarly, by its very nature, this world lacks the requisite שְׁלֵמוּת.

Not so with Phinehas.

He encompassed both worlds, the *olam hazeh* and the *olam haba.*

For he was a *shaleim.*

He bridged two worlds, personally encompassing seemingly opposite characteristics and using them in tandem.

As a *shaleim,* he was a proper vessel to "take his reward" — even in this world.

וַיְדַבֵּר ה׳ אֶל מֹשֶׁה לֵּאמֹר: נְקֹם נִקְמַת בְּנֵי יִשְׂרָאֵל מֵאֵת הַמִּדְיָנִים אַחַר תֵּאָסֵף אֶל עַמֶּיךָ

Hashem spoke to Moses, saying,
"Take vengeance for Bnei Yisrael against
the Midianites; afterward you will be gathered
unto your people" (31:1,2).

Moses is told to take vengeance against the Midianites — and then (only afterward) he is to die. This juxtaposition is puzzling. Is it just a matter of one last mission needed to be completed before Moses passes on? Or, do we look at it in the opposite way: It is inevitable that Moses will die at a certain point in history; perhaps there's something about taking vengeance upon the Midianites that makes it the most appropriate antecedent to his death.

I would like to suggest an idea that is something along the lines of what I read in a certain *sefer.*

The author is commenting upon the legend that when Jacob told Esau that Abraham had just died, Esau was shocked: He cried out, "What? Divine Justice has decreed that even my grandfather would die? There's no justice and there's no judge!" A voice then called out from heaven, "Esau, don't cry for this dead one (Abraham). Weep instead for the one who is yet alive — Esau!"

Esau's words are astounding! Did he not know that in the end, all men are to die? After all, Esau grew up in the households of Abraham and Isaac — where the inevitability of man having to ultimately meet his Maker was a constant focus of their *avodas Hashem*!

What was the surprise?

What kind of excuse is this for throwing off the yoke of Heaven?

Allow me to suggest the following: When faced with an enemy who hates him, tries to harm him personally, and seeks to destroy everything he represents, there are few satisfactions as great as seeing this person's ultimate downfall. Let me explain how this applies to our case.

Esau received news of Abraham's death upon his return from killing Nimrod. Nimrod was Abraham's enemy, having thrown Abraham into the fiery furnace — and also his antithesis:

שְׁלֹמֹה מַבִּיט בְּכָל הַדּוֹרוֹת וְרוֹאֶה דְּבָרִים שֶׁמַּגִּיעִים לָרְשָׁעִים מַגִּיעִים לַצַּדִּיקִים וְאָמַר הַכֹּל כַּאֲשֶׁר לַכֹּל, מִקְרֶה אֶחָד לַצַּדִּיק זֶה אַבְרָהָם שֶׁנֶּאֱמַר "כִּי יְדַעְתִּיו לְמַעַן אֲשֶׁר יְצַוֶּה וגו'," וְלָרָשָׁע זֶה נִמְרוֹד שֶׁהִמְרִיד כָּל בָּאֵי עוֹלָם עַל הַקָּדוֹשׁ בָּרוּךְ הוּא זֶה מֵת וְזֶה מֵת הֱוֵי מִקְרֶה אֶחָד לַצַּדִּיק וְלָרָשָׁע

(יַלְקוּט שִׁמְעוֹנִי קֹהֶלֶת רֶמֶז תתקפט).

... King Solomon looks at all the generations and sees that what happens to the reshaim happens to the tzaddikim as well.

Who is an example of a tzaddik? It is Abraham, about whom it is written, "For I have loved him, because he

> *commands his children and his household after him that*
> *they keep the way of Hashem, doing charity and justice"*
> *(Bereishis 18:19).*
>
> *Who is an example of a rasha? It is Nimrod, who tried*
> *to make the entire world rebel (moreid) against Hashem.*

Abraham personified the ideal of a *tzaddik;* Nimrod, that of a *rasha.* Certainly, thought Esau, Abraham will get great satisfaction from hearing the news that his nemesis is now dead, killed by Esau's hand. Esau therefore ran home, eagerly anticipating the pleasure he would be bringing his grandfather with the great news.

Abraham could now pass from the world, secure in the knowledge that his enemy had been vanquished.

So thought Esau.

And then Esau was shocked; things did not turn out according to plan.

Abraham had died first. Actually, we don't know whether or not he died first. But, he did die without having first heard the news regarding his nemesis.

Esau's reaction was: לֵית דִּין וְלֵית דַּיָּין , *There's no justice and there's no judge.*

So, why did Abraham die before having heard Esau's news?

According to *Chazal,* he died prematurely so that he would not see the extent to which his grandson had taken up "bad ways." This is precisely the reason why the voice called from the heavens, "Esau, don't cry for this dead one (Abraham). Weep instead for the one who is yet alive — Esau!"

We are now ready to revisit our original question: The verse reads: *Hashem spoke to Moses, saying, "Take vengeance for Bnei Yisrael against the Midianites; afterward you will be gathered unto your people."* Our question was why Hashem said that Moses should take vengeance against the Midianites — and then he will die.

I would like to suggest that when Hashem was announcing to Moshe that his time had come to die, he was offering words of consolation as well. He said: Before you die, you shall merit to witness the destruction of those who hate your people: נְקֹם נִקְמַת בְּנֵי יִשְׂרָאֵל.

Moses would have accepted the Divine decree regarding his death with or without this opportunity for consolation. However, Hashem wanted his *simchah* at carrying out the decree (the commandment that he die) to be even greater.

We have seen the consideration that *HaKadosh Baruch Hu* showed when speaking to Moses. I would like to add a further thought along these lines.

Our *parashah* begins, וַיְדַבֵּר מֹשֶׁה אֶל רָאשֵׁי הַמַּטּוֹת לִבְנֵי יִשְׂרָאֵל לֵאמֹר זֶה הַדָּבָר אֲשֶׁר צִוָּה ה', *Moses spoke to the heads of the tribes of the Children of Israel saying, "This is the matter that Hashem has commanded."* Moses spoke to the רָאשֵׁי הַמַּטּוֹת, heads of the tribes. Why refer to them in this way? Wouldn't it have been more appropriate to refer to them as נְשִׂיאֵי יִשְׂרָאֵל, the Princes of Israel?

Allow me to suggest the following: Moses is speaking to a group that will have the authority to compel the Jewish people to follow Hashem's law. They will have the power to enforce judgments handed down from the *beis din* as well.

Note that the verse says אֶל רָאשֵׁי הַמַּטּוֹת לִבְנֵי יִשְׂרָאֵל לֵאמֹר. Maybe what this means is that Moses is saying, "Even though you will be the ones with the sticks (הַמַּטּוֹת) — in other words, the authority to compel the Jewish people — resort to physical force is not the right way. Rather, *speak* to them, use *words*, use reason, use kindness — not raw authority.

Immediately following our verse is: אִישׁ כִּי יִדֹּר נֶדֶר לַה' ... לֹא יַחֵל דְּבָרוֹ כְּכָל הַיֹּצֵא מִפִּיו יַעֲשֶׂה, *If a man takes a vow to Hashem ... he shall not profane his word, according to whatever comes from his mouth shall he do.* This marks the beginning of the section that describes some of the laws of vows and oaths. It immediately follows וַיְדַבֵּר מֹשֶׁה אֶל

רָאשֵׁי הַמַּטּוֹת ... לֵאמֹר, *Moses spoke to the heads of the tribes ...* **saying**. I believe that the connection is quite clear: *Speak.*

Words have great power. In the form of a vow or an oath, a few words can transform that which is permitted into that which is forbidden. The words of a Kohen can transform that which is *tahor* to that which is *tamei.*

Therefore, at least as the first step — even when trying to enforce compliance with the law — use verbal persuasion.

And spare the rod.

מַסְעֵי

אֵלֶּה מַסְעֵי בְנֵי יִשְׂרָאֵל ...

**These are the journeys
of the Children of Israel ... (33:1).**

T he Torah lists forty-two segments of the journey — and
tells us the names of each and every station. Why?

Perhaps it is because these physical travels are metaphors
for the stages of man's journey through life. More specifically, they
are symbolic of the challenges we face along the way. In some instances, we will "pass." Other times, we will "fail."

Let us discuss the "failures."

Some accept failure with resignation and disappointment. For
others, it could be a "learning experience" — a catalyst for better
understanding oneself and for personal growth. Rather than simply see failure as inevitable — or delude oneself into denying that
he has failed at all — one could honestly see it as an outgrowth
of some personal deficit. And then, after properly taking account

of oneself, one could use the new insight to correct what needs to be corrected.

Human nature is such that we generally choose not to acknowledge our failures. Or, we try to quickly forget them. We focus instead on our successes. Unfortunately, because we prefer to forget (or deny), significant opportunities for growth are lost.

This is true on both the individual and the national scale.

Accordingly, the Torah lists forty-two stations; their names correspond to what occurred there rather than to their geographic locale. By listing the places according to these significant incidents, the Torah is teaching us to not forget them. More specifically, it is teaching us to learn from them.

Torah was given in a מִדְבָּר, in a wilderness, and these recorded "growth opportunities" occurred in the *midbar* as well. This points toward the theory that the *midbar* symbolizes an ideal educational environment. What this means is that the optimal atmosphere for development is one that is free of secular influence.

Another lesson of the *midbar* is to remind us that we are living in *galus*, in a *midbar* of the nations, and we should not forget that this is not our true home. Rather, it is but one stage of a journey that will ultimately bring us to Eretz Yisrael.

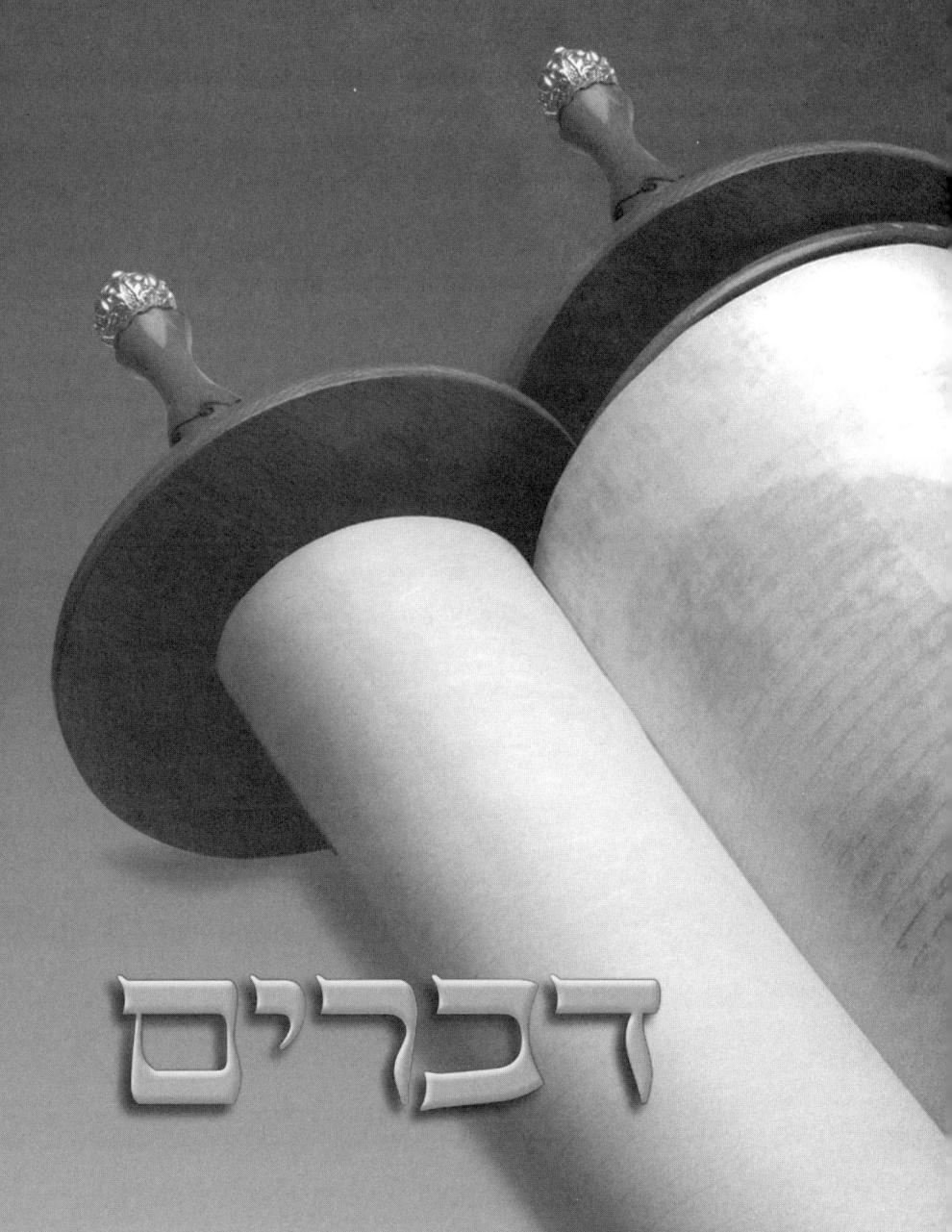

דברים

דְּבָרִים

וַתָּשֻׁבוּ וַתִּבְכּוּ לִפְנֵי ה'
וְלֹא שָׁמַע ה' בְּקֹלְכֶם וְלֹא הֶאֱזִין אֲלֵיכֶם

***Then you wept again before Hashem,
but Hashem did not hear your voice
and did not give ear to you (Devarim 1:45)***

O*nkelos* translates this verse as: וְתַבְתּוּן וּבְכִיתוּן קֳדָם ה' וְלָא קַבִּיל
ה' צְלוֹתְכוֹן וְלָא אַצֵּית לְמֵלֵּיכוֹן, *And Hashem will not accept your
prayers nor listen to your words*. *Rashi* says: כִּבְיָכוֹל עֲשִׂיתֶם מִדַּת
רַחֲמָיו כְּאִילוּ אַכְזְרִי, *So to speak, you have made the attribute of His
mercy as if it is cruel*.

Rashi seems to be answering the question as to why Hashem did
not "give ear" to their voice and "listen" to their words. He says that
the impediment was that they had "made the attribute of His mercy
as if it is cruel." This seems to say that Hashem would have listened
to their words, but He did not because He was not relating to them
through *Middas HaRachamim*.

This *Rashi* enables us to see one of the distinctions between *Middas HaRachamim* and *Middas HaDin*.

This is not true when *Middas HaDin* is operative.

Then, Hashem is like a judge, making His decision whether or not to help strictly according to objective criteria. He is unmoved by the mere fact that a supplication is being made. Rather, He has to hear the content of the request and decide purely on its merits. Perhaps, He will help to a great extent; perhaps, not at all.

This is the meaning of *Rashi's* explanation of וְלֹא שָׁמַע ה' בְּקֹלְכֶם. His comment was that they had made the attribute of His mercy as if it is cruel. And therefore, He would not listen to them. More specifically, it is as *Targum Onkelos* rendered it, that the "not listening" means וְלָא אַצֵּית לְמֵלֵיכוֹן, *That Hashem did not listen to their* words. Hashem listened to what they had to say — using *Middas HaDin* — and decided not to grant their request.

Abba Shaul says: אֲדֻמֵּה לוֹ: מַה הוּא רַחוּם וְחַנּוּן, אַף אַתָּה רַחוּם וְחַנּוּן, *How does one fulfill the obligation of, "I will imitate Him"? Just as He is* רַחוּם וְחַנּוּן, *compassionate and gracious, so should you be* רַחוּם וְחַנּוּן (*Mechilta d'Rabbi Yishmael, Parashas Beshalach*).

Our context helps to understand this *Chazal:* In what way can we possibly be like Hashem? He is חַנּוּן, having decided to help simply because a request has been made, even though He has not yet heard the words. So, too, should we respond, prepared to help simply because we know that another Jew is asking. Yes, we, like Hashem, must hear the content of the request to determine exactly what kind of help to offer. But, like Hashem, the issue is not *whether* we will extend our hand, but only *how* we will do so.

When juxtaposing the words, "חֶסֶד וֶאֱמֶת", the Torah's sequence is invariably חֶסֶד וֶאֱמֶת. This shows that there must first be חֶסֶד, and only afterwards can there be אֱמֶת. It means that the first step toward achieving אֱמֶת is to have a sincere commitment to do חֶסֶד. Once one has this initial desire to do חֶסֶד, then one can figure out the best way to help. One will thereby achieve אֱמֶת.

One might think that he could do the opposite and start with אֱמֶת. He could begin by carefully evaluating a situation. He could meticulously weigh the pros and cons. Should he help? Should he not? Should he decide in the affirmative, he could then determine just what type of help to give and to what degree. He believes that, in the end, this will be the optimal path toward ultimately achieving חֶסֶד.

In fact, he will discover that not only will חֶסֶד suffer, but אֱמֶת will suffer as well.

For this is not the way of Hashem.

אֶעְבְּרָה נָּא וְאֶרְאֶה אֶת הָאָרֶץ הַטּוֹבָה
אֲשֶׁר בְּעֵבֶר הַיַּרְדֵּן הָהָר הַטּוֹב הַזֶּה

Let me, I pray, cross over and see the good land
on the other side of the Jordan (3:25).

And Hashem has not given you a "heart" to know ... (29:3):
  Said Shmuel bar Nachmani: Moses said this to them
[the Jewish people] for his own sake. How is this to be
understood? HaKadosh Baruch Hu decreed two things:
one regarding Yisrael and one regarding Moses.
  The one regarding Yisrael was decreed when they made
the Golden Calf ... as it says: "Let me alone and I will destroy
them and blot out their name from under the heavens, and I
will make you a nation far greater than they" (9:14).
  The one regarding Moses: When he wished to enter
Eretz Yisrael, HaKadosh Baruch Hu said to him, "You will
not cross the Jordan."

Moses asked God to cancel both these decrees. Hashem did cancel the decree on Yisrael, but He fulfilled the one on Moses.

How do we know this? Because when Moses wanted to enter Eretz Yisrael, he said: "Let me, I pray, cross over and see the good land on the other side of the Jordan" (3:25).

Hashem said to him: "Moses, I have already canceled Mine and sustained yours. I said, 'I will destroy them,' and you said, 'Forgive them.' Your [objection] was accepted. Now (however), I intend to fulfill Mine [against the Jewish people] and to cancel yours" (meaning that now he "would" be allowed to go into Eretz Yisrael, but the Jewish people would be destroyed).

HaKadosh Baruch Hu said to him, "Moses, you don't know what to do. You want to grasp the rope at both ends. If you wish to enter Eretz Yisrael, cancel your request of 'Forgive them.' If you wish that I fulfill your request of 'Forgive them,' then cancel your request to enter Eretz Yisrael."

Rabbi Yehoshua ben Levi said: Once Moses our Teacher heard this, he said, "Master of the Universe, let Moses and one hundred like him die, and don't harm even one fingernail of the Jewish people."

Rav Shmuel bar Yitzchak said: When Moses was about to die and they [the Jewish people] did not pray on his behalf for mercy, namely that he should be allowed to enter Eretz Yisrael, he brought them in and began to reproach them. He said to them, "One individual could redeem 600,000 [as regards the Golden Calf] but 600,000 could not redeem one individual?' Therefore, we can see that וְלֹא נָתַן ה' לָכֶם לֵב לָדַעַת, Hashem has not given you a heart to know. Don't you remember how I led you in the Wilderness for forty years...?" (Devarim Rabbah 7).

*T*his Midrash amazes me. Why would the *tefillah* of Moses our Teacher that he be allowed to enter Eretz Yisrael be considered, "trying to grasp the rope at both ends"? Why are the two requests interdependent — that it's one or the other?

I would like to propose an answer.

It seems to me that in the wake of the incident of the Golden Calf, Hashem told Moses that the Jewish people deserved to be destroyed. A new nation would take their place, descended from Moses. He then prayed that the decree be nullified and *Klal Yisrael* pardoned.

One might wonder as to the efficacy of one person's praying that someone else be forgiven; those desiring forgiveness are expected to make that request on their own. How would someone else's prayer help them? After all, he is not them.

While that rule might be true generally, our case is different.

In relation to *Klal Yisrael*, Moses was no ordinary third party; his soul was bound up with theirs. This was evidenced in his prayer. Should *Klal Yisrael* be decimated, *chas v'shalom*, Moses' life would be no life at all. It would be as if he, too, had just been judged for destruction.

Because their fates were so interconnected, and because Moses certainly did not deserve this inevitable punishment, *Klal Yisrael* could not rightfully be destroyed. It would simply be unjust.

Moses had already tied his own fate to theirs through his prayer: וְעַתָּה אִם תִּשָּׂא חַטָּאתָם וְאִם אַיִן מְחֵנִי נָא מִסִּפְרְךָ אֲשֶׁר כָּתָבְתָּ, *Now, if You will forgive their sin [well and good]; but if not, erase me from Your Torah, which You have written* (*Shemos* 32:32). He was not a private citizen; he defined his life strictly as an extension of *Klal Yisrael's*. For him, there was only the *Klal*, no *Prat*.

Through this prayer, he had already committed himself to destruction were they to be wiped away. As long as Moses was inextricably tied to them, and remained innocent of sin, *Klal Yisrael* would live. He was an extension of them.

Why, then, when they proceeded into the land, was he not allowed to join them? Was he a part of the *Klal* or was he not?

The answer is that, in fact, his not going into the land was because of the *Klal* as well. וַיִּתְעַבֵּר ה' בִּי לְמַעַנְכֶם, *And Hashem was wrathful with me because of you* (3:26).

One could homiletically read this as saying the following: It is not that he was punished because of them (as the verse seems to read), but that he did it לְמַעַנְכֶם, *for their benefit*. Perhaps, they needed a different type of leader once they got to Eretz Yisrael. And Moses would not be the right one. At least, not for this particular generation.

If that's the case, then when he prayed to enter the land, he was not doing so as the leader of *Klal Yisrael*. Rather, he was doing so as Moses, private citizen. For himself. Not for the sake of the *Klal*.

And that is why Hashem's reply was, "You cannot grasp the rope at both ends." He meant, "You cannot be Moses, private citizen acting according to personal interests (possibly against the best interests of the *Klal*), and simultaneously be Moses our Teacher, having no essence other than as an extension of the *Klal*. One prayer says that you are them and they are you, and the other says that, independent of what is best for the *Klal,* you wish to enter the land."

"Of course," says Hashem, "your merits are great and you are entitled to be rewarded for them independent of the *Klal*. But, you must choose. They are being spared punishment only because you are a part of them.

"Your two requests are תַּרְתֵּי דְּסָתְרֵי אַהֲדָדֵי, *mutual contradictions*."

We are now ready to understand the last part of the Midrash:

> *Rav Shmuel bar Yitzchak said: When Moses was about to die and they [the Jewish people] did not pray on his behalf for mercy, namely that he should be allowed to enter Eretz Yisrael, he brought them in and began to reproach them. He said to them, "One individual could redeem 600,000 [as regards the Golden Calf] but 600,000 could not redeem one individual?"*

Klal Yisrael could have saved him. What was needed was that they tell Hashem, "Our souls are tied up with his. We want him with us in Eretz Yisrael. We need him as our leader. We cannot live without him."

Had they done this, the situation would no longer have been one of תַּרְתֵּי דְסָתְרֵי אַהֲדָדֵי, *mutual contradictions.*

However, they did not.

And that is why the Midrash continues with Moses saying, *"We can see that Hashem has not given you a heart to know."*

This brings to mind another puzzling Midrash that can now be explained. It is based on the verses, *I pleaded with Hashem at that time, saying, "O, Hashem, You had begun to show Your servant Your greatness and Your mighty hand"* (3:23-24).

These verses deal with the prayer Moses offered in the hope that Hashem would cancel the decree that he not enter the land. The Midrash says that Moses used the obligation of *dalet minim,* the Four Species taken on Succos, as the basis of his claim, as follows: אַתָּה הַחִלּוֹתָ לְהַרְאוֹת אֶת עַבְדְּךָ — The *hei* in הַחִלּוֹתָ stands for *hadas;* the *lamed in* לְהַרְאוֹת stands for *lulav;* the *aleph* in אֶת stands for *esrog;* the *ayin* in עַבְדְּךָ stands for *aravah.*

A Gemara in *Maseches Succah* (38a) speaks of one who took the Four Species and said, "Let this be an arrow in the eye of the Satan."

What is the meaning of this strange statement?

When all factions among the Jewish people unite to become as one man, one heart, then the Satan (meaning the angel of death) has no dominion over them. Had Moses' request penetrated *Klal Yisrael's* hearts, and therefore they would have prayed on his behalf, saying that they are nothing without their shepherd, then Moses' *tefillah* would have set aside the Divine decree.

And that's what Moses meant when he said, וַיִּתְעַבֵּר ה' בִּי לְמַעַנְכֶם (3:26). Rather than the standard reading of the verse, understand לְמַעַנְכֶם to mean, "בִּשְׁבִילְכֶם" — נָתַן לָכֶם לֵב לָדַעַת שֶׁלֹּא, *for He has not given you a "heart" to know.*

וָאֵפֶן וָאֵרֵד מִן הָהָר וָאָשִׂם אֶת הַלֻּחֹת
בָּאָרוֹן אֲשֶׁר עָשִׂיתִי וַיִּהְיוּ שָׁם ...
וּבְנֵי יִשְׂרָאֵל נָסְעוּ ... שָׁם מֵת אַהֲרֹן וַיִּקָּבֵר שָׁם
וַיְכַהֵן אֶלְעָזָר בְּנוֹ תַּחְתָּיו ...

*I turned and went down from the mountain
and placed the luchos into the Aron that I had
fashioned, and they remained there ...*

*The Children of Israel journeyed ... Aaron died
there, and was buried there, and Elazar, his son,
ministered in his stead ... (10:5,6).*

Moses interjects a reference to his brother's death right in the midst of an extended retelling of the story of his breaking the *Luchos,* the Tablets. The reference seems out of place — almost a non sequitur — as the breaking of the *Luchos* and the death of Aaron occurred almost forty years apart.

Aaron died in the fortieth year of *Klal Yisrael's* journey from Egypt; the breaking of the *Luchos* occurred in the first year.

This unexpected juxtaposition is noted by *Chazal*, who offer that it comes to teach an important insight: אָמַר רַבִּי יוּדָן בִּי רַבִּי שָׁלוֹם: לָמָּה סָמַךְ הַכָּתוּב מִיתַת אַהֲרֹן לִשְׁבִירַת הַלּוּחוֹת? לְלַמֶּדְךָ שֶׁמִּיתָתָן שֶׁל צַדִּיקִים קָשָׁה לִפְנֵי הַקָּדוֹשׁ בָּרוּךְ הוּא כִּשְׁבִירַת לוּחוֹת, *R' Yudan son of R' Shalom said: "Why did the Torah juxtapose the account of Aaron's death with the account of the breaking of the Luchos? It was in order to teach that the death of tzaddikim is as difficult to HaKadosh Baruch Hu as the breaking of the Luchos" (Yerushalmi, Yoma* 1:1*).*

The metaphor of *Sheviras HaLuchos* might be extended to other events as well. It is also emblematic of the destruction of the First and Second Temples.

Perhaps, the idea is that *Sheviras HaLuchos* serves as the symbol of סוֹתֵר עַל מְנָת לִבְנוֹת, destroying for the sake of building anew.

One could say that at the time of the Giving of the Torah, the Jewish people had not reached a very high level independently, on their own. Rather, they had achieved this high level through Divine assistance. They thereby grew to rely on this type of assistance rather than strive to accomplish on their own.

Yes, they were standing at the peak.

But, their position there was somewhat shaky, as it utterly depended on *HaKadosh Baruch Hu's* holding on to them. They were left highly vulnerable, subject to losing their perch once they lost that support. Even the slightest change — and they would be gone.

This is precisely what happened when Moses went on high to receive the first set of *Luchos.*

The *Luchos* he brought back that first time had to be smashed. Actually, to be more precise, they had to to sculpted anew. The new *Luchos* would have to be commensurate with *Klal Yisrael's* level of *kedushah* — not beyond it.

The verse tells us what would happen to this first set: They would go into into the Ark built by Moses. And why would they go there?

Because that is where they belong, for this Ark was built expressly for these Tablets, with a holiness of intent that matched the holiness of what was to be placed inside them.

Getting back to our main point, I wish to suggest that the *Batei Mikdash* were destroyed because, rather than rise to the level of the *Beis HaMikdash*, the Jewish people relied upon the *korbanos*. Rather than raise their personal holiness to that of the *Mikdash*, they relied upon the atonement that the *korbanos* could effect on their behalf. They relied upon the holiness of the place rather than upon the holiness of themselves.

So, too, in the case of our relationship with great *tzaddikim*. Rather than seek to emulate them, striving to attain their spiritual level, we rely upon them instead. We want them to do everything on our behalf. And that is why Hashem eventually takes them away, denying us the opportunity to continue this dependency. This is what is meant by the comparison between the death of the *tzaddik* and the breaking of the *Luchos*.

This dependence on the *tzaddik* was manifest at the incident of the Golden Calf. Aaron was not the first to see what was happening. Others, some of them great *yirei Shamayim* themselves, must have been there as well.

Yet, they did nothing and said nothing.

Everyone looked to Aaron; it was all left to him. Evil was in their midst. Yet, they looked on from afar.

Therefore, the *tzaddik* had to be removed from the scene.

When Moses was speaking to the people here, retelling the episode of the breaking of the Tablets and mentioning the death of Aaron, he was saying that Aaron did not die in the fortieth year from their having left Egypt.

Rather, he died in the first year — when they made the Golden Calf.

רְאֵה אָנֹכִי נֹתֵן לִפְנֵיכֶם הַיּוֹם בְּרָכָה וּקְלָלָה. אֶת הַבְּרָכָה
אֲשֶׁר תִּשְׁמְעוּ אֶל מִצְוֹת ה' אֱלֹהֵיכֶם אֲשֶׁר אָנֹכִי מְצַוֶּה
אֶתְכֶם הַיּוֹם. וְהַקְּלָלָה אִם לֹא תִשְׁמְעוּ אֶל מִצְוֹת
ה' אֱלֹהֵיכֶם וְסַרְתֶּם מִן הַדֶּרֶךְ אֲשֶׁר אָנֹכִי מְצַוֶּה אֶתְכֶם הַיּוֹם
לָלֶכֶת אַחֲרֵי אֱלֹהִים אֲחֵרִים אֲשֶׁר לֹא יְדַעְתֶּם

Behold: I am putting before you today a blessing
and a curse: the blessing, when you will listen to
the commandments of Hashem, your God, which
I command you today; and the curse
if you won't listen to the commandments of
Hashem, your God, and you will turn from the way
that I command you today, to go after other gods
that you have not known (11:26-28).

This *parashah* begins with Moses telling the Jewish people that he is placing before them two possibilities: a blessing and a curse. However, the phrasing is not equally balanced. The blessing is to occur *when* they will listen to the commandments; the curse will occur *if* they will not. Also, the conditions for the curse include an extra level of asymmetry: The blessing will occur when they listen to the commandments, but the curse is not only expressed in the converse (if they *won't* listen), but also that *"you will turn from the way that I command you today, to go after other gods that you have not known."*

What accounts for this asymmetry?

Tehillim 1:5 says: עַל כֵּן לֹא יָקֻמוּ רְשָׁעִים בַּמִּשְׁפָּט וְחַטָּאִים בַּעֲדַת צַדִּיקִים, *Therefore, the wicked will not survive judgment, nor will sinners, in the assembly of the righteous.* *Ohr Shraga,* by Rav Shraga Feish, asks, "Isn't this perfectly obvious? Would we have thought otherwise?"

Rav Feish answers that by looking at the verse in a new way, one might find an answer to this question. Rather than say that the second part of the verse, וְחַטָּאִים בַּעֲדַת צַדִּיקִים, refers to *sinners* who would be standing in the assembly of the righteous, we could read the word more literally and say that it refers to *sins* that will be found among the righteous. The righteous are human; it is unrealistic to expect that they will be free of sin. Just as the wicked have sins, so too do the *tzaddikim.* This will not, however, be the cause for denying the *tzaddikim* their reward. Nor will it mitigate the punishment of the wicked: לֹא יָקֻמוּ רְשָׁעִים בַּמִּשְׁפָּט, *they will not survive judgment.*

Why is this so? When Hashem judges an individual, he looks at the person's overall attitude. Yes, an individual might occasionally falter. However, does he basically strive to do good? Or, is his basic attitude one of *resha,* wickedness?

This accounts for why the *rasha* will not survive judgment — and for why the *tzaddik,* despite his occasional sin, will. It is a matter of whether the sin was consistent with one's overall behavior — or, an aberration.

We may now return to our original question: Why, when Moses refers to the blessing, he says it will occur *when* they will listen to the commandments, but the curse will occur *if* they will not?

One answer is that it comes to emphasize just how distinct the path of בְּרָכָה, *blessing,* is from that of קְלָלָה, *curse.*

The path of *berachah* is "אֲשֶׁר תִּשְׁמְעוּ אֶל מִצְוֹת ה' אֱלֹהֵיכֶם אֲשֶׁר אָנֹכִי מְצַוֶּה אֶתְכֶם הַיּוֹם" — and not "אִם תִּשְׁמְעוּ". The path of *berachah* is when one unquestioningly fulfills the mitzvos. It is one of unflinching commitment to follow the way of Hashem. This is the way of the *tzaddikim.* They are absolute in their commitment. Yes, they might sometimes falter. But, their resolution to follow Him is unhesitating. They do not even consider אִם תִּשְׁמְעוּ.

The path of קְלָלָה is just the opposite. It is all about אִם תִּשְׁמְעוּ.

The path of קְלָלָה begins where one entertains the question, "*Should I listen — or should I not?*"

כִּי הָאָדָם עֵץ הַשָּׂדֶה
Are the trees of the field human?
... (alternatively) Is man a tree of the field? (20:19).

Man is created from אֲדָמָה, *earth;* he carries within him everything that is earthly. He has desire and ambition. He has the faculty to discern. And, he has the capability of interpreting the words of Hashem.

He also possesses a שֵׂכֶל אֱלוֹקִי, *a Godly soul.* Hashem therefore saw to it that, despite its being formed from *adamah,* his body would be compatible with his Godly soul.

Adam HaRishon added to what Hashem had told him, and subtracted from it as well. He was never told that he could not touch the Tree of Knowledge, but innovated such a prohibition anyway. When telling Eve of this new prohibition, he never made clear that it was his own rule rather than that of Hashem. By not making this distinction, he ultimately wound up undermining what Hashem wanted for this world.

The snake pushed Eve against the tree. She had touched it, yet did not die. She had now become more susceptible to the snake's promise that no punishment would result from eating of the fruit itself.

When "adam" was then punished, the adamah was punished as well, for it too had not followed Hashem's command. The earth also added and subtracted from the word of Hashem (Bereishis 1:11-12).

Adam had acted in a way that ultimately caused an apparent diminution of Hashem's commandment. The adamah was then punished in kind: Its capabilities were diminished as well. The non-fruit-bearing trees would no longer be edible; their utility would be restricted to use as building material and kindling.

We translated the verse according to its traditional reading, כִּי הָאָדָם עֵץ הַשָּׂדֶה, *Are the trees of the field human?* Works of *mussar* sometimes use an alternate reading: *Man is a tree of the field.*

I would like to extend this latter reading of the verse to demonstrate a principle of Torah education.

Zerizus, alacrity, is a wonderful character trait. It entails doing things without delay, hesitation, or procrastination. It is the initial stage of attaining holiness and a prerequisite to *ruach hakodesh*.

It is not to be confused with recklessness.

The mishnah in *Avos* says, הֱווּ מְתוּנִים בַּדִּין, *be deliberate in judgment.* This means that when forming judgments, one must exercise wisdom and extreme care. However, once one has reached a conclusion and is confident that it expresses the word of Hashem, he must rush forward, eager to implement what he has just decided.

There is also such a thing as excessive caution, to the point that one becomes paralyzed. It sometimes stems from a lack of clarity as to what Hashem wants done in a particular situation.

Excessive hesitation caused by lack of understanding opens the door to sin. The Torah therefore warns that we should neither add to the Torah nor take away from it. This situation is only tempo-rary, though.

When the *aretz* will once again be filled with wisdom, in the time of Mashiach, this sin will find its correction. The barren trees will become edible or begin bearing fruit.

When Hashem saw His Creation, the *pasuk* says, וַיַּרְא אֱלֹהִים כִּי טוֹב, Hashem saw that the world was good, for man would have the abil-ity to discern, to make the right decisions, and thereby to bring the *aretz* to its state of completeness as desired by Hashem.

לֹא יָבֹא עַמּוֹנִי וּמוֹאָבִי בִּקְהַל ה' גַּם דּוֹר עֲשִׂירִי לֹא יָבֹא
לָהֶם בִּקְהַל ה' עַד עוֹלָם. עַל דְּבַר אֲשֶׁר לֹא קִדְּמוּ אֶתְכֶם
בַּלֶּחֶם וּבַמַּיִם בַּדֶּרֶךְ בְּצֵאתְכֶם מִמִּצְרָיִם וַאֲשֶׁר שָׂכַר עָלֶיךָ
אֶת בִּלְעָם בֶּן בְּעוֹר מִפְּתוֹר אֲרַם נַהֲרַיִם לְקַלְלֶךָ

Neither an Ammonite nor a Moabite may enter
the congregation of Hashem. Even the tenth
generation may not enter the congregation of
Hashem, forever, because they did not greet you
with bread and water along the way as you left
Egypt and because he hired Balaam son of Be'or,
from Petor, Aram Naharaim, to curse you (23:4-5).

The verse says that the Ammonite and Moabite are for-ever barred from "entering the congregation of Hashem." This means that, even if they were to fully convert to Judaism, the males are still forever barred from marrying a Jewish woman.

The reason? *Because they did not greet you with bread and water along the way as you left Egypt and because he hired Balaam ... to curse you.*

Because they did not greet you with bread and water? Is this truly so great a sin? Doesn't it sound more like a lack of *tzidkus*, righteousness, than a tremendous moral flaw? And, why is it that its mark does not disappear, even one hundred generations later, long after the original ancestor who committed this "sin" has departed the face of the earth?

Is it their lack of *chessed* that disqualifies them? If so, what are we to do with the other nations? Haven't we been terribly oppressed by so many of them throughout the ages? Lack of *chessed*? That's our complaint? We should consider ourselves fortunate when they choose not to murder us!

Yet, there's no such prohibition against marrying a convert from any of the other nations!

One further question: What is the connection between their lack of showing *chessed* and their having hired Balaam to curse us?

Regarding the first question, in my opinion, the reason we may not marry them has nothing to do with their failure to act like the friendliest of neighbors. In fact, it wasn't even that they had failed to act in the interests of *Klal Yisrael*. Rather, it is that they failed to act in the interests of — *themselves*!

After having heard about the miracles done for the Jewish people at the Splitting of the Sea, it is said of the nations:

שָׁמְעוּ עַמִּים יִרְגָּזוּן חִיל אָחַז יֹשְׁבֵי פְּלָשֶׁת. אָז נִבְהֲלוּ אַלוּפֵי אֱדוֹם אֵילֵי מוֹאָב יֹאחֲזֵמוֹ רָעַד ... תִּפֹּל עֲלֵיהֶם אֵימָתָה וָפַחַד.

Peoples heard — and they shuddered. Shaking seized those who dwell in Philistia. Then, Edom's chiefs were terrified; the chiefs of Moab were seized with trembling ... Terror and fear came over them (15:14-16).

Logic dictates that Ammon and Moab would be very much interested in greeting the Israelites with bread and water. Not out of courtesy or *middos tovos*, but purely as a matter of self-interest, if not self-preservation. Clearly, the Jewish people were favored by Hashem. And the verse says that the people of Ammon and Moab were well aware of the great miracles He had done to punish *Klal Yisrael's* enemies.

Yet, they refrained to come forward.

Why?

The question becomes even more compelling. Why didn't they try to capitalize on a certain advantage they had — they were *mishpachah*! [Ammon and Moab were descended from Lot, Abraham's nephew.] So, why didn't they go out to greet their "cousins"?

I would suggest that it had to do with hatred. A hatred so intense that they would even sacrifice their own well-being rather than show any favor whatsoever to a people they despised.

The object of their hatred was, of course, *Klal Yisrael.*

They could have chosen to forge a bond, or at least to pretend they wished their brethren well.

No. Better to die.

It wasn't their failure to bring bread and water *per se* that was the basis for Ammon and Moab being banned from our midst. Rather, it was their intense hatred.

The incident with the bread and water merely served to reveal how deeply the hatred was embedded within them. The Torah's claim against then was not that they lacked certain *middos tovos*. Instead, it was the fact that their hatred was so profound that it superseded mankind's natural interest in self-preservation.

Perhaps we could say something in their favor. After all, they must have been people of principle. The Torah itself often admonishes us to act out of principle rather than self-interest. Not only must we forfeit great sums of money for the sake of not violating certain mitzvos, but we must even be prepared to give up our lives for certain others.

What was their principle? Perhaps, it was to not be hypocrites. They felt that one must be consistent, that the desire of one's heart and the words coming out of one's mouth should be as one.

If that's the case, why shouldn't we be able to marry them once they convert? Once they've decided to join the Jewish people, they would no longer be facing these internal contradictions. Their actions would improve and they should be able to put their sordid past behind them.

The answer is: וַאֲשֶׁר שָׂכַר עָלֶיךָ אֶת בִּלְעָם ... לְקַלְלֶךָ — *they hired Balaam ... to curse us.*

What is the significance of this?

Its significance is that it belies any claim of their not wishing to betray their principles by acting hypocritically.

"עַל כֵּן יֹאמְרוּ הַמֹּשְׁלִים" (במדבר 21:27) זֶה בִּלְעָם וְאָבִיו שֶׁשְּׂכָרָן
סִיחוֹן לְקַלֵּל אֶת מוֹאָב

"Therefore the bards would recite" — this refers to Balaam and his father, who were hired by Sichon to curse Moab (Bamidbar Rabbah 19, quoting Bamidbar 21:27).

We see that Moab was not the first nation to hire Balaam to lay a curse on an enemy. Sichon had done so as well. In that case, Moab was the object of the curse.

Yet, this did not stop them from turning around and hiring Balaam, the one who had cursed their own nation, to do their bidding against *Klal Yisrael.*

In this instance, they were willing to swallow their pride. Despite their hatred of Balaam, they were prepared to honor him. They were prepared to hide their true feelings. They could be polite, gracious, and respectful, despite what they were really thinking. Quite obvious to every observer, they were very well capable and willing to be hypocrites.

But not to the Jews.

That's how great was their hatred and their resentment of *Klal Yisrael's* extra measure of holiness.

They couldn't even bring themselves to offer them bread and water.

And that is why they are not permitted to marry into the Jewish people. It wasn't the fact that they did not bring water; it was what this behavior revealed about the sickness that was within their souls.

וְהָיָה כִּי תָבוֹא אֶל הָאָרֶץ אֲשֶׁר ה' אֱלֹהֶיךָ
נֹתֵן לְךָ נַחֲלָה וִירִשְׁתָּהּ וְיָשַׁבְתָּ בָּהּ

When you enter the land that Hashem,
your God, gives you a heritage,
and you possess it, and dwell in it (26:1).

Sifri to this verse says: כִּי תָבוֹא אֶל הָאָרֶץ — *perform the mitzvah referred to here, **for you will enter the Land as its reward.*** The phrasing seems somewhat strange. It seems to be saying that they will enter the Land as reward for having performed the mitzvah about to be mentioned, namely that of *bikkurim*, first fruits. However, how could one do this mitzvah *before* having entered the Land? *Bikkurim* are done only *inside* the Land — not outside of it! One must first inherit the Land and dwell there!

In expounding this teaching, perhaps the *Chachamim* were troubled as to why, instead of saying, וְהָיָה כַּאֲשֶׁר תִּירַשׁ, *when you inherit* [*the Land*], which would seem more logical, the Torah said, וְהָיָה כִּי תָבוֹא, *when you enter* [*the Land*] which seems much less clear.

I would like to suggest that the intent is as follows: It is possible that one could inherit the Land, conquer it, and physically enter it — yet still remain among those who have never *arrived* there.

What do I mean?

When does one truly become among those who dwell upon the Land? After he has taken the first fruits grown upon his land and brought them to the *Beis HaMikdash*, the place chosen by Hashem. He hands them to the Kohen and this is what the Torah describes:

וְהָיָה כִּי תָבוֹא אֶל הָאָרֶץ אֲשֶׁר ה' אֱלֹהֶיךָ נֹתֵן לְךָ נַחֲלָה וִירִשְׁתָּהּ
וְיָשַׁבְתָּ בָּהּ. וְלָקַחְתָּ מֵרֵאשִׁית כָּל פְּרִי הָאֲדָמָה אֲשֶׁר תָּבִיא מֵאַרְצְךָ
אֲשֶׁר ה' אֱלֹהֶיךָ נֹתֵן לָךְ וְשַׂמְתָּ בַטֶּנֶא וְהָלַכְתָּ אֶל הַמָּקוֹם אֲשֶׁר יִבְחַר
ה' אֱלֹהֶיךָ לְשַׁכֵּן שְׁמוֹ שָׁם. וּבָאתָ אֶל הַכֹּהֵן אֲשֶׁר יִהְיֶה בַּיָּמִים הָהֵם
וְאָמַרְתָּ אֵלָיו הִגַּדְתִּי הַיּוֹם לַה' אֱלֹהֶיךָ כִּי בָאתִי אֶל הָאָרֶץ אֲשֶׁר נִשְׁבַּע
ה' לַאֲבֹתֵינוּ לָתֶת לָנוּ.

It will be when you enter the Land that Hashem, your God, gives you as an inheritance, and you possess it, and dwell in it, that you shall take of the first of every fruit of the ground that you bring in from your Land that Hashem, your God, gives you, and you shall put it in a basket and go to the place that Hashem, your God, will choose, to make His Name rest there. You shall come to whomever will be the Kohen in those days, and you shall say to him, "I declare this today before Hashem, your God, that I have entered the Land that Hashem promised to our forefathers to give to us" (26:1-3).

וּבָאתָ אֶל הַכֹּהֵן — *You shall come to the Kohen ... and say to him,* הִגַּדְתִּי
הַיּוֹם לַה' אֱלֹהֶיךָ כִּי בָאתִי אֶל הָאָרֶץ אֲשֶׁר נִשְׁבַּע ה' לַאֲבֹתֵינוּ לָתֶת לָנוּ *I declare*

this day before Hashem, your God, that I have entered the Land that Hashem promised to our forefathers to give to us.

What is the significance of הִגַּדְתִּי? It means: I hereby demonstrate through my actions. What is the significance of כִּי בָאתִי אֶל הָאָרֶץ אֲשֶׁר נִשְׁבַּע ה' לַאֲבֹתֵינוּ לָתֶת לָנוּ ? It tells us when the individual is considered to have truly *come* to the Land: with the acknowledgment that it is the Land of the *Avos*. The word תָבוֹא is composed of the same letters as the word אָבוֹת.

This idea is seen as well in *biur ma'aseros* and *vidui ma'aser sheni*, which also appear in this *parashah*. And, one sees it in the blessings and curses at Har Eival and Har Grizim. After pronouncement of the curses, the Torah says (28:47), תַּחַת אֲשֶׁר לֹא עָבַדְתָּ אֶת ה' אֱלֹהֶיךָ בְּשִׂמְחָה וּבְטוּב לֵבָב מֵרֹב כֹּל, *Because you did not serve Hashem, your God, with gladness and goodness of heart, when everything was abundant.*

This statement is truly amazing. One could have meticulously obeyed every one of the commandments that apply to him and still be subject to the curse. Why? Because he did not do it with joy.

How could this be? What it means is that mitzvah performance was inadequate, incomplete. While he might have been scrupulous as to the details, the spirit with which he did the mitzvos was greatly lacking, as it was bereft of *simchah*. Such an attitude will ultimately lead to distortion of the mitzvah itself.

And that seems to be the theme.

Physically coming into the Land is insufficient. It is superficial. And so is the superficial performance of a mitzvah, doing so with no regard to its inner meaning. Serving Hashem without *simchah* is tantamount to serving Him only partially.

When one enters the Land in such a fashion, without regard for the inner essence of Eretz Yisrael, it is as if he has not yet entered.

כִּי הַמִּצְוָה הַזֹּאת אֲשֶׁר אָנֹכִי מְצַוְּךָ הַיּוֹם לֹא נִפְלֵאת
הִוא מִמְּךָ וְלֹא רְחֹקָה הִוא. לֹא בַשָּׁמַיִם הִוא לֵאמֹר
מִי יַעֲלֶה לָנוּ הַשָּׁמַיְמָה וְיִקָּחֶהָ לָּנוּ וְיַשְׁמִעֵנוּ אֹתָהּ וְנַעֲשֶׂנָּה.
וְלֹא מֵעֵבֶר לַיָּם הִוא לֵאמֹר מִי יַעֲבָר לָנוּ אֶל עֵבֶר הַיָּם
וְיִקָּחֶהָ לָּנוּ וְיַשְׁמִעֵנוּ אֹתָהּ וְנַעֲשֶׂנָּה. כִּי קָרוֹב אֵלֶיךָ
הַדָּבָר מְאֹד בְּפִיךָ וּבִלְבָבְךָ לַעֲשֹׂתוֹ.

For, this mitzvah that I am commanding you today;
it is neither elusive nor distant from you.
It is not in the heavens, that you should say,
"Who will go up to the heavens on our behalf
and acquire it for us, and tell it to us, and we will
fulfill it?" Nor is it across the sea, for you
to say, "Who will cross to other side of the ocean
on our behalf and acquire it for us, and tell it to
us, and we will fulfill it?" For the matter
is extremely close to you, in you mouth and in
your heart, for you to fulfill it (30:11-14).

amban explains that "הַמִּצְוָה הַזֹּאת" refers to the mitzvah of *teshuvah*. In other words, he is saying that the commandment mentioned here, the one that is neither elusive nor distant, the one that does not demand the sending of an agent across the oceans or up to the heavens, is that of *teshuvah.*

His profound explanation deserves careful study. On a superficial level it seems somewhat puzzling. After all, was it necessary for the Torah to tell us this? Wasn't it already well established that *teshuvah* requires nothing more than *charatah, kabbalah,* and *viddui?* Why would Moses have thought that *Bnei Yisrael* would one day believe that they would need his intervention to ascend to the heavens and cross the sea on their behalf?

Allow me to present an interpretation of my own.

The mitzvah of *teshuvah* has two levels: basic *teshuvah* and a higher level known as *teshuvah sheleimah* or *teshuvah gemurah,* complete *teshuvah.* Basic *teshuvah* is where one commits oneself to no longer perform a certain transgression. While this is certainly praiseworthy, it would not be called *teshuvah sheleimah,* as he has not yet sought to uproot the *reason* that caused him to sin, that is, the inner need that drove him to sin in the first place.

Earlier in this *perek,* the Torah urges *Bnei Yisrael* to seek out the root cause of what would ultimately lead either to blessing or curse:

וְהָיָה כִי יָבֹאוּ עָלֶיךָ כָּל הַדְּבָרִים הָאֵלֶּה הַבְּרָכָה וְהַקְּלָלָה אֲשֶׁר נָתַתִּי
לְפָנֶיךָ וַהֲשֵׁבֹתָ אֶל לְבָבֶךָ בְּכָל הַגּוֹיִם אֲשֶׁר הִדִּיחֲךָ ה' אֱלֹהֶיךָ שָׁמָּה.
וְשַׁבְתָּ עַד ה' אֱלֹהֶיךָ וְשָׁמַעְתָּ בְקֹלוֹ כְּכֹל אֲשֶׁר אָנֹכִי מְצַוְּךָ הַיּוֹם אַתָּה
וּבָנֶיךָ בְּכָל לְבָבְךָ וּבְכָל נַפְשֶׁךָ. וְשָׁב ה' אֱלֹהֶיךָ אֶת שְׁבוּתְךָ וְרִחֲמֶךָ וְשָׁב
וְקִבֶּצְךָ מִכָּל הָעַמִּים אֲשֶׁר הֱפִיצְךָ ה' אֱלֹהֶיךָ שָׁמָּה.

It will be that when all these things come upon you
— the blessing and the curse that I have presented before
you — then you will take it to your heart among all the
nations where Hashem, your God, has dispersed you;

*and you will return unto Hashem, your God, and listen
to His voice, according to everything that I command you
today, you and your children, with all your heart and all
your soul. Then Hashem, your God, will bring back your
captivity and have mercy upon you, and He will return
and gather you in from all the peoples to which Hashem,
your God, has scattered you (30:1-3).*

The verses speak of *Klal Yisrael's* having to "take to heart" why
Hashem would disperse them and how, after their *teshuvah,* He
would gather them in again.

The First Temple was destroyed due to the lack of honor shown
to Torah and its scholars. Once their respect for Torah had lapsed,
they regressed from one failure to the next, ultimately transgressing
even the most serious of transgressions, namely idol worship, murder, and illicit relations.

How could this be?

How could the same people who unquestioningly accepted the Torah, saying *na'aseh v'nishma,"* now disparage that very same Torah?

Perhaps the reason is that, when they accepted the Torah, they felt
that they had done so without free will. In a sense, with the mountain
suspended above, the Torah had practically been forced upon them.

Ultimately this might have led to resentment, manifested by the
way they treated Torah and its scholars.

And the *Beis HaMikdash* would be destroyed.

They would need to do *teshuvah.*

And not basic *teshuvah,* but *teshuvah sheleimah.*

The sin would therefore have to be uprooted at its very source.
They would have to address the very issue that led them to sin in the
first place.

And that was the resentment in their hearts over their feeling that
the Torah had been forced upon them.

There was only one remedy: They would need to receive it a second time.

Voluntarily.

But hadn't the Torah already been given?

Perhaps they would need to send someone to request it once again. They might thereby accept it entirely as an expression of their own free will. Their emissary would have to ascend to *Shamayim*. Who better than the sages of the generation to accomplish this on their behalf? After all, these *rabbanim* could then teach it to them once again.

The cycle would then be complete. And they would have thereby addressed the root cause of their sins — not just its manifestation.

The Second Temple was destroyed due to causeless hatred. The Jewish people had divided into separate groups, each suspecting the other. Even their shared misery, having been mutually oppressed by foreign rule, did not unite them.

This seemed to mirror their experience in Egypt.

As they stood at the shore of the sea, trapped by an army that was poised to destroy them, they divided into factions.

One group said, "Let's go back to Egypt!"

Another said, "Let's fling ourselves into the sea!"

We can now understand why Moses anticipated in our *parashah* that they might one day wish to have someone cross the sea for them once again: In order to address the causeless hatred and factionalism prevalent in their own time, they would need to do this crossing once again.

This time, however, it would be as one united people.

Their "replaying" of the crossing of the sea would be similar to their "replaying" of accepting the Torah, motivated by a desire to repair the root cause of why they were now being punished.

Moshe answered them:

לֹא בַשָּׁמַיִם הִוא לֵאמֹר מִי יַעֲלֶה לָּנוּ הַשָּׁמַיְמָה וְיִקָּחֶהָ לָּנוּ וְיַשְׁמִעֵנוּ אֹתָהּ וְנַעֲשֶׂנָּה. וְלֹא מֵעֵבֶר לַיָּם הִוא לֵאמֹר מִי יַעֲבָר לָנוּ אֶל עֵבֶר הַיָּם וְיִקָּחֶהָ לָּנוּ

וְיִשְׁמָעֵנוּ אֹתָהּ וְנַעֲשֶׂנָּה. כִּי קָרוֹב אֵלֶיךָ הַדָּבָר מְאֹד בְּפִיךָ וּבִלְבָבְךָ לַעֲשׂתוֹ.

What this means is, "Yes, you are correct; your sins must be addressed. It is necessary for you to accept the Torah again, this time with love. And it is important for you to unite with one another. However, you need not reenact these two episodes the way you think. For, you do not need any kind of agent. And, you don't need to cross the sea or ascend to heaven. All that is necessary is that the Torah should be בְּפִיךָ וּבִלְבָבְךָ, that is, *in your mouth and in your heart*.

"You must learn it with the greatest of dedication, your goal being that the Torah should be בְּפִיךָ, *in your mouth*. And you should love one another, בִלְבָבְךָ, *in your heart* (as expressed both in our verse and in *Vayikra* 19:17, לֹא תִשְׂנָא אֶת אָחִיךָ בִּלְבָבֶךָ, *you shall not hate your brother in your heart*).

"If you do as I say, then it will be as if you had, in fact, crossed the sea and ascended the heavens.

"For your sins are not part of your essence, burned into your character. All that is needed is that you change the way you *think*."

This is what is written in *Hoshea* (14:2-3):

שׁוּבָה יִשְׂרָאֵל עַד ה' אֱלֹהֶיךָ כִּי כָשַׁלְתָּ בַּעֲוֹנֶךָ. קְחוּ עִמָּכֶם דְּבָרִים וְשׁוּבוּ
אֶל ה' אִמְרוּ אֵלָיו כָּל תִּשָּׂא עָוֹן וְקַח טוֹב וּנְשַׁלְּמָה פָרִים שְׂפָתֵינוּ.

Return, O Israel, unto Hashem Your God; for you have stumbled in your iniquity. Take with you words, and return to Hashem; say to Him: Forgive all iniquity, and accept that which is good; so we will render for sacrifices the offering of our lips.

Let us play close attention to the words of the prophet. He is saying, *Return, O Israel unto Hashem your God*. And how are they to do it? *Take with you words*, meaning *the offering of our lips*.

What is needed is to repair our thoughts and appropriately use our words. We do this through prayer and by redirecting our aspirations.

וַיֵּלֶךְ

וַיֵּלֶךְ מֹשֶׁה וַיְדַבֵּר אֶת הַדְּבָרִים הָאֵלֶּה אֶל כָּל יִשְׂרָאֵל

***Moses went and spoke these things
to all of Yisrael (31:1).***

וַיֵּלֶךְ מֹשֶׁה וַיְדַבֵּר אֶת הַדְּבָרִים הָאֵלֶּה אֶל כָּל יִשְׂרָאֵל, אֵין וַיֵּלֶךְ אֶלָּא
לְשׁוֹן תּוֹכָחָה שֶׁנֶּאֱמַר (תהלים מו:ט) "לְכוּ חֲזוּ מִפְעֲלוֹת ה' אֲשֶׁר שָׂם
שַׁמּוֹת בָּאָרֶץ" (מדרש תנחומא [ורשא] פרשת וילך סימן א).

*The word וַיֵּלֶךְ means "reproof," as we see in Tehillim 46:9,
"Come (לְכוּ), behold the works of HASHEM, Who has made
desolation (שַׁמּוֹת) in the earth" (Midrash Tanchuma
Vayeilech).*
*R' Eliezer said: Do not read it as שַׁמּוֹת (destruction);
rather, read it as שֵׁמוֹת (names) (Berachos 7b).*

Our *parashah* begins with the word וַיֵּלֶךְ. Its simple meaning is "to go." However, there is a *Midrash Tanchuma* that
says that its real intent is "reproof." The Midrash uses a verse

from *Tehillim* to demonstrate this. There, לְכוּ is used in association with שַׁמּוֹת, whose simple meaning is "destruction," from the word שְׁמָמָה.

There is a Gemara, however, in *Maseches Berachos*, that says that one should not read the verse in *Tehillim* as שַׁמּוֹת (destruction), but as שֵׁמוֹת (names).

It could be said that Moses caused a שְׁמָמָה, *destruction*, on the last day of his life. And, it should serve as a source of reproof for us all, something that should stir us to *teshuvah*. Just look at what he accomplished in that one, final day! After a lifetime of greatness, he finished it with giving us *V'zos HaBerachah* and *Ha'azinu*! Even on that last day, he moved higher and higher, from one level up to the next.

How is that a reproof to us?

Look at us. We could squander a lifetime, or major portions of it, on foolishness and just "killing time." Yet, see how much we should actually value every day, not wanting to waste even a moment. Just look at what Moses accomplished in a day.

And he was already starting from a much higher place!

Reading this, how could we dare to not do *teshuvah*?

What is the connection between these various *derashos*?

Perhaps we could understand them as follows: The first step toward *teshuvah* is to recognize which values are genuine and which are false.

When we consider whom we consider "wealthy," do we see an image of the millionaire or do we see that of a *talmid chacham*? When considering the meaning of the word "*gibor*," do we think of the commando, or do we think of one who has overpowered his own instincts?

What do we consider "bad"? And what do we consider "good"?

Do we think about that which is transitory, meaning that which will be gone tomorrow? Or, do we think about those things that will be forever?

Perhaps this is the double meaning of לְכוּ חֲזוּ מִפְעֲלוֹת ה' אֲשֶׁר שָׂם שַׁמּוֹת בָּאָרֶץ.

Those who realize the correct שֵׁמוֹת (*names*), meaning *values*, can cause שַׁמּוֹת (destruction).

Of what? Of the מִפְעֲלוֹת (works) of those whose lives are driven by vanity, jealousy, idleness, and pursuit of pleasure.

כִּי שֵׁם ה' אֶקְרָא הָבוּ גֹדֶל לֵאלֹהֵינוּ
When I call out the name of Hashem,
ascribe greatness to our God (32:3).

רש"י: **כִּי שֵׁם ה' אֶקְרָא** – הֲרֵי כִּי מְשַׁמֵּשׁ בִּלְשׁוֹן כַּאֲשֶׁר, כְּמוֹ (וַיִּקְרָא
כג, י) "כִּי תָבֹאוּ אֶל הָאָרֶץ", כְּשֶׁאֶקְרָא וְאַזְכִּיר שֵׁם ה' אַתֶּם הָבוּ גֹדֶל
לֵאלֹהֵינוּ וּבָרְכוּ שְׁמוֹ. מִכַּאן אָמְרוּ שֶׁעוֹנִין בָּרוּךְ שֵׁם כְּבוֹד מַלְכוּתוֹ
אַחַר בְּרָכָה שֶׁבַּמִּקְדָּשׁ.

RASHI: WHEN I CALL OUT THE NAME OF HASHEM
— *The word* כִּי *is used here to mean* כַּאֲשֶׁר *(in other words,
it means "when" rather than "if"), just as* כִּי תָבֹאוּ אֶל הָאָרֶץ
*means, "When you enter the Land." When I call out and
mention the name of God, you should bring greatness to
our God and bless His Name. From here we see that we
answer* בָּרוּךְ שֵׁם כְּבוֹד מַלְכוּתוֹ *after [hearing] a blessing in
the Mikdash.*

*I*mmediately prior to our verse, Moses begins *Ha'azinu* with:

הַאֲזִינוּ הַשָּׁמַיִם וַאֲדַבֵּרָה וְתִשְׁמַע הָאָרֶץ אִמְרֵי פִי.
יַעֲרֹף כַּמָּטָר לִקְחִי תִּזַּל כַּטַּל אִמְרָתִי כִּשְׂעִירִם עֲלֵי דֶשֶׁא וְכִרְבִיבִים
עֲלֵי עֵשֶׂב.

*Give ear, O heaven as I declare, let the earth hear the
words I utter! May my instruction flow like rainfall, let my
saying drip like dew; like storm winds on young growth,
and like raindrops on grass.*

Rashi comments on the words: יַעֲרֹף כַּמָּטָר לִקְחִי, May my instruction flow like rainfall — *This is the testimony you shall give: That I
declare before you that the Torah that I have given Yisrael is life to the
world like the very rainfall, which is life to the world when the heavens
flow with dew and rainfall.*

Rashi continues, on the words תִּזַּל כַּטַּל, Drip like dew — *With
which all rejoice, while rainfall brings dismay to some, for example,
wayfarers, or someone with a cistern filled with wine.*

Hashem's Torah is "life to the world." It is compared to rainfall,
dew, and strong winds. Like dew, it can be a source of blessing to
all. However, like rainfall, it can also be a mixed blessing, in certain
circumstances, bringing dismay to some.

It can be a source of *simchah*. And, it can also be like "storm winds
on young growth." *Rashi* interprets this last phrase to mean, *Just as
the winds fortify vegetation and nurture it, so do the words of Torah
nurture those who study them.*

Allow me to suggest a different approach: Strong storm winds can
overturn much of what lies in their path. What was below could
wind up above; what was above could wind up below. Under certain
circumstances, the uprooting could be a cause of destruction; under
others, it could be a catalyst for new life.

How can this be compared to the way of Torah?

The answer is, כִּי שֵׁם ה׳ אֶקְרָא הָבוּ גֹדֶל לֵאלֹהֵינוּ, *When I call out the Name of Hashem, ascribe to greatness to our God.*

The שֵׁם ה׳ (י-ה-ו-ה) is indicative of Hashem's *middas harachamim*, Attribute of Mercy. Thus, we can read the verse as expressing the thought that, when we pray to Hashem asking for *rachamim*, let us not forget to also praise His *middas hadin*, Attribute of Justice, alluded to by the words הָבוּ גֹדֶל לֵאלֹהֵינוּ (אֱלֹהֵינוּ is indicative of *middas hadin*). While we are accustomed to relate to His *middas harachamim*, we must remember to relate to His *middas hadin* as well.

The very next verse says: הַצּוּר תָּמִים פָּעֳלוֹ כִּי כָל דְּרָכָיו מִשְׁפָּט אֵל אֱמוּנָה וְאֵין עָוֶל צַדִּיק וְיָשָׁר הוּא, *His deeds are flawless. All His ways are just. A Faithful God; never false. True and upright is He!*

The blessing brought to the earth by the mild dew (*middas harachamim*) is quite apparent; that brought by the strong winds (*middas hadin)* is much less so. Therefore we must especially remember that His *din* is perfect as well.

**וּלְכֹל הַיָּד הַחֲזָקָה וּלְכֹל הַמּוֹרָא הַגָּדוֹל
אֲשֶׁר עָשָׂה מֹשֶׁה לְעֵינֵי כָּל יִשְׂרָאֵל**

*And for all the great might and awesome power
that Moses performed before the eyes
of all Israel (34:12.).*

n a *shiur* on *Parashas Bereishis,* I explained that the unique quality of *Sefer Bereishis* is how it reveals the latent potential of the *beriyah.* The word רֵאשִׁית describes what is paramount about a given thing. אֲשֶׁר בָּרָא אֱלֹהִים לַעֲשׂוֹת, *that God created "to make"* (*Bereishis* 2:3), means that it is our task on earth to actualize that which is latent within every created thing and thereby draw out its full potential.

Similarly, this is what is meant when the verse says, וּלְכֹל הַיָּד הַחֲזָקָה וּלְכֹל הַמּוֹרָא הַגָּדוֹל אֲשֶׁר עָשָׂה מֹשֶׁה לְעֵינֵי כָּל יִשְׂרָאֵל, *And for all the great might and awesome power that Moses performed before the eyes of all Israel.* The phrase מוֹרָא הַגָּדוֹל אֲשֶׁר עָשָׂה praises Moses for the contribution he made in actualizing Hashem's Creation, before the very eyes of *Bnei Yisrael,* a model for them to follow.

Everything stems from בְּרֵאשִׁית בָּרָא אֱלֹהִים, meaning from the potential infused within every created thing by *HaKadosh Baruch Hu.* Every miracle and wonder that Moses performed was also part of the original creation. All of these lay hidden, awaiting Moses' actualization of them at the proper time.

In another of my *shiurim,* I developed the association between יִרְאַת שָׁמַיִם, *fear of Heaven,* and רְאִיַּית שָׁמַיִם, *seeing of Heaven.* It seems to me that the phrase יִרְאַת שָׁמַיִם actually comes from רְאִיַּית שָׁמַיִם. What I mean is that for everything we see on this earth, we also have to see its emanation from that which is most high. As the Gemara says in *Chullin* 7b: אֵין אָדָם נוֹקֵף אֶצְבָּעוֹ מִלְמַטָּה אֶלָּא אִם כֵּן מַכְרִיזִין עָלָיו מִלְמָעְלָה, *Man does not even tap his finger unless it had already been decreed from Above.*

Everything comes from Above, meaning from Hashem. We are supposed to recognize this, that is, to *see* it. And, in other words, יִרְאַת שָׁמַיִם really means רְאִיַּית שָׁמַיִם, *seeing* Hashem's Hand in every created thing and in all that happens.

The *sefer Imrei Avraham* says that the phrase: אֲשֶׁר עָשָׂה מֹשֶׁה לְעֵינֵי כָּל יִשְׂרָאֵל (כֵּלִים), *that Moses performed before the eyes of all Israel,* refers to the keilim. A favorite theme of mine has always been how the Torah is not only a book of law, but also a guide as to how to teach the law. In other words, it consists not only of laws, telling what is forbidden and what is permitted, but contains within it the *keilim* with which to effectively show how to make Torah the guide to our lives. Our leaders, who bear responsibility for imparting Torah to *Klal Yisrael* in a meaningful way, are obligated to search within it for the pedagogic tools most appropriate to their generation.

Moshe exemplified that.

His praise was that he uncovered within the Torah the methods to make it relevant and alive for each and every Jew — מֹשֶׁה לְעֵינֵי כָּל יִשְׂרָאֵל (כֵּלִים).

We are now prepared to discuss *Rashi*.

רש"י: לְעֵינֵי כָּל יִשְׂרָאֵל – שֶׁנְּשָׂאוֹ לִבּוֹ לִשְׁבּוֹר הַלּוּחוֹת לְעֵינֵיהֶם, שֶׁנֶּאֱמַר (לְעֵיל ט, יז) "וָאֲשַׁבְּרֵם לְעֵינֵיכֶם", וְהִסְכִּימָה דַעַת הַקָּדוֹשׁ בָּרוּךְ הוּא לְדַעְתּוֹ, שֶׁנֶּאֱמַר (שְׁמוֹת לד, א) "אֲשֶׁר שִׁבַּרְתָּ", יִישַׁר כֹּחֲךָ שֶׁשִּׁבַּרְתָּ.

RASHI: BEFORE THE EYES OF ALL ISRAEL — *That he decided to break the Luchos before their very eyes, similar to where it says, "And I will break them before their very eyes." God agreed with Moses' idea, as it says, "Which you have broken"; you were correct in breaking them.*

Why did Moses think that the *Luchos* should be broken? And why did *HaKadosh Baruch Hu* agree? And, what does this have to do with our verse?

One answer could be as I have explained up to now: The job of the *Chachamei HaDor*, the sages of each generation, is to educate and guide the generation, using the methods most appropriate to the needs of that particular generation. What was right for one might not be the right thing for the next. Perhaps the new generation will have a different mentality, a different culture. Their needs will therefore be different. Their teachers will need to adjust; their students might need a different approach.

And that is why Moses broke the *Luchos*.

They no longer were the right tools for transmitting Torah to that particular generation.

For, these *Luchos* were *ma'aseh Elokim*, the handiwork of God.

Which is why they were the right tools for the generation that departed Egypt. But it is also why they were not the right ones for the generation that Moses was leading right now.

Let me explain.

The previous generation was extricated from Egypt through a series of miracles and wonders, all by the Hand of God. They miraculously went from slavery to freedom, taken from among one nation to become one of their own. Their existence was *min haShamayim*, from Heaven.

And that's why their *Luchos* were *min haShamayim* as well, *ma'aseh Elokim.*

Their *Luchos* reflected their needs.

The new generation was different.

They had just made an *eigel*, a Golden Calf.

Therefore, their needs would be different.

They had exercised independence. They were no longer living in fear of taskmasters — or ruled by an Egyptian despot.

This was the generation that would be accepting the Torah and would be charged with passing it down to subsequent generations. They would be the ones passing it down. And, they would acquire it, not as a gift, but through their investment in its struggle. They would need to work at it themselves. It was now up to them.

Moses recognized that they would therefore need *Luchos* that reflected this new reality and this new mentality.

וַיֹּאמֶר ה' אֶל מֹשֶׁה פְּסָל לְךָ. Therefore Hashem said to Moses, "*You make the Luchos; you, yourself!*"

The Torah is forever. And it does not change.

But its *keilim*, the pedagogic tools one must use to effectively transmit it, can change from one generation to the next.

Depending upon the need.

Indexes

Index by Topic

Index by Parashah

Bereishis

PARASHAS BEREISHIS
Sefer Bereishis: Sefer HaYashar /
Potential / Reward Plus Punishment
Free Will / Chinuch / Kiruv / Eternity /
Light vs. Darkness / Olam Hazeh /
Berachah of Hamotzi / Actualizing Our
Potential / Definition of Eretz /
Greatness / Chinuch / Striving for
Perfection / Man vs. Beast / Yetzer
Hara / Dominion of Man / Imposing
Restrictions / Oaths and Vows

PARASHAS NOACH
Righteousness / Consistency / Chizuk /
Empathy / Consolation and Comfort /
Cruelty / Human Nature / Unity

PARASHAS LECH LECHA
Universal Brotherhood / Blessing /
Emulating Hashem / Building for Klal
Yisrael / Not Investing for Other Nations /
Relocating to a New Place / Leaving
Your Home / Kiddush Hashem /
Techeiles / Chalitzah / Honor /
Bris Milah / Influencing Others /
Conforming

PARASHAS VAYEIRA
Tzedakah / Hachnasas Orchim /
Self-effacement / Leadership / Faith in
Hashem / Never Say Impossible / Proper
Chessed / Leadership / Strict Justice /
Giving Thanks / Chinuch / Servitude to
Hashem / Sacrifice Our Spirituality

PARASHAS CHAYEI SARAH
Ruling Over Oneself / Faithfulness /
Consistency / Man's Potential / Life's
Purpose / Distress / Chessed / Working
for Klal vs. Chinuch of Your Children /
Misplaced Honor / Chinuch and
Transmitting Mesorah

PARASHAS TOLDOS
Chinuch and Transmitting Mesorah /
Chinuch for Generations / Tefillah /
Pure Intentions / Self-analysis /
Torah Study / Yeshivah / Searching /
Striving for More / Written Torah–
Oral Torah / No Enthusiasm

PARASHAS VAYEITZEI
Impact of Torah / Influence on Others /
Anti-Semitism / False Peace / Divine
Presence / Torah Life /
Silent Contemplation / Tefillah /
Determination

PARASHAS VAYISHLACH
Living Among the Nations /
Assimilation / Going to Eretz Yisrael /
Materialism / Influence of Galus /

Discord / Unity / Living in Galus /
Returning to Eretz Yisrael

Parashas Vayeishev

Galus / Lack of Unity / Accepting
Culpability / Attitude / Our Role in
Society / Lack of Appreciation

Parashas Mikeitz

Emes / Speech / Strict Justice / Truth /
Higher Standard / Spirituality /
Chanukah / Shabbos

Parashas Vayigash

Warfare / Appeasement / Tefillah /
Reaching Another's Heart / Expressing
Feelings / Communication / Mutual
Affection / Brotherhood

Parashas Vayechi

Life Is Unpredictable / Instilling
Middos / Mesorah / Hidden Miracles /
Societal Influence

Shemos

Parashas Shemos

Actualizing Your Potential /
Environment / Connection to Family /
Eternal Influence / Middah Keneged
Middah / Assimilation / Fighting
Oppression / Chessed / Kohanim /
Middah Keneged Middah / Royalty /
Emes and Chessed / Divine Providence
and Faith / Strict Justice / Bris Milah

Parashas Va'eira

Knowing Who You Are / Listening

Parashas Bo

Integrating Faith / Mitzvos / Fear of
Death / Teshuvah / Renewal / Yetzer
Hara / Bondage / Chinuch

Parashas Beshalach

Faith / Trust / Faith / Seeing the Whole
Picture

Parashas Yisro

Inculcating What We Hear

Parashas Mishpatim

Civil Courts / Laws of Torah / Spiritual
Assent / Transition of Chol to Kodesh

Parashas Terumah

Yeshivah / Building Torah /
Development of Self / Love of Fellow
Jew / Fear of Hashem / Torah: Source
of All Wisdom

Parashas Tetzaveh

Sin / Kedushah / Avodah / Bigdei
Kehunah–Their Inner Meaning

Parashas Ki Sisa

Shabbos / Separation / Holy–Profane

Parashas Vayakhel

Kilayim / Distancing Oneself from Bad
Things / Good Name /
Spiritual Damage

Parashas Pekudei

Tzedakah / Heavenly Assistance

Vayikra

Parashas Vayikra

Dedication to Hashem / Korbanos /
Theft / Aspiration

Parashas Tzav

Day Follows Night / Trust in Hashem

Parashas Shemini

Will of Hashem / Service of Hashem /
Energy / Death and Life

Parashas Tazria

Bris Milah / Birth / Tumah / Nature of
a Person